COMMUNAL THREAT TO SECULAR DEMOCRACY

COMMUNAL THREAT TO SECULAR DEMOCRACY

Ram Puniyani

KALPAZ

Communal Threat to Secular Democracy

Rs. 860

ISBN: 978-81-7835-861-1

Published in 2010 in India by
Kalpaz Publications
C-30, Satyawati Nagar,
Delhi-110052
E-mail: kalpaz@hotmail.com
Phone : 9212729499

Lasser Type Setting by: Rudra Computer Graphics, Delhi
Printed at : Chawla Offset Press, Delhi

Contents

Preface

Indian democracy-secularism is facing a grave threat from the politics in the rame of religion. This politics began in the wake of Shah Bano Judgment, Ram Janmbhumi and other identity related issues in the decade of 1980s. The offshoot of this campaign/politics started challenging the very edifice of our Constitution, 'the values of freedom movement. The communal forces took full advantage of the weakness of the ruling party, Congress, in implementing the secular policies. The weakness and opportunism of Congress was projected to be the weakness of secularism itself. A section of middle class and even others lapped up this criticism of secularism, the formulation of appeasement of minorities, loyalty of Muslim minorities to Pakistan etc.

With the demolition of Babri mosque the propaganda against Muslim minorities, the propaganda based on communal interpretation of history, the propaganda deriving form the poverty and illiteracy of the community, the propaganda taking advantage of the hold of conservative Maulanas on the community became the part of social common sense. The hapless community, battered by the scars of partition tragedy became the victim of social humiliation. Along with this came the issues related to economic survival, equity, the violence during communal episodes and the heightened importance to identity issues. The basic issues of community, education, employment and livelihood took the backseat and the issues related to burqa, triple talaq, and polygamy dominated social debates.

It is in this background that the articles and essays compiled in this volume were written and later modified for inclusion in this volume. These contributions have been the major focus of democratic values, the application of democratic norms in a grossly uneven society and the backdrop where the pluralism of the country came under attack from the communal elements. The communal politics has an advantage that it can arouse the sentiments, emotions in which the underlying core issues get swept off. The identity issues also distract the attention from the basic issues of society.

The other unfair advantage which communal politics takes is by homogenizing the whole community in a single entity. Here the economic and social diversity and differences of interests gets submerged in the religious identity. This politics is to the advantage of the privileged sections of society and tbe poor of both communities suffer as their issues get marginalized. The ascendance of communal politics leads to the dampening of the democratic spirit and democratization process of society. Since the communal politics creates a sort of hysteria, in the din of this the issues related to human rights get bypassed, which is a big advantage of vested elements of society.

The communal violence accompanying this politics further worsens the scenario by polarizing the communities along religious lines and thereby weakening the national integration. Along with this the demonization of minorities goes up and a process of ghettoization takes precedence over the intermixing of communities in the democratic atmosphere.

While this process of onslaught of communal politics was on, some major incidents shook rhe society. After Babri demolition, the ghettoization of Muslim community went up very badly. Pastor Graham Stains' burning came as a big shock for two reasons. One, it made us aware that the propaganda and hatred spread against minorities has gone to what extent, and two now Christian communities also became the target of communal politics. The Gujarat carnage set new lows in the national dynamics and the role of state, the nation realized as to what happens if the state is ruled by communal elements, to what extent the acts of commission and omission can go became glaringly obvious.

The tragedy of 9/11 opened another front of the global politics in the name of identity. The deeper dynamics of terror attack apart, the popularization of the word "Islamic Terrorism" by American media played its own sinister role in the society.

Today we stand at a pass where the real causes of terrorism, politics of control over oil wells, are becoming apparent to all. The real goal of politics in the name of religion is also becoming apparent to large sections of society. This book a small attempt to deal with the issues involved the themes of contemporary politics.

I wish to thank my comrades-in-arms, Asghar Ali Engineer, Harsh Mander, Shabnam Hashmi, Lajja Shanker Hardenia and Irfan Engineer for their invaluable association and for their contributions in encouraging the struggles for secular values.

I also wish to thank of Kalpaz Publications for his interest in publishing this book.

Ram Puniyani,
All India Secular Forum
Mumbai 2010

Introduction

The decades of 1980s saw a shift in the language of political discourse. Starting with Ram temple movement, which came in the form of rath yatras and culminated in the demolition of Babri mosque, it also saw an intensification of communal violence and broadening and deepening of myths against minorities. It did give a severe jolt to the human rights movement. Accompanying this onslaught was a whole set of 'understandings', myths and stereotypes about minorities, challenge to the prevalent notions of secularism, personal laws and the very concept of nationalism itself.

The rising communal phenomenon challenged the concept of Indian nationhood and propagated that ours is a Hindu nation. The weaknesses in the practice of secularism by the then ruling party were attributed to the defects in the concept of secularism. Secularism was branded as a western concept, unsuitable for the Hindu India. It was asserted that this notion has been the cause of weaknesses of Indian society. It has led to appeasement of minorities at the cost of interests of Hindus. The major project of the communal forces was to occupy the social space, in which the myths about minorities, their loyalty to India were questioned along with an increased intimidation and violence against them.

Over a period of time the demonization of minorities went on increasing. On one hand the Muslim minority was labeled as anti National, violent, conservative, sticking to separate laws for themselves, and also that they are terrorists, as demonstrated by the acts of AL Qaeda, Bin Laden and what have you. There is a whole list of such malicious accusations against the Muslim minority and this list has become fairly acceptable to the large sections of population. These deeply set notions provide the fertile ground on which the communal violence stalks the streets.

The debate about the need for Uniform civil code, uniform laws for all the religious communities began as a step towards equal rights for the women. In due course the question of gender justice was side tracked and the issue was given the communal color. When given some thought it becomes clear that most of the prevalent civil codes are male centric and undermine the rights of women in a serious way. This dimension of the issue needs to be highlighted in most of the debates on this aspect of law.

Linked with the issues related to medieval history, places of worship, Ayodhya temple and whole lot of things came up, rupturing the communitarian bonds between the majority community, and the two big minorities, Muslims and Christians. The communal historiography introduced by British did look at Indian history from the view point of religion of the ruling Kings. It did help them to sow the seeds of divide and rule and planted the stereotypes which strengthened the communal political streams, Muslim League and Hindu Mahasabha; RSS, during freedom struggle. It left many a sore points which are currently playing havoc with the social amity, providing the much needed ammunition to these forces. The whole Ram Temple movement is a sad reminder to this fact.

The issue of conversions in the history, conversion to Islam was supplemented by the threat currently being projected, the one of conversion to Christianity. Many a state governments rushed to pass legislations to ban the conversions, leading to intimidation of Christians in general and Christian missionaries in particular. The very concept of secularism, religion being a private matter, came under the chopping block of communal politics. The language and intent of this politics was not easy to make out at the surface. The most visible part of this started getting its manifestation in the regular occurrence of violence. Amongst the saddest incidents of these, the society helplessly witnessed the ghastly post Babri violence of Mumbai and Surat. It saw the brutal burning of Pastor Graham Stains on the charge that he is converting the gullible Adivasis into Christianity and that he is a threat to Hindu religion. Nation also painfully witnessed the state sponsored anti Muslim pogrom of Gujarat of 2002. All this hit the social psyche in no uncertain terms, at the same time polarizing the society along the religious lines and ghettoizing the minorities at places.

The deeper agenda of this politics, that of suppressing the human rights of weaker sections of society, Dalits, women, workers, adivasi and minorities also started getting visible by and by. The manifestations of this were quite different in different cases but the result was there for all to see and feel in the form of gross abuse of Human rights of these sections of society. To add salt to the communal wounds, the real culprits, the organizers of pogroms, the ethno-preneures, unleashing the violence trough their foot soldiers have rarely been given the punishment. The reports of most of the inquiry commission reports indicate towards forces behind the carnage, but as the matters stand these individuals are too powerful to be convicted and the role of police and judiciary is also not above board as for the convicting the guilty of the riots are concerned.

The NDA governments (BJP led coalitions) coming to power in different stretches of time gave official facilities and space to the process of communalization. The peak of this was visible in the form of withdrawing the NCERT text books written by rational and progressive authors in the decades of 70s and 80s. These were replaced by the ones written from the angle of communal interpretation of events, which surely would have the divisive effect on the Nation as a whole.

There are serious and profound analyses of these phenomena, of its Indian vehicle, the ideology of Hindutva and the associated aspects related to law, sociology and most of the disciplines, which help us understand this divisive politics. While the outstanding academic worth of these contributions is laudable, the conduit of reaching these understanding to the average person of the society has been lacking so far. Human rights groups have been grappling to develop these techniques, content and form of the ideas, which need to be taken at popular level.

The decade of 1980s saw a rapid turn around in many a fields. The socialist economies collapsed under the weight of inner contradictions of lack of proper control, lack of inner democracy and external pressures of the arms race and pressures of the western assertions. The Iranian revolution, coming to power of Ayatollah Khomeini, the defeat of US puppet, Raza Shah Pehlavi and the imperialist lust for oil made it focus its attention in the West Asia, where already the seeds of problem were sown with the promotion of Zionism and formation of Israel. US assured of its unrivalled power with the collapse of socialist states, changed its swan song to 'oil is too important' to be left to the natives in West Asia', took up the tactics to control and dominate this oil zone. The language which was devised was that Islam is the new threat, succeeding the threat of Communism as the threat to freedom and democracy. The ideological propaganda was unleashed in full swing to demonize Islam and Muslims. With collapse of socialist state multiple phenomena took place and this was the major transition in the language of global politics.

The foremost of this was the emergence of United States as the only super power in the world. Its policies now had no brakes and it went on to undermine the authority of United Nations, which was an attempt towards democratic relations amongst the nations of the world. Now US felt its' might can go unchecked and it launched its economic offensive in the form of globalization at the new level in which the adverse impacts of its implementation were too severe, the welfare measures by states were downgraded and privatization became the mantra which the industrial houses were to take full advantage of by plundering the industrial sectors run by public sector. The type of economy unleashed was the one where GDP raises to high level along with social differentiation, riches for the top few and pauperization for the bottom majority.

The unemployment started rising, underemployment was the key and the biggest victim of this was the agricultural sector. The farmer's suicides have become the major phenomenon and in a way express the major part of the problem of the way globalization is rampaging the lives the people. The economic disparity, economic deprivation is also leading the people to desecration and some of them get drawn to the rising breed of Babas and Acharyas. The rise in the religiosity in society in general and a proactive promotion of events around religion are significant. Amongst the middle classes the rising fondness for Yoga, the discourses of long robed one's with bald head or flowing manes seems to be the core around which the tense nerves are clamed.

A section from the deprived groups forms the ideal fodder to recruit the foot soldiers of the violence which is unleashed by communal forces. The economic instance heightens the identity politics in a subtle way. It is during this period that different social strife's are assuming the religious language, wearing the cloak of religion.

At global level the phenomenon of terrorism has affected all the nations in some way or the other and the global war on terror, is the overarching slogan for hiding the imperialist ambitions for oil hunger. It is also the expression of unresolved ethno national issues. Terror as such is not an abstract concept. Today it is a product, retaliation against the global imperialist policies, the ethnic aspirations gone sour and also response to the communal violence. Lately one is also witness to the competititive terrorism, resorted to by majoritiarian groups also. Most interestingly terrorism, though not well defined, has been brought to the fore as a religious phenomenon. The turning point of such insane acts of violence came with the formation of Al Qaeda by CIA through ISI of Pakistan through the indoctrination of Muslim youth in Madrassas. The cancer sown in these Madrassas, used initially to fight to Soviet occupation by US is visiting us in different forms and at different places. This is the additional point in demonizing of Muslims and Islam. The global conflicts, war against Afghanistan, Iraq and the threat to Iran, Syria are stalking the global consciousness while the UN has been effectively emasculated by the superpower.

This global phenomenon around Islam has created all the perceptions where Islam, the religion of peace, has been presented as the religion of violence, the bane of human society. The Huntington thesis of clash of civilizations has been the doctrine guiding the policy of the major power of the world. The atrocities in Iraq, Afghanistan etc. are being palmed off as the price to be paid to protect democratic values. One had seen the fate of export of socialism' by the USSR and now one is witness to the export of democracy! Can democracy be 'imposed from outside? The very concept of democracy flows from below upwards; it is internal phenomenon in society. The claims of concern for democracy and so this aggression doesn't hold any water under critical scrutiny.

This book is compilation of my essays/articles on the themes manily around communalism in India. One essay has also been incorporatd to see the linkages of the global phenomenon of terror with the changing political dynamics in the country. This tries to give a broad canvass of the problems related to politics and terrorism in the name of religion.

1

Religion and Modern Society

1. Theology: Term-History

The term theology literally means sayings of God. In due course the word was applied to study, sayings of God, to talk about God. While theology began with Christian tradition, its application in different situations and religions had similar or parallel meaning. Aristotle included discussion of the nature of the divine in this term. Drawing on Greek sources, the Latin writer Varro distinguished three forms of such discourse: mythical (concerning the myths of the Greek gods), rational (philosophical analysis of the gods and of cosmology) and civil (concerning the rites and duties of public religious observance). (Wikepedia, http://en.wikipedia.org/wiki/Theology)

It also came to mean discourse on the gods or cosmology at times. For Aristotle it became discussion of the nature of the divine. In some medieval Greek and Latin sources, *theologia* (in the sense of "an account or record of the ways of God") could refer simply to the Bible. It a sense, theology has meant the rational study of the teachings of a religion or of several religions, that lies behind most modern uses. Though it also means a discussion specifically of a religion's or several religions' teachings about God.

In Buddhism, the prefered word is Buddhist philosophy as Buddhism does not have the concept of God. There is, within Hindu philosophy, a solid and ancient tradition of philosophical speculation on the nature of the universe, Darshana (meaning, view or viewpoint). In Islam, theological discussion which parallels Christian theological discussion is named "Kalam" (This section baed on Wikepedia).

2. Religion; Politics and Conflicts

The world scene has seen immense and horrific violence in recent times. Two planes ram into the World trade center, nearly three thousand people perish into oblivion, an "Islamic terrorist" Osama bin Laden thanks Allah for this act. US President George W. Bush launches an attack on Afghanistan to catch hold of Osama bin Laden and calls this attack as crusade. Separated by thousands of kilometers, in another part of the World, in Gujarat, India, a train coach catches fire. After 'instant investigation' Chief minister of the state, Narendra Modi, concludes that it was an act of Islamic terrorists in collaboration with local Muslims. His associates give the call that Hindus are in danger and will take 'revenge' and Modi signals that revenge process will not be disturbed. Modi instructs his staff not to stop the violence. His administration goes a step further and assists the rampaging marauders out to kill Muslims. Two thousand people loose their life. Just a few years ago people in Bosnia and Rwanda died in thousands for belonging to the 'wrong' religion.

Last three decades have seen the violence world over under the flag of religions. At the same time Islam has been projected as the religion promoting violence and Muslims, the terrorists, violent people. Is this violence due to Religion, Islam? Is the current politics in the name of religion done to protect the moral values, *din*, ethics, and *dharma* of the particular religions? Is this violence done to save the traditions and communitarian ethos of the followers of those religions? How are religions related to the massive violence, which goes on in their name?

One recalls that even in medieval times the phenomenon of crusades, jihads and *dharmayudhs*, which, kings undertook on the pretext of religion. Were these meant to expand religion or were they meant to expand their empires. One recalls that the identity of religions is associated more with the clergy and less with the moral values of the religions. It does not require too much of knowledge to realize that in pre-industrial society the clergy, the most visible part of religion was associated with the landlords and the kings in different forms. Also there was another set of people associated with religions, the saints, who were away from the power centers. These were the saints, the bhakti saints in Hindu tradition, the Sufi saints in Islamic tradition and mystiques and later liberation theologian in Christian tradition, were away from the centers of power and were close to the poor, exploited and oppressed sections of society.

The rulers did not tolerate the saints. The clergy, the official upholders of the religion, were hostile to *bhakti* saints, who were killed in various ways. The two facets of religion were always counter-posed to each other. Since the traditions close to power are more dominant, the Church, Ulema and Brahmins are presented as the vehicles of religion. The parallel traditions of saint's remains on the margins were snubbed by the social and political powers.

Religion: Rise of different Religions

Human life is close to 4 million years old. Human life made slow transitions in the beginning and later went on making strides with ever increasing rates. The discovery of fire, wheel and the like, helped the human society to make the life more comfortable and gradually with the change in the pattern of production and social relationship, the pattern of life went on changing. It is nearly 60000 years ago that we get the first evidence of the spirituality and faith in the supernatural; the genesis of religion can help us understand some core aspects of the phenomenon. Nature worship was the predominant aspect of early belief systems. The information about early stages of religion comes from the archeological sources. The consciousness of ancient human beings was oriented more towards practical matters, which did not have religious connotations or expressions. This can be called as pre-religion. "Some Soviet scholars maintain that the period of pre-religion lasted a long time, until the end of Early Paleolithic period, also covering the Mousterian Period (c.100000-40000 years ago) when Neanderthal man hunted cave bears and other animals." (Tokarey, Moscow, 1986, 9) This understanding is contrasted to the understanding, which asserts that religion was inherent in man from the outset.

Belief in the supernatural dates from 60000 years back in time. "Archeological evidence reveals that Neanderthal man in Near East buried his dead with flowers, tools and jewelry." (Harlombos, Delhi 1994, 455) The archeological researches also make it clear that Earth, as mother and Mother Goddess were the most initial objects of worship. The mysteries of Nature and that of childbirth were most striking phenomenon in the imagination of human beings and that's how these two became the initial objects of veneration. "In southern France the image of Mother of Laussel on the rock seems to be amongst the earliest of images." (Sharma, New Delhi, 2003, p.18) During

Neolithic period the pregnant women's sculptures with big breasts have been found. Later with the realization that Man is also part of the reproductive process, the concept of Sky as father came into being.

In the mystery of nature, the fright and fascination, man came to worship the forces of nature, fire, sun, rain, water and the like. With this worship the clerical elements came into being. This pattern is quiet common in different civilizations like, in Sumer-Anu, Babylon-Inlil, Egypt-Aton, Greece-Zeus, Rome-Jupiter, East Europe-Thor and Japan-Iznagi came to represent Sky, Rain etc. With man's coming into "civilization, the life changed drastically. The urban culture came into being, personal selfishness was introduced, patriarchy, personal property, class divisions, slavery became the hallmark of this society. The position of women was relegated to secondary status, and the new concept of God, the single almighty one came into being. He was attributed to be the creator, almighty and gave reward or punishment for the deeds of Man" (Sharma, p.19)

It was probably in Sumerian civilization that the concept and worship of Gods began. Around 3500 BC God Asur, Goddess Neena and spirits were worshipped. Around this time the worship of Gods started in Babylon and Egypt. Magic, sacrifices and rituals also started taking birth at the time. The concept of supernatural power evolved along with the progress in the production techniques and the related social relationships. The feeling of insecurity might have played a crucial role in the concept of development of supernatural powers. For protection of crops, for better crops and well being in the society the concepts of Gods started becoming rooted more firmly. Three major components of religions started coming into being with this transition in the techniques and methods of production. The transition from matriarchy to patriarchy brought in the concept of private property, the sense of insecurity for future generations, and the tendency for acquisition for more and more wealth. This also created a situation of disorderliness and religions played the role of creating the norms for social relationships, the code of conduct so to say. The concept of reward and punishment, heaven and hell was a step in this direction. Most of the religions originated in the situation of adversity, where social affairs were intimidating and religions came with a message of harmony amongst people. Roughly it is to eradicate the blind faith and crass injustices that religions came into being, it is another matter that in later periods the same religious institutions became the vehicles of the evils of social and political power. Rituals and external identity gradually became the most powerful symbols of religions and clergy emerged as the biggest authority in religious matters.

Before the religions took the clear cut institutional forms the religious beliefs were present in the form of Animism and Naturalism. The pattern of evolution of religions has changed over a period of time. Same religion also does change over a period of time. Though the following patterns are recognized it is difficult to say that they succeeded each other. But it may give a rough pattern of the trajectory of religions. The evolution of different religions can be summarized as follows.

Animism

Many social scientists do not recognize animism as religion. It can be called a culture as well. Animism is the most prevalent form amongst the tribal. Animism means belief in the spirits. Animism derives from man's attempt to answer two questions related to difference between living and the dead and what are the human shapes appearing in dreams? According to this understanding "soul is a spirit being, which leaves the body temporarily during dreams and visions and permanently once one is dead. Once invented, the idea of spirit was applied not simply to man, but also too many aspects of natural and human environment." (Harlombos, 1994, 454) "Animistic images are spirits of deceased ancestors, souls of living people and personification of forces of nature. The spirits of elements could be benevolent, or, on the other hand they could threaten the well being of mankind. That is why small sacrifices were offered to them, when it was deemed necessary." (Progress Publishers 1985:19) Animism is quite close to the Naturism, a belief that forces of nature have supernatural powers. It is likely that awed by the power of nature early man might have transformed abstract natural forces into personal agents, nature personified. Wind, lightening, rains and many such phenomenon became deified and do continue to hold that status in many a religions.

Ethnic Religions:

Historically these came later than the animistic beliefs. The common features of these religions are, their being based on clans. Historically they emerge with the emergence and rise of agricultural society in particular. They also reflect the consolidation of various ethnic groups and later Nations. Judaism, Hinduism, Shintoism and Confucianism are some of the religions belonging to this group. One of the factors here is the detailed ritualistic daily practice, like the way food is taken, the rules of hygiene, performance of ablution rites and prescription of rules and taboos in interaction with intra-group segments as well as the outsiders.

Universal Religions:

These religions were founded around the teachings of prophet. There may not be much in common between one and the other. These are prevalent in different parts of the world, cutting across the geographical boundaries. Many of these do not have a concept of Supernatural power, God. Over period of time the followers of these religions made the prophets themselves as the God. Jainism and Buddhism are the major examples of these. Today this classification may not hold much water, as religions reflect the social reality many of the categories get mixed up.

Concept of Supernatural

The concept of supernatural power has been major component of religions. Even in tribal cults the animistic spirits are having powers, which transcend the limitations of human being perceived at that point of time.

Polytheism

Many an earlier religions venerate many gods-goddesses. This phenomenon generally begins with the disintegration of primitive society. These many gods generally represent core functions of society; a sort of division of labor prevails in these. Between different deities there is hierarchy as well. Hinduism, Religions of Ancient Greece and Rome are major examples of this. "A typical feature of Egyptian religious belief was deification of animals and birds. The town of Memphis had the cult of bull god, Apis, and hawk headed sky God, Horus, who was worshipped in many towns. In India we see a plethora of such Gods-Goddesses: cow, snakes, trees, rains, air. In Babylonian society the spirits of local rivers and canals and the spirits of dead were worshipped. Ancient Iran had mountains and animals as gods. In China the Nature worship revolved around earth and mountains." (Puniyani, 33, 2005)

Tritheism

Some religions and religious traditions show the intermediate phase of transition from polytheism to monotheism through tritheism. In these there are three major Gods, the creator; maintainer and destroyer who regulate the functioning of the world. Between the three of them the Universe revolves its activities. Brahma Vishnu Mahesh. in Hindu tradition and Father Son and Hoy Spirit are two such examples. It is in this stage that the supernatural assumes the male identity and this male identity continues in the concept of Monotheism as well.

Monotheism

Here single God substitutes the multiple Gods of polytheism. Judaism, Christianity and Islam adhere to this concept. The initial concept of a single God revolves around the physical being of the almighty. In due course a concept of God regards Him as a supreme power, which is formless. Many a legends have attributed the status of Godhood to some of the values they cherish. like truth and non-violence (Gandhi) and Daridranarayan, The God as an embodiment of poor (Swami Vivekanand).

Major Religions of the World:

Hinduism

While Jerusalem has seen the rise of three major religions, India also witnessed the rise of an ethnic local Hindu religion, and three World (Prophet based) religions, Jainism, Buddhism, and Sikhism. Hinduism started developing from 3-4 Thousand years ago. The word Hinduism first was used when Alexander attacked India (327-325BC). But this was not widely prevalent at that time. Nearly a thousand years later with Mohammad bin Kasim attacking Sind (712AD), this word became widely prevalent. These Persian aggressors and traders pronounced S as H so the people on this side of river Indus came to be called as Hindus. Initially Hindus were called Aryans or Bharatvanshi later many a sects came up under this umbrella. In due course Brahmanism became the most dominant sect of Hinduism and also became synonymous with the same.

Vedas are the earliest holy books later to be added by various other Puranas, Upanishad, and Brahmans. Ramayana and Mahabharat also acquired the holy status. Gita has a special place in the Hindu pantheon. As such Hinduism is a conglomerate of various trends but lately Political Hinduism, Hindutva is the one at thc fore of this religion. The caste system, Brahmins and rituals became the most visible symbols of this religion. The caste system came to be supplemented by the jati system where the specificity of occupation is central to the status and identity of the communities. Shankaracharya, eighth century, came into establish the hegemony of Brahmanism after Buddhism challenged it.

Shankaracharya's central philosophy was that World is the illusion and Brahma is the only reality. "Hinduism retained many elements from primitive beliefs: veneration of "sacred" animals, natural phenomenon, ancestor worship etc. Hinduism does not have a single authoritative organization and its creation cannot be attributed to specific founder. The existence of sects and diverse interpretations of religious tenets are allowed, Hinduism has a complex range of religious and philosophical ideas and also a code of prescriptions, which specifies man's rights and obligations from birth to death. Great importance is attached to rituals." (A dictionary for Believers and non Believers, Progress Publishers, Moscow 1989)

To put the understanding in a linear way: "The Hindu religion as it is described today is said to have its roots in the Vedas. In any case, whatever we call the religion of these nomadic clans, it was not the religion that is today known as Hinduism. This (Hinduism in its current version) began to be formulated only in the period of Maghadha-Mauryan State, Buddhism and Jainism (as well as the materialist Charvak tradition) were equally old-Hinduism as we know it, was in other words, only one of the many consolidations within a diverse sub-continental cultural tradition, and attained social and political hegemony only during the sixth to tenth century A.D., often after violent confrontations with Buddhism and Jainism". (Gail Omvedt, Dalit Visions, Orient Longmans, Hydrabad, 1995, p 7-12)

As per Gail Omvedt this Brahminic Hinduism adopted and identified with the authority of the Vedas and Brahmans.

Material base of this system was the caste structure of the society. Its co-optive power was qualified to the extent that dissidents had to accept their place in the caste hierarchy. The masses of people did not have the identity of 'Hindu'. Multiple local gods and traditions existed side by side forming the base of popular culture. Later, only during colonial period this identity of 'Hindu' was constructed for all the inhabitants of this land except those who were followers of Islam or Christianity. This construction was thrown up by English scholarship and by Indian elite. Gail posits that, "In the nineteenth century, people like Lokmanya Tilak adopted the 'Aryan theory of Race', claimed a white racial stock for upper caste Indians and accepted Vedas as their core literature. Tilak was also the first to try and unite a large section of the masses around Brahminical leadership with celebration of Ganesh festival." (Omvedt, 8) One gets a clear idea that Sangh Parivar has succeeded in perpetuating a perception amongst Hindus to forge a communal solidarity through elective projections of the past, and this does involve a deliberate reformulation of history. Emergence of nation-state does bring in a homogenization of religion. In case of India this evolution of "national religion and Hinduism has mainly been defined in opposition to the Muslim 'other'"(Omvedt, 10).

Buddhism

This religion came into being in India in opposition to the caste system and the Brahmanical values persisting at that time. Its founder Mahatma Gautam Buddha (Siddharta) lived around Sixth-fifth century B.C. Buddhism developed in the conditions of fierce class struggle in northern Indian principalities, for example in Magadha in sixth and fifth centuries BC. social contradictions reached extreme. The luxurious and soft life of the wealthy slave owners, Brahmans, Khastriyas and the princes contrasted with the poverty of slaves serfs and lower castes. Rivalry and struggle for power existed between the upper castes, the Brahmans and Kshatriyas." (Sergei Tokarey, History of Religion Progress Publishers Moscow, 1989, 304) The evolution of military dynasties of Khastriyas boosted the power of Brahmans and the traditional world outlook faced a severe crisis. Questioning of caste system became the norm.

Emergence of Buddhism stemmed from the massive changes in Indian society and collapse of clan and tribal ties and customs. The oppression of lower classes was intensified and simultaneously the large slave owning states emerged. The prevailing social contradictions could not be addressed by the tribal religions, while Brahmanism stood for the oppression of the lower castes.

Buddha's doctrines were essentially moral-ethical one's, not getting trapped in the debate of the supernatural, which was the forte of Brahmins, instead focusing on the problems of this world, and the blatant miseries of the society. Illness, sorrow, old age and failure to achieve one's goals were addressed in an ethical way, by defining the norms of human conduct. Metaphysical questions were relegated to the margins and ethical questions were highlighted. Buddha is mainly atheist, though he did not deny the existence of Brahmanic Gods, at the same time stating that these Gods are powerless to help man, who can be helped by his own efforts.

In India the stabilization of agricultural system and caste system progressed. Buddhism spread very much all over India. Ashoka sent his preachers to spread this religion. Eight century onwards the Brahmanism and the beneficiaries of caste system rallied around Shankaracharya and ideological and social attack on Buddhism resulted in the banishment of Buddhism from India and consolidation of Brahmanism. Somewhere along the Bhakti tradition did held sway on the section of people, but overall

Brahmanism remained dominant. With the coming of British and the rise of reform movements, Jotiba Phule; Ambedkar and the movement of Dalits the landlord Brahman combine came up with the political Brahmanism called Hindutva, which is the current major politics of section of society opposing the democratic norms and values.

Christianity

Christianity came up in the backdrop of the formation of Roman Empire and its oppressive structure. It suppressed the small provinces and imposed a despotic structure on the society. Increase in taxation and absence of civil rights led to discontent not only amongst slaves but also amongst other sections of society. Unsuccessful rebellions of slaves and of oppressed people of Rome increased the general sense of helplessness and dejection. "... Any resistance of individual small tribes or cities was futile. Where was the way out, where was salvation for the enslaved, oppressed and poverty-stricken, a way out, common to all these various groups of people with various interests that were either alien to one another or even opposite" (Marx, p. 330) The severe conditions of slave owning society resulted in the development of newer social consciousness. "Already in the epoch of the early empire fundamentally new notions developed along with aristocratic ideology that showed disdain for poverty, slavery and manual labor. These new ideas involved respect for the "little man" with his modest requirements and interests; including the slave and his human dignity...Thus early Christianity was the religion of slaves and the oppressed. (Tokarey, 332)

In the initial phases this religion was characterized by the struggle against established order and was subjected to repression by the state. This was also the phase when Church emerged and got consolidated. Christianity can be periodized into three major phases, the first one when it had to face a lot of prosecution in the hands of the rulers. This phase lasted till third century. This was a very liberal phase of Christianity. 'During the first century due to the affectionate and liberal attitude of Saint Barnabas and Saint Paul many a Jews and Pagans converted to Christianity. The prevalent Clergy and rulers boycotted them. During the era of Roman emperors Severus and Decius they were tortured and harassed." (Geetesh Sharma, 62)

Later with the adoption of Christianity by the Emperor Constantine, it was declared as the state religion and it started becoming more orthodox and conservative. Religion and sword came together. The attitudes stiffened. From ninth century the King-Pope alliance was consecrated, and Church became the legitimizer of political power. With the division of Roman Empire into two the Church also bifurcated into Roman Catholic and Eastern Orthodox. Later 11^{Th} -12 centuries saw the struggle between the clergy and supporters of secularism. During this period itself saints like St. Columbia and St. Augustine, through their modesty and attitude of service were able to spread Christianity in Britain. After renaissance the nature of Church changed and it concentrated more on the service aspect of the religion.

Islam

Islam, the second major World religion developed in Saudi Arabia in seventh sanctuary. It literally means submission. The Arab at that time was the roving tribes, very backward. They had many wars amongst themselves and were worshiping different idols. These were Semitic tribes, settled around oases and cities. "Arabia was economically and culturally connected with neighboring countries, Mesopataia, Syria, Palestine, Egypt and Ethiopia. One of the important trade crossovers was in the Meccan oasis, near the coast of Red sea. The tribal community of Koerish people profited a great deal from this trade... Caravan trade of Arabia began to decline in the sixth century, since trade routes switched to the east, Sassanid Iran. This upset the economic balance that had existed for centuries. The nomads who lost their incomes from caravan trade began to settle down and take to farming. The need for land grew and thus the clashes increased amongst the tribes." (Tokarey, 369)

The rising clashes brought in the need for unification. This is what led to the to merging of tribal cults into a community worshipping single god, Allah. In these situations Mohammad's preaching began and got a good response from the society. Essential to these teachings was the principle that there is no God but only one God, Allah, "There is no God but He: That is the witness of God, his angels and those enbued with knowledge, standing firm on justice. There is no God but He, the exalted in power, the wise. The religion before God is Islam..." (Holy Quran 3:16-17) Initially there was a big mistrust about his teachings all around. His community Koreish tribe also did not accept it easily. Merchants feared that it will reduce the imporatance of Meccaca as a trade center. This led to Mohammad and his followers going to Medina for some time, where they gathered new followers and returned to Mecca later. With the acceptance of this new religion the importance of Mecca grew all over. While many scholars see Islam as the movement of this or that group, it is better understood as a religion of various social groups in the Arab community. As per Engels, Islam was a religion, on one hand, intended for city dwellers engaged in commerce and crafts and on the other hand, for nomad Bedoins." (Engels, 1974 p. 450)

The teachings of Mohammad came in this backdrop and received hostile reception from the chief of different tribes. Some of the tribes were armed and opposed Mohammad's preaching. Mohammad formed his own army for defense and preaching. Islam in the prevailing context of society came as the revolutionary principle and united the Arab tribes into a single religious community, creating the feeling of brotherhood, resulting in emergence of Arabs as a major force. Later many a sects emerged in this religion and it spread far and wide.

The common pattern discernible in the rise of most of these religions has been a response to prevalent injustices, violence and rise in the suffering of the oppressed sections. In due course those controlling social power recognize the religion, and the institution of religion becomes and accomplice of the political powers. The saints who are not very powerful but have a substantial following amongst the poor and oppressed strata of society tend the ethical and moral component.

The period of origin of these religions is also very important. We see many of the religions coming into being in the few centuries BC to first half of first millennium AD. Very broadly one can say this was the period of massive changes in the social and political structure of society. They did mark the new era in the history of society. The pace and nature of these changes was not similar all over the world.

Last two decades have witnessed an increased abuse of religion for the political goals of imperialism and the dominant sections of society. In India the rise of RSS combine, the RSS and its offshoots working for the agenda of Hindu nation, have created an impression as if it is the Islam and Muslim which are creating the problem. In India both the religious communities have interacted and lived with each other for centuries. While the Ulema and Pundits have a particular version of other religions, the Sufi saints from Islam and Bhakti saints from Hinduism have preached harmony amongst the people. The life of religious communities had been thickly interwoven all through. The preceding decades were the one's which tried to posit the progressive values but currently the superficial religiosity and blind faith connect up and have created a mass consciousness about the Islamic terrorism along with a negative image and projection of Muslims. The social and political factors controlling the lives of religious communities are relegated to the backdrop and only religious identity and religious language is put to the fore. The history of Islam is projected to be the one of violence between two religions.

Freedom Movement and Rise of Conflicts in the name of Religion:

With the formation of Indian National Congress and it's representation of the cause of 'rising classes', and it's methods of 'protest' vis-a-vis loyalty, he (Sir Syed) got alarmed and kept aloof from this. Instead he set out to organize the Jagirdari elements amongst Muslims, and along with his followers, he propagated that Congress is meant for the interests of the Hindus and 'low born' classes. In contrast to Congress demand for representation he was for nomination of elite by the British and said that the British are the best guardians of the Muslim interests in India. Later these efforts culminated in the formation of Muslim league, which stood for the interests of Muslim landlords and Nawabs of Riyasats.

Simultaneously the principles of the Indian National Congress (INC) were being opposed by another section also. This again was the section of Hindu Jamindars, traditional tradesmen (*baniyas*) and the Rajas of Riyasats (Princely states). From 1870's , a section of Hindu zamindars, moneylenders and middle class professionals began to arouse anti-Muslim sentiments, simultaneously opposing the Congress goal of a single nation, of a common nation irrespective of religious identities. They talked of tyrannical rule of Muslim rulers and of the role of British in giving liberation from that. They came up with the formulation, that ancient, pre-Mughal, age was the golden age of India. The leader of Arya Samaj, Pandit Lekh Ram went on to condemn all forms of Islam and demanded that Muslims should be expelled from India or converted to Aryanism. They founded 'Punjab Hindu Sabha, were hostile to Indian National Congress. According to them INC's role of uniting people of different religions into a single nation meant sacrificing Hindu interests to appease Muslims. As per them Hindu is a Hindu first and than an Indian. The culmination of these efforts led to the formation of Hindu Mahasabha and later Rashtriya Swayamsevak Sangh.

British rulers realized the differences between Hindu and Muslim elite and embarked on the policy of divide-et-empera (divide and rule). With the formation of Indian National Congress, they were very uncomfortable with its' demands. Sir Syed's opposition to these demands came in handy for them and they encouraged Sir Syed and his elite followers in their 'communal demands'. British played their cards well and taking advantage of Hindu Muslim divide, they tried to snub the INC times and over again. They recognized a group of Muslim Nawabs and Jagirdars (Shimla delegation) as the representative of Muslims, and similarly encouraged the Hindu Mahasabha and RSS. None of the organisations undertook any anti-British agitation, neither were they subject repression by the British.

The declining sections of elite, Landlords and Kings resorted to the politics in the name Islam or Hinduism and that led to communal violence. This led to partition and then persistence of violence, which resurfaced in more dangerous form from the decade of 1980.

It was not religion due to which the clashes, violence and later the partition tragedy took place, it was the political interests of the declining sections of society which were couched as religious interests.

Terrorism

In the aftermath of various acts of terror, a prevalent formulation that all Muslims are not terrorists but all terrorists are Muslims is doing rounds and has become part of social common sense, but it has nothing to do with truth. Terrorism is a political process resorted to by a section of people whose democratic rights are strangulated, who perceive that the injustice which has been perpetrated on them will not get justice in the times to come and that revenge is the only option in such a situations. It is a political process and religion or a religious community has nothing to do with it. Neither any religion teaches to kill the innocents (that is what the terrorists do) nor are the terrorists the people chosen by that religious community to undertake such ghastly acts on their behalf.

The definition of terror is also not well formulated, the person appearing as terrorist, for some may sound as freedom fighter for anther set of people. The examples of Bhagat Singh, the Kashmiri militants and LTTE are few such. We have seen the ghastly terrorist acts by Khailstanis, the ULFA, the likes of Timothy McWeigh; who dropped a bomb on Oklahoma out of frustration, we also know of a Jewish bomber dropping a bomb on a Hotel in Cairo in 1942 and Buddhist monks indulging in such violent acts in Srilanka and Thailand. The backdrop of these countries will tell us the political nature of the acts and that these are not meant to serve any religion.

The trajectory of terrorism in which some Muslims have participated has roots in the oil politics at global level, in the Kashmir problem and in the rising communal problem in Indian context. The formation of Al Qaeda by U.S. to drive away the Russian armies from Afghanistan is too well known by now. The Kissinger doctrine, 'Asians should fight Asian' was employed to train Al Qaeda by CIA to fight the Soviet occupation of Afghanistan. Special Madrasas were set up, which indoctrinated a section of Muslim youth in to Jihad. The meaning given to this word was that jihad is killing of non believers, communists in this case, an innovation which worked wonder for US policy. The Muslim youth were dangled the carrot of 72 virgins in Jannat once they lay down their life in pursuance of the US goal of capturing Afghanistan after evicting the Soviet armies.

The demonization of Islam and Muslims began with the US propaganda in the wake of Ayatollah's revolution in Iran and it was systematically built up with every US intervention in the West Asia, attack on Iraq, the occupation of Afghanistan the occupation of Iraq and also after the Al Qaeda attack on WTC. The demonization of Islam and Muslims has been a very systematic process akin to demonization of communists in the cold war era, McCarthyism and the accompanying propaganda. Noam Chomsky explains this doctrine as 'manufacturing consent' for the goals of US foreign policy, which are achieved by US administration through various mechanisms, media being the central key to this doctoring of mass consciousness. This and other means employed by US administration to demonize Muslims has been outlined very well by Mahmood Mamdani's 'Good Muslim Bad Muslim' and by Tariq Ali in 'Clash of Fundamentalisms' and 'Bush in Babylon', where both these researchers have given the details of US policymakers documents and the mechanism to demonize the targeted country and the people.

The earlier goal of offsetting the Soviet influence and to keep hegemony on the world was achieved by all methods of propaganda where by Communists who were fighting for various anti- colonial, anti imperialist goals were presented as the enemies of democracy and freedom. Now in pursuance of the goal to dominate the West Asian oil zones, anti Muslim, Anti Islam has become the central point of propaganda. The 'ideological' foundation of this was laid by Samuel Huntington who in his book Clash of Civilizations puts forward the thesis that the backward Islamic civilization is the real threat to the advanced and democratic western civilization. This global anti Islamism of US finds its supplement in the RSS ideology. Incidentally when US was hunting communists, at that time RSS chief was writing to the home minister in his mercy petition to seek release from the jail in the aftermath of Gandhi's murder by RSS trained swayamsevak. The Sarsanghchalak of RSS that time wrote that if he is released from jail he will give all the cooperation to the Govt to fight against the communists. Today again, the US designs of anti Islamism match very well with the RSS designs here in India.

The popular psyche is shaped by multiple factors. There is not much time to get to the roots of the issues and so the superficial incidents form the basis of judgments and understanding of the people at large. While those with motives and agenda for dominating the world/ society play their games from behind the curtain, an Osama or a Kashmiri militant is visible as holding the AK47 or RDX in his hands, and here the popular understanding takes a full stop unable to see that Osama is the creation of US, or a petty terrorist is insanely avenging the stifling of democracy or violation of the treaty of accession in Kashmir, or a volunteer of Gujarat Muslim Revenge group is insanely avenging the genocide perpetrated against his community. Interestingly in this discourse there is no place for the bomb makers of Bajrang Dal, the RSS affiliates, in Nanded and so the powers that be prefer to sleep on the issue and keep arresting hundreds of Muslim youth, as by now the popular psyche, Government machinery and more particularly police has imbibed the myth that Islam promotes terrorism and that all terrorists are Muslims!

Themes of Relevance:

The major confusion in study of religion is the confusion created by the language of politics. It has tried to project as if there is a clash between the religions, between civilizations. On the contrary the civilizations have been interacting and adopting to each other, learning from each other. While the precise theological elaboration may be expressed differently in different religions, the values enunciated by different religions have a good deal of overlap and similarity. These are values of love, compassion, brotherhood, peace and justice find their expression in most of the religions. So while theology has to be understood in the proper light, the emphasis has to be on the values of that religion. The emphasis has to be to see the teachings of the founders of these religions before they get institutionalized by the clergy, which becomes a vested interest group and associates with those in power to maintain the exploitative political system. The spirituality of the religions as expressed by the saints of that religion again are very accommodating and respectful of others religion. Most of the Saints of the religions expressed this spirituality and attracted the people from all the religions to their fold.

At the same time the kings distorted and appropriated the religious institutions for continuation of their powers. They also used the words like crusade, jihad and dharmayudha for their ambitions of power. Same way today's politics managed by the superpowers is using religion for its selfish goals. Humanity as such has picked up from different religious values and moved on to recognize the equality of people of all religions, it has also recognized that there is amity amongst different people cutting across their regions and religions.

Religions: Clash or Alliance

Most of the religions came as a set of moral vales to guide the people to cultivate the feelings of love for mankind. There began a process of institutionalization of religions to ensure that these values are sustained and percolated to the broad layers of people. At the same time the emphasis on rituals began to be heavier while the focus and emphasis on moral values took a back seat. There have been numerous attempts to ensure that the basic unity between people of different religions is sustained though the efforts of saints and others who preached the values of humanism in right earnest. Today the vested interests have launched the efforts to suppress the weaker section of society and weaker nations for the sake of their material interests. As these attempts are undertaken in the name of religion a feeling of alienation amongst people overtakes the real spirit of religion.

Here at home those associated with RSS and politics in the name of Hindutva have been spreading the hate amongst different communities. The result is there for all to see. In India this hate has been spread against Muslims and Christians both. World wide and in India Muslims have been projected to be fanatics, aggressors, having more wives, converting through sword etc. This has resulted in a broad social common sense which see Muslims as the 'other', there demonization, the consequent violence at different places even on the smallest of pretexts, the fear and insecurity leading to their ghettoisation. At global level the US has been resorting to War against terror which is a ploy to attack the areas in oil rich countries and to create a global Islamophobia. World wide this hate against Muslims is on the rise. In India the problem is worst confounded as the US goals worldwide and RSS goals at home match and worsen the problem.

In India even the tiny minority of Christians has been accused of conversions through allurement and fraud. As matter of fact the population of Christians is declining from last four decades (1971-2.60%, 1981-2.44%, 1991-2.32% and 2001-2.30 %), despite that a sustained scattered attacks on Christian missionaries is on the rise.

The responsible people of different faiths do realize that this is not in tune with the spirit of their religion. They are watching helplessly this whole process of demonization of certain religious communities and the social rifts being created due to that. Faith in the values of humanism is paramount in the values of religion. This current scenario is pushing back the aspirations of poor people and so it is needed that the situation is overcome for the sake of better world, for the sake of peace and amity. While the political forces bent upon creating this mayhem are very powerful and almighty, have control over resources of different types and on media, the people with genuine faith in human values need to come forward to ensure that this dark phase of human history is overcome in the spirit of dialogue. The need for inter community relations and dialogue was never needed more than at present times.

The isolation due to this political process is not only creating emotional walls amongst different communities, it is also resulting in the retardation of social development. The kernel of present efforts for peace lies in the process of building bridges amongst communities and that process can be started only by a genuine dialogue amongst people of different faiths, by coming close to each other by abolishing the artificial boundaries created by the politics of hate being practiced by various forces, globally and locally.

These dialogues amongst different religious communities are needed at all the levels, starting from the basti, mohalla (localities) to the leadership of religions, scholars of religions, the activists engaged in dispelling hate from the society, and those working for human rights, all of them need to be involved in this process of dialogue. The present impasse which is presenting religions as the separating points need to be overcome and the understanding that religious differences and plural ways of life are a strength not an obstacle to peace.

We need to look into the recent high level committee of UN which went on to counter the thesis of Clash of civilizations put forward by the US professor Samuel Huntington. This thesis forms the cover for US ambitions for its aggressions in West Asia. The UN committee (http://www.unaoc.org/repository/report.htm) has put forward that there is no clash between civilizations, as a matter of fact civilization have an alliance for a better tomorrow. On the similar lines one will like to say that there is no clash between the moral values of religions, it is the alliance between these values that the human race can look forward to a better future, a future which will eliminate poverty, hunger, disease and misery from the world. It is this alliance which will ensure that the focus of world policies has to be brought back to the issue of Human rights of weaker sections of society. Nothing short of a genuine dialogue amongst people of different faiths can overcome the obstacles created by the political forces misusing the religious identity for their political goals.

Future Directions:

With the realization that theologically the primacy is that of moral values and that the present scenario is due to political factors, we can ensure that religious communities interact with each other and promote amicable atmosphere. The issues like Kashmir, Indo Pak relations have to be resolved in a peaceful manner with dialogues and respect for each others faith and values. The promotion of study of humane aspects of religions will go a long way to ensure the amity between people across different countries and the religions. It is necessary the people across the World put a brake on the politics of intimidation and aggression leading to the genesis of terrorism. With this an enhanced sense of security will bring in the peace and theology will have its real moral impact on the society. Society and state should focus on the values given by religions and these values should be made the base of dialogue on equal footing.

References

Engineer Asghar Ali, Medieval History and Communalism, Center for Study of Society and Secularism, 1996 Mumbai,

Fredrich Engels, Zur Geshinchte des Unchristentums, in Karl Marx, Fredrichs Engels, Werke, Band 22, Dietz Verlag, Berlin, 1974 p. 450

Gail Omvedt, Dalit Visions, Orient Longmans, Hydrabad, 1995, p 7-12

Geetesh Sharma, Dharma Ke naam Par, Rajkamal, New Delhi, 2003, p.18

Karl Marx and Fredric Engels, Collected Works (Russian Edition, Vol 22, p.483, quoted in Tokarey, p. 330

M.Harlombos, Sociology: Themes and Perspectives, OUP Delhi 1994, 455

Progress Publishers, A dictionary for Believers and non Believers, Moscow 1989

Puniyani; Ram, Religion Power and Violence, Sage, New Delhi, 2005

Sergi Tokarey, Progress Publishers Moscow, 1986, p. 9 http://en.wikipedia.org/wiki/Theology

2

Religious Pluralism and Peaceful Coexistence

During last three decades Worldwide in general and in India in particular, there has been a great deal of intolerance for others' religious tradition. Globally the theory of clash of civilizations is based on the clash between religious traditions, and locally the politics of RSS combine, the Hindutva also builds itself on the dislike, demonization and hate for others religious traditions.

Medieval Times

As such India has been a country with multiple religious and cultural traditions living and interacting peacefully in the society. While kings had been fighting with each other for the sake of power the average people interacted with each other, cutting across religious lines and created the humane syncretic traditions.

The diversity of Indian society has been a rich source of strength and resilience of the community. Though it is true that kings fought amongst each other for larger control of Territories, the average people, the toilers, the downtrodden of both the religions celebrated the interaction with each other. While the kings had bigger preoccupations with expansion or preservation of their kingdoms for their material benefit, the large chunk of society derived the pleasure from their social and community life. While different sectors of nobility were more interested in consolidating their political powers and humiliating the other, different creative layers of society: poets, laureates, architects, performing artists, folk artists and painters integrated the other streams into their art, and went on to enrich the art itself in the process.

RELIGION: Biggest synthetic trends are discernible in the popular religions, Bhakti from Hindu side and Sufi from the side of Islam are the major religious trends to have come up in this period. Kabir, Nanak and Tulsidas reflected the synthetic trends and the influence of both major religious trends to have come up in this period. Kabir, Nanak and Tulsidas reflected the synthetic trends and the influence of both religions in their lives and works.

Kabir, rejected Sanskrit, the language of elite Brahmins and communicated with people in simple Hindi and reflected the building of bridges between the two communities. In one of his *Sabda* he goes on to say that just as ornaments are different manifestation of some basic product, gold, so Allah, Ram, Rahim, and Hari were all different names of the same god. *Puja* offered by Hindus and Namaz offered by Muslims are just different methods of adoration of the same God. Kabir was a harsh critic of institutionalised religions and the religious traditions which divided people. He was a critic of the mullahs and pandits in equal measures, and the social evils which had infested the society in the name of religion like caste system and untouchability :his teachings spread amongst vast followers of major religious trends to have come up in this period. Kabir, Nanak and Tulsidas reflected the synthetic trends and the influence of both religions in their lives and works teachings spread amongst vast sections of weavers and others, cutting across both the religions.

Tulsidas another poet sage of this time in an autobiographical couplet shows how the religious synthesis was operating at this time:

> A slave of Ram is Tulsi,
> What ever they say let them say.
> On alms I live, the mosque is my refuge,
> my give and take with the world is done.
>
> (Tulsidas: from Kavitavali)

One of the biggest Ram bhakts of the time was living in a mosque, from where most of his devotional works for lord Ram emanated. Guru Nanak was for peace in the society, influenced by ideas of Kabir and was a strong proponent of syncretism. He tried to unite Hinduism and Islam by adopting beliefs from both these religions, borrowing from Islam, it believes in one God Islam by adopting beliefs from both these religions. Borrowing from Islam, it believes in one God and prohibits image worship. From Hinduism it adopted the theory of reincarnation and karma according to which a persons actions determine his fate in future incarnations. It was against the caste system. Their holy- book Adi Granth quotes extensively from Kabir and Sufi saints like Baba Farid. Also one of the Sufi saints Mir Miyan was requested to lay the foundation stone of the Golden temple.

Sufis attracted a large following among the lower classes and castes. It was their unorthodox and simple lifestyle which attracted large number of low castes to convert to Islam. Their majors (holy places) were open to all irrespective of their religious following. Sufis were basically upholding the spiritual side of Islam, and it can be said that it was a revolt against the rigidities of Islam, propagated mainly by the Ulema. One of the great Sufi saints Muhiuddin Ibn Arabi founded the doctrine of Wahahdat-al-wujud i.e. Unity of being, which promoted spiritual universalism, in turn demolishing the barriers of caste founded the doctrine of Wahahdat-al-wujud i.e. Unity of being, which promoted spiritual universalism, in turn demolishing the barriers of caste and creed. This doctrine states that the real being is One and we are all its manifestations, this brought in harmony amongst followers of different religions.

It is interesting to note that Sufi saints writings were very close to the people. Baba Farid wrote poetry in Punjabi and his writings are a part of Granth Sahib, the holy book of the Sikhs. Baba Farids most distinguished follower was Nizamuddin Auliya, who proudly used to say that there were as many ways of worshipping God as there are particles of sand. He was very fond of listening to bhajans, being touched equally by bhajans and quawallis. His respect for local traditions was tremendous. One small story will illustrate as to how he was away from Islamic orthodoxy and had great respect for local traditions.

"One day he was passing through the bank of Jamuna in Delhi, along with his disciple, the famous poet Khusrau, and saw some Hindu women bathing in the Jamuna and offering prayers to the sun. To this his disciple, the famous poet Khusrau, and saw some Hindu women bathing inthe Jamuna and offering prayers to the sun. To this Hazrat Nizamuddin said, O Khusrau, these women are also praying to Allah; they have their own way of prayer; and then he recited a verse from Quran: "And every one has a direction to which one turns, so vie with one another in good works" (from A.A Engineer, Sufism and Interfaith Harmony: Institute of Islamic Studies, March 4, 95)

Asghar Ali Engineer points out "Ulema often denounced all those who followed religions other than Islam as kafirs, where as sufis respected similar spiritual practices in all other religions and showed utmost respect for them" (A.A Engineer, above paper). Similarly Mazhar Jan-I-Janan was a Sufi theologian of repute who was again a great upholder of respect for others traditions. Dara Shikoh, the heir of Jahangirs throne, who was murdered by his own brother for the sake of power was a great Sanskrit scholar who had studied the Hindu scriptures at depth and had written a book called as Majmaul Baharayn (The meeting of the two great oceans, Hinduism and Islam). In this book he compared the Islamic and Sufi Phraseology and that of Hinduism and shows that there is much in common between the two.

The interaction of the practice of these two religions has been very well summarised by well known scholar Dr.B.N Pandey, "Islam and Hinduism which appeared at the start so antithetical, at last intermingled, each one stirred the profoundest depth of the other and from their synthesis grew the religion of Bhakti and Tasawwaf, the religion of love and devotion, which swept the hearts of millions following different religions and sects in India. The current of Islamic Sufism and Hindu Bhakti combined into a mighty stream which fertilised old desolate tracts and changed the face of the country. It was this spirit of India which achieved apparently an impossible task of reconciling the puritanical severity and awe inspiring transcendence of Islam into luxuriant fullness and abundance of form and the intuitive perception of there immanent unity with Hinduism, and created those monuments of art, luxuriant fullness and abundance of form and the intuitive perception of there immanent unity with Hinduism, and created those monuments of art, literature, painting, music and poetry and love inspired religion which are the heritage of Indian History, during the middle ages."

CULTURE: Due to interaction of the Muslim kings, Islam and local culture there developed a whole stream of synthetic culture in all walks of life, in music khayal, ghazal and thumri are outstanding contributions of these interactions. North Indian classical music as known today is a thorough blend of Hindu and Muslim elements achieved over 500 years. Ibrahim second Adishahi of Bijapur (1580-1626) had 300 Hindu singers in his court. To popularise this music among Muslims he himself composed Kitab-e-Naurang in Urdu (a book containing 59 poems) and of those the first one is an invocation of goddess Saraswati). Chaitanya Maha prabhu and most of the Vaishnav saint poets influenced many Muslims to write in their idiom. Rahim and Raskhan are among the very popular Hindi poets who have written in Brij-bhasha in praise of lord Krishna. Syed Wazid Shah wrote Hir-Ranja the greatest classic of medieval times. Sheikh Mohammed has greatly contributed to Marathi literature and Shivaji's guru (saint teacher) Ramdas said that Sheikh Mohammed has greatly contributed to Marathi literature and had special words of praise for him.

Mixture of Persian dialect with Western Hindi spoken in and around Delhi produced a new language which later on came to be called as Urdu. There were great Hindu scholars who took to Urdu not only as administrative language but also wrote and contributed to Urdu literature. Hindu architecture was masked by profusion of intricate sculptured detail, while Islamic architecture was notable for elegance and lightness. The fusion of the two got manifested in different architectural marvels which came up during this phase. This fusion is seen in Jodhabais palace in Agra fort, in Fatehpur Sikri, and in arches of Kuwat-ul-Islam mosque. The influence of this mixture is discernible far and wide in the havelis of Rajasthan and Madhya Pradesh and the Indo-Saracenic architecture of Jodhpur, Bikaner and Jaisalmer. Similarly fusion of Persian techniques and brilliant Hindu colors resulted in the type of miniature painting marked by beauty and lyricism. by beauty and lyricism.

One of the most valuable relics of the harmony of mediaeval society which has survived the onslaughts of different communal forces is Sufi dargah (shrine). These dargahs are scattered in many a cities, managed by Hindu or Muslim families and visited by people of all religions, unmindful of the communal venom being poured by practitioners of communal politics. Right near Mumbai, Haji Malang shrine is a very good expression of syncretic ethos of medieval times. The hereditary trustee of the shrine is the Kailashnath Gopal Ketkar (a Brahmin). The offerings given at the shrine are a mixture of Hindu and Muslim traditions. Devotees offer chaddars, coconuts, flower and sheets of flower. To add on to this the many a Christian churches also became a place of pilgrimage for people of all the religions like Mount Mary Church in Mumbai amongst many others.

Such examples are numerous and scattered all over. Today there is a conscious attempt to downplay such a valuable tradition and to harp upon the differences of the elite and the rulers. There is a need to look at the truth as a whole. There is a need to observe the richness of these syncretic traditions which are a rich tribute to our communities love, respect and tolerance for each other. These syncretic traditions which are a rich tribute to our communities love, respect and tolerance for each other.

Modern India

The concept of Indian Nationalism began with the introduction of modern industries and modern education system. These profound changes in India resulted in the rise of many new social classes, businessmen–industrialists, educated classes and workers. They formed their associations; the political expression of these new classes was Indian National Congress.

With the formation of this political outfit, which strove for the interests of these new rising classes, the declining classes of landlord, kings and associated clergy of both the religions, Hindus and Muslims, came together to form United India Patriotic Association (UIPA), which pledged its loyalty to British rule and opposed the formation of Congress on the ground that 'our' religion teaches us to be loyal to the king (queen in this case) and the action of Congress tantamount to disloyalty to British.

It is from this period on that communal violence started in India and foundations of communal politics were laid. This formation, UIPA later gave birth to religion based communal streams, Muslim League, Punjab Hindu Sabha and Hindu Mahasabha. Later from amongst the Brahmins, RSS came into being. People like Bhagat Singh (Hindustan Socialist Republican Association) Dr. Bhimrao Babasaheb Ambedkar (Republican Party of India, and Maulana Abul Kalam Azad, Mahatma Gandhi, Annie Besant etc (Indian National Congress) strove for democratic/socialist nationalism and contributed in different ways for the freedom of the country and participated in the freedom movement. While people like Mohammad Ali Jinnah (Muslim League) Vinayak Damodar Savarkar (Hindu Mahasabha) and RSS (Hindu Rashtra) talked of the old glories of their religions and opposed the movement for secular Indian nationalism. Savarkar was anti British revolutionary till 1906, but after getting himself released from Andmans, he never participated in the anti British movement. Jinnah initially joined Congress but later when Gandhi gave the call for non cooperation movement he distanced himself from Congress and much later joined and led Muslim League.

People like Bhagat Singh, Gandhi and Ambedkar saw India as a nation in the making while Muslim league argued that Muslims are a nation from the time since Mohammad bin Kasim attacked and ruled Sindh from 8th Century. Savarkar argued that Hindus are a nation from times immemorial and RSS later went to say that Muslims have to live here as a subordinate nation. The streams deriving their identity from religion acted as the ideal foil for British policy of 'divide-and-rule'. The average people of India did not support communal streams. Only an insignificant section of Muslim supported Muslim league and the demand for Pakistan. Similarly a miniscule section of Hindus supported Hindu mahasabha. The partition tragedy took place mainly due to British policy of divide and rule supplemented by the decisive politics spread by ML, HM and RSS. Since these streams did not get popular support they started spreading hate against the other community.

Muslim League, Muslim communalists propagated that Hindus are cowards, we ruled them, they kafirs etc. Hindu Mahsabha/RSS picked up from British historiography to propagate through various mechanisms and more so through Shakha baudhhis that Muslim kings destroyed Hindu temples, Islam was spread by sword, Muslims committed lot of atrocities on Hindus, they marry four times, produce many children and kill cows that are an object of worship for Hindus. These myths about other communities were the ground on which communal violence stood and social and political atmosphere started getting vitiated and communal violence and divisive atmosphere started affecting the national scene. This aided in the partition process. This propagation about other community totally ignored the plural and diverse nature of Indian society. It totally bypassed the syncretic values, bhakti-Sufi of Indian tradition and harped on the differences of the elite.

Indian constitution came to express the values of freedom movement and was based on the concepts of Liberty, Equality and Fraternity. The communal streams believe in the hierarchy of caste and gender, though in a subtle form. Muslim elite inherently believed in the Ashraf, Azlaf and Arzal at caste level and the inferiority of women at gender level. The hierarchy of Hindu caste system, Brahmin, Khstriaya, Vaishya and Shudra was put forward as the glorious way of organizing the society and inferiority of women was reflected in the word, Rashtra Sevaka Samiti the subordinate women's organization where the word swayam is missing, in contrast to Rashtriya Swaymaseva Sangh which is the real controller of the other subordinate hindutva organizations.

Pakistan, the result primarily of British machinations was formed on the basis of Islam, and India on secular grounds. Pakistan toeing the religion based nationalism broke into two, Pakistan and Bangla Desh, while India though formed on the grounds of secular democracy is being severely threatened by the growing strength of RSS, Hindu nationalism and its impact on the cultural and political arena in India. It got manifested in the form of ascendance of divisive politics, demolition of Babri masjid, post demolition violence, burning of Pastor Stains, Gujarat carnage, and the blasts all around. The concept of secular democracy has been maligned, efforts are being made to demonize the minorities, their being part of Indian society is being questioned and in the whole milieu the social progress is being retarded.

Current Times

In India one has seen the intensification of violence in the name of religion more so from last two decades. After Babri demolition a wave of violence rocked the nation. In 1998, a Pastor working amongst leprosy patients was burnt alive along with his two innocent sons. Anti Christian violence has been the marker of our times. The burning of Sabramati express in Godhra followed by the massive anti Muslim violence, the genocide, was another blot on the national life. The 9/11 events, resulted in the death of close to three thousand people of all religions. Along with this came the thesis that current time is the one of clash of civilizations, the backward Islamic civilization is out to destroy the advanced Western civilization. One can see the underlining element of the attempt to relate the violence and religion in some form or the other.

Along with this came the misunderstanding about other religions. This misunderstanding has assumed mammoth proportions today and it provides the base for the violence and the policy of aggressions/acts of violence and terror. There is a clear need to understand the difference between religion and politics, there is a need to understand the rise of violence from these misconceptions.

Most of the religions came as a set of moral values to guide the people to cultivate the feelings of love for mankind. There began a process of institutionalization of religions to ensure that these values are sustained and percolated to the broad layers of people. At the same time the emphasis on rituals began to be heavier while the focus and emphasis on moral values took a back seat. Over a period of time the institutional rigidities and ritual, identity part of religion has undermined the moral values of religions. There have been numerous attempts to ensure that the basic unity between people of different religions is sustained though the efforts of saints and others who preached the values of humanism in right earnest.

Today the vested interests have launched the efforts to suppress the weaker section of society and weaker nations for the sake of their material interests. As these attempts are undertaken in the name of religion a feeling of alienation amongst people overtakes the real spirit of religion.

Here at home those associated with RSS and politics in the name of Hindutva have been spreading the hate amongst different communities. The result is there for all to see. This hate has been spread against Muslims and Christians both.

Muslims have been projected to be fanatics, aggressors, having more wives, converting through sword and being more loyal to Pakistan. This has resulted in a broad social common sense which sees Muslims as the 'other', their demonization, the consequent violence at different places even on the smallest of pretexts, the fear and insecurity leading to their ghettoisation. At global level the US has been resorting to War against terror which is a ploy to attack the areas in oil rich countries and to create a global Islamophobia. World wide this hate against Muslims is on the rise. In India the problem is worst confounded as the US goals worldwide and RSS goals at home match and worsen the problem. In many a Muslim majority countries similar processes are going on against the other religious minorities.

In India even the tiny minority of Christians has been accused of conversions through allurement and fraud. As a matter of fact the population of Christians is declining from last four decades (1971-2.60%, 1981-2.44%, 1991-2.32% and 2001-2.30 %), despite that a sustained scattered attacks on Christina missionaries is on the rise. Similarly the myths against Muslim minorities have no truth but have captured the minds of people, the destruction of holy places done by kings in the past for the sake of power and wealth is being presented as the insult of faith, the conversions in the past are being presented as due to coercion, the demographic profile which is due to social factors is being shown to be due to religion, the loyalty to other nations is a mere propaganda meant to suit their political goals, and that all Muslims are terrorists also does not hold any water as neither is terrorism due to religion nor all terrorists belong to Muslims.(LTTE, ULFA, Khalistainis, Irish Republican Army and so on)

Way to Humane Future

The responsible people of different faiths do realize that this is not in tune with the spirit of their religion. They are watching helplessly this whole process of demonization of certain religious communities and the social rifts being created due to that. Faith in the values of humanism is paramount in the values of religion. This current scenario is pushing back the aspirations of poor people and so it is needed that the situation is overcome for the sake of better world, for the sake of peace and amity. While the political forces bent upon creating this mayhem are very powerful and almighty, have control over resources of different types and on media, the people with genuine faith in human values need to come forward to ensure that this dark phase of human history is overcome in the spirit of dialogue. The need for inter community relations and dialogue was never needed more than at present times.

The isolation due to this political process is not only creating emotional walls amongst different communities, it is also resulting in the retardation of social development. The kernel of present efforts for peace lies in the process of building bridges amongst communities and that process can be started only by a genuine dialogue amongst people of different faiths, by coming close to each other by abolishing the artificial boundaries created by the politics of hate being practiced by various forces, globally and locally.

These dialogues amongst different religious communities are needed at all the levels, starting from the basti, mohalla to the leadership of religions, scholars of religions, the activists engaged in dispelling hate from the society, and those working for human rights, all of them need to be involved in this process of dialogue. The present impasse which is presenting religions as the separating points need to be overcome and the understanding that religious differences and plural ways of life are a strength not an obstacle to peace. The dialogue amongst religions needs to be supplemented by the cooperation in the field of social work to alleviate the pain and misery of the mankind, there is a need to encourage and coordinate in the field of struggles for the human rights of deprived sections of society. We aspire for peace and we remind ourselves that the peace desired by us can not be achieved without justice for the people. Justice is a mandatory prerequisite for peace. The spirit of service to mankind has to prevail over the current assault on the basic human values in the name of religion.

We need to look into the recent high level committee of UN which went on to counter the thesis of Clash of civilizations put forward by the US professor Samuel Huntington. This thesis forms the cover for US ambitions for its aggressions in West Asia. The UN committee (http://www.unaoc.org/repository/report.htm)has put forward that there is no clash between civilizations, as a matter of fact civilization have an alliance for a better tomorrow. On the similar lines one will like to say that there is no clash between the moral values of religions, it is the alliance between these values that the human race can look forward to a better future, a future which will eliminate poverty, hunger, disease and misery from the world. Religions should be standing for love and peace. One posits that there cannot be peace without justice and so the implication is that religions should address the issues not only of poverty but also of the system which creates poverty, it just does not talk of superficial manifestation of the problems but to go to the root of prevalent problems and to raise the voice against perpetrators of injustices. Religions have to raise the issues of human rights of all people of the World. It is this alliance which will ensure that the focus of world policies has to be brought back to the issue of Human rights of weaker sections of society. Nothing short of a genuine dialogue amongst people of different faiths can overcome the obstacles created by the political forces misusing the religious identity for their political goals.

India is essentially a plural, multicultural, multi-religious nation. The tasks for secular movement are huge, we need to retrieve the values of freedom movement from the clutches of communal politics, politics in the name of religion. We need to reconnect with the plural, mixed heritage and cultural diversity of the country. We need to strengthen the syncretic aspects of religious traditions, the traditions which look at religion as a uniting force, not a divisive disrupter.

3

Secularism, Secularization and Human Rights

Current times have seen the rise of new paradigms in the arena of political discourse. The accepted terminologies got challenged and new one's got rooted in the popular psyche. The established norms, Secularism, democracy got challenged by the politics of Hindu right. The talk of Hindu nation, Hindutva came to the fore. The concept of duties started getting more prominence. The compromising practices of ruling party were distorted to put doubts on the very concept of the gains of India's freedom movement, the one's related to secular democracy.

What does secularism mean, is it is western, or is it modern? Is it alien to Indian values? Secularism as a social phenomenon emerged with the rise of industrial society. From 17th century discoveries of science were challenging deeply held beliefs and faiths, which were integral part of the broad canvas of religion. The application of these technologies and rise of industrial societies necessitated the change in social equilibrium, which was then prevalent. The earlier society where agriculture was the dominant production activity and 'feudal' mode of production was prevalent; the major sectors of society were tied to land as poor peasants. Demands of newly developing industries required the peasants to be freed from land. What tied them to land was feudal social structure and the concomitant ideological constructs, which were again part of the religion in the broad sense of the term. The clergy (Church is the most organized form of the same but similar role is played by Brahmins, and Mullahs also) supplemented the feudal structure, 'kingdoms' and fulfilled the need to ensure firm implementation of the ideology, which supplemented the feudal production norms. This was the time when social life was revolving around the dictates of the clergy.

Industrialization

With onset of industrialization process, the earlier ideological chains proved to be obstacles to the emerging industrial society. It is in this realm that one has to understand the loosening hold of clergy and some religious traditions in social life. One has to understand the social norms developing around modern rationality, ideas from science i.e. the beginning of 'age of reason', in contrast to 'age of faith'. The farmer having its roots in science and technology and later in the clergy's interpretation of the word of God, clergy's imposition of ideologies in the name of religion, clergy's use of emotions of people for smoothening the exploitative social system of feudalism. Historically this process first occurred in clear form in West, where the above phenomenon manifested itself in the struggle between church and the state. Church stood for the declining social force of feudal lords, stood for age of faith, while the emerging nation state" (vis-à-vis kingdom) stood for 'age of reason', for industrialization process based on science and technology, concretizing newer social relations (industrialists and the workers) in the process. This process which was called

'Enlightenment' and is a part of secularization process began as radical rationalist critique of some facets of religion, especially those pertaining to the mediation between people and God by the clergy. This process assumed the undisguised role of displacing aspects of religion and faith (manufactured by clergy) to the private lives of people, freeing the social life from the constraints of orthodoxy and obscurantism towards the emerging realms of modernity.

Secularism

Thus secularism is a product of social movement of industrial bourgeoisie and landless peasants, manifested initially (in West) as Renaissance and Enlightenment, being the expression of man's urge to live life of his own, independent of the domination by Church, which was prevalent feature of medieval society. Starting from this premise secularism assumed a socio historical context in mid nineteenth century, shaped by circumstances and philosophy of the time. Secularism was based on the values, which recognized the contribution of science as a major source of knowledge and considered technological progress, social amelioration and human welfare as the goals of life. The goals of life shifted to this world (secular, profane) from the other world (sacred). With crumbling of dogmas and supernaturalism under the wheels of science and reason, the repository of dogmas, the clergy took a back seat and modern secular democratic states began to occupy the 'drivers' seats. Secular ethos is not concerned about the other world (leaving them as a merry hunting ground for the custodians of dogmas, the clergy). In a sense secularism is the policy of modern nation-state, it is philosophy of secularization process. A process through which man becomes a free person from his earlier domination by the blind faiths imposed on the society by the clergy to ensure the smooth running of kingdoms, which require divine legitimacy, conferred on them by clergy, to continue their crass exploitation of the peasantry, which is the main source of their wealth. Secularization introduces instrumental values, rational procedures and technological methods, which bring along urbanization, pragmatism, profanity, pluralism and mutual respect. Secularization process brings in the ideas that all value systems are a product of historical circumstances, without any claims of finality. As a part of the package, science replaces supernatural explanation of things with those in terms of natural laws and an intellectual attitude in which reality is accounted from worldly mode of thinking.

Colonization

Those nations, which industrialized initially, went out to colonize other countries, especially in Asia, Africa and South America. India was colonized mainly by British, small portions by Portuguese and French. British 'plunder project' aimed at taking away the raw materials from here and creating markets for their goods. In order to do these, they set up new ventures here in agrarian, commercial and industrial arenas. In these, Indians first acted as subordinates but soon took to modern technologies and with this a new class of merchants, bankers, landlords, industrialists, plantation owners and brokers came into being. Introduction of English education in 1835 was meant to produce a class of clerks and administrators. This changing social dynamics laid the foundation of the new phenomenon of 'nationalism'. In a very elementary form this changed scenario formed the backdrop for rise of different reform movements and new associations and unions of economic, social and political nature on the western pattern. In due course, the intelligentsia started demanding widening of franchise, simultaneous examinations for administrative services, Indianization of services. And in this demand of theirs' emerging industrialists supported them adding their own demands for increased facilities for industrialization in India. A spirit of Indian consciousness started emerging for the first time and this was due to a combination of various factors like material demands of newly emerging classes (professionals, businessmen, industrialists).

Modern education, communication (railways, telegraphs, free press), hatred for British racial arrogance, economic exploitation, weaknesses of judiciary were the initial features of British rule. The process unleashed by British was pregnant with contradictory features. Free press created a strong impetus for the rise of national consciousness. This led to the formation of many local regional associations aimed at voicing the grievances of emerging elite and projecting their vision of 'nation'.. Some of these associations were, the Bombay association, Madras natives association, Pune Sarvajanik Sabha and Madras Mahajan Sabha. The major meeting of these associations started taking place and the one such which took place in Calcutta in 1883 was the precursor of the formation of the INC (Indian National Congress) in 1886.

India: Nation in the Making:

Indian National Congress expressed the ambitions of these associations and rising classes and asked for holding of Indian civil service exam in India, more facilities for the Industry and commerce and land reforms. The basic principles of INC (Indian National Congress) were eradication of race, creed and provincial prejudices, and encouragement of natives in the political process.

In reaction to this Sir Syed and Raja Sheo Prasad of Kashi formed United India Patriotic Association (August 1888). The aim of this association was to convey to the British that all communities and aristocracies are not with Congress, to convey the views of Hindu and Muslim organisations to the British Parliament and to strengthen the rule of British in India, to wean away people from Congress. Many a people associated with this association were later to be part of Muslim League and Hindu Mahasabha. The mix of these processes and secular organisation being thrown up was described by Surendranath Banerjea and Lokmanya Tilak as '***India is a nation in the making***' meaning thereby that it is a representation of common interests of Indian people vis-a-vis the colonial power. At this time reformers like Rammohan Roy were asking for abolition of abominable practices like Sati. Phule at this time was calling for taking to modern education and women's education. Pandita Ramabai took up the cause of women's education. Phule also laid the foundation of a Non-Brahmin movement aimed against the social power of Jamindar-Brahmin nexus. Later Ambedkar was to pickup the threads of this movement and struggle for the rights of the untouchables.

Communalism:

Rise of communalism has been a very complex process. Colonial policies generated the growth and economic domination of merchant-money lenders (by and large Hindus). Hindus could take maximum advantage of modern education and accordingly, a place in bureaucracy. Post 1857 anti Muslim bias of British gave slight edge to Hindus, who took to modern enterprises/ professions with great keenness. British Historians used the categories Hindu, Muslim, and Brahmin etc. Indian Historians picked up only two of these categories, Hindu and Muslim. Indian leadership used religious consciousness to inculcate 'Modern nationalism amongst the people, e.g. Ram Rajya, Khilafat. This resulted in two processes: (a) arousal of nationalism (b) arousal of communalism. We will shortly see that communalism arose due to the politics of Muslim feudal lords, Hindu Jamindars and British policy of divide and rule.

The secularization of society though slow, its political reflection in the freedom struggle and the National movement was dominantly secular, though communal (Muslim and Hindu) nationalisms also came up in the wake as a reaction to the growth of secular nationalism. Initially secularization process got reflected in movements of Jotiba Phule, Savitribai Phule and other radical reformers. Secular nationalism was finding expression in the politics of Gandhi and Nehru while Muslim communalism found expression in the politics of Muslim league and Hindu communalism was manifested in Hindu Mahasabha and RSS. Some of the Hindu nationalists were the part of Indian National Congress as well. The social base of Muslim Communal nationalism was Muslim zamindars and moneylenders; similarly Hindu communal nationalism had its base in Brahmin, Bania (caste level), Hindu zamindar & moneylenders (at class level). Secular nationalism was rooted amongst the nascent industrialists, newer professionals and, vast sections of peasantry and the low castes. It was the aspirations of these classes, which gave strength to freedom struggle and were translated in the foundation of Indian State and its constitution. Thus secularism as a principle of this society was not an artificial graft but a result of the struggles of the rising industrial class and the section of peasantry and the dalits.

Secularism- Western or Modern

To see secularism as a principle of Christian west is a very simplistic way of looking at social phenomenon. It is true that for a brief while church possessed state power and controlled it, kings of Europe were subordinate to it for some time and then they revolted against the authority of the church to set them free. As pointed out above secularism is an outcome of secularization process, which is a comprehensive term for the changes in social values with the advent of industrialization and accompanying social relations, introduction of science, technology and rationalist thinking in society. Secularism in that sense is a marker of modernity, overcoming of feudal relationships and value system and thereby is a battle cry of newer social classes interested in overthrowing the feudal relationships and the accompanying baggage of constraining ideologies which find their vehicle in the religious clergy. It is the political expression of democratic values, Liberty, Equality and Fraternity. So secularism is a must for India. As it has entered the modern era with the introduction of industrialization and accompanying rationalism the logical values are those of secularism. Those propagating the above myth are the sections of society who stand to loose in the liberal ethos which are an accompaniment of secularism, those are the social elements who hold to religious nationalism in contrast to modern, secular democratic nationalism. No country can be a stagnant pool and with dynamic changes in society in progressive direction secularism comes in as an outcome of struggle of rising industrialist, poor peasant, worker and women against the obscurantist, dogmatic values and the feudal social system and further provides the base for enhancement of struggles of exploited and subalterns.

During freedom movement the major political tendencies which came up were due to two main group of classes, one the rising one's, due to industrialization and education and two the declining classes, the landlord and associated clerical one's. From the former came up the political streams of Indian national Congress, Revolutionaries of the type of Bhagat Singh and Dr, Bhimrao Baba Saheb Ambedkar. While from the declining classes and declining ideologies came up Muslim league, Hindu Mahasabha and RSS.

During freedom struggle itself secularism was emerging as the most dominant principle of the 'Nation in the making', India. The leaders of Indian National Congress Gandhi, Maulana Abul Kalam Azad, Nehru and others were deeply committed to the ideal of secularism though its expression was very different in all of them. It is not to be denied that some of the Hindu Nationalists also joined Congress and some other leaders in Congress were having ideologies colored by communalism of different hue, but it is undoubted that Congress did represent secular ideology to a large extent.

The constituent assembly debates clearly reveal that it reflected the national aspirations of the time. Secularism does not suppress religion. Secularism as principle is the outcome of the deeper social process called as secularization. As seen above with change in the material conditions, with change in social relations of production, with introduction of science and technology, society comes to newer equilibrium in which the hold of religion especially as mediated through the mediation of clergy changes in the society. It is important for us to understand that religion is a collation of multiple components like institutional, ritualistic experiential, doctrinal, mythical and ethical ones.

The social dynamics was very complex. The process of secularization/industrialization was going on at slow pace, not completed. At this stage, though constitution was secular, state apparatus: bureaucracy, judiciary, army and police, was infiltrated by Hindu communal elements. The Congress Government, though predominantly secular, was having many leaders in important positions that were influenced by Hindu communal ideology. This resulted in a social development, which was mixed; on one hand secularism thrived and on the other communalism though remained dormant, was never dead. With social changes during late 70's and early 80's communalism got a strong boost and it started attacking secularism in a big way. Its expression surfaced first through the policies of Indira and Rajiv, but in due course the Ram Janm Bhumi was taken up by BJP and during the course of this secularism came under severe attack.

Freedom Movement:

India won freedom under the aegis of secular democratic movement led by Indian National Congress, with the leadership

Table
Introduction of Education: Industrialization: Changes in Social Values, Relationships

1.	Rise of New classes of Businessmen-Industrialists, Workers, Educated classes	1.	Decline of Landlords, Kings and section of clergy associated with them
2.	These Groups form Associations, Bombay Association, Madras mahajan Sabha etc.	2.	This groups looks at new changes with fear and suspicion
3.	Their political expression in the form of Indian National Congress	3.	Fearful of the rise of new classes and INC, they form United India Patriotic association UIPA to Promote loyalty to British
4.	In due course other political streams expressing the values of this group come up, Hindustan Socialist Republican Association, (Bhagat Singh and Friends), Republican Party of India	4.	UIPA gave rise to Hindu Maha sabha, Muslim League. Later RSS came up as an ideology inspired by leaders of Hindu Mahasabha
5.	This stream was conceptualizing for India as 'a nation in the making'.	5.	Muslim League held that they Are a Muslim Nation since the advent of Mohammad bin Kasim Hindu Mahasabha/RSS held that We are a hindu Nation since times immemorial

(Contd.)

(Contd.Table)

6.	This group held the values of Liberty, Equality and Fraternity. Equal rights to people of all religions, by All caste and both genders	6.	Ideology was based on hierarchy of caste and gender, as sanctified the organized religion, clergy
7.	Participated in freedom Movement and Process of social change	7.	Totally aloof from freedom movement and opposed to social change

of people like Mahatma Gandhi and Jawaharlal Nehru and Maulana Abul Kalam Azad. Secularism was the guiding principle of anti-colonial struggle and it thereby succeeded in mobilizing vast sections of this plural society. It was recognized as an essential element of platform for multi-religious, multi-caste, poly-ethnic population of the subcontinent, as an instrument for unity of the people at large. It did act as a vehicle for transmitting the common aspirations of colonially oppressed people into a broad, powerful movement targeted at achieving independence from the clutches of colonial masters.

The different strata of society, which were the main bulwark of this movement, were modern, i.e. industrial bourgeoisie, urban proletariat, poor peasants, shudras and modern intelligentsia. This core was able to mobilize sections of other population. After Independence, Constituent Assembly was formed which framed the constitution, which was diverse in nature, and represented the aspirations of majority of population. The constitution thus framed after prolonged debates made different provisions, which formed the base of secular practice. These secular provisions of Indian constitution are,

i) State by itself shall not espouse or establish or practice any religion,

ii) Public revenues will not be used to promote any religion,

iii) the state shall have the power to regulate any economic financial or other secular activity associated with religious practice (Article 25 (2) (9) of constitution),

iv) every individual person will have an equal right to freedom of conscience and religion.

Thus, "ours is a secular state which has no particular religion of its own and must observe neutrality and equality in respect of all religions prevalent in the country. The state cannot discriminate between one religion and the other, or between their respective followers — regardless of their numerical strength in the country. At the same time constitution guarantees to individual and groups/sections of citizens the fundamental right to religious freedom in all its facets. Thus, secularism, equality of religions and neutrality of state to various religions within the constitutional limits are the basic features and part and parcel of unalterable basic structure of constitution of India." (Mahmood, 1996, 1) Jawaharlal Nehru explained it thus "What it means is that it is a state which honors all faiths equally and gives them equal opportunities; that as a state, it does not allow itself to be attached to one faith or religion, which then becomes the state religion...In a country like India, no real nationalism can be built up except on the basis of secularity...narrow religious nationalisms are a relic of the past age and no longer relevant today" (Nehru, 1961)

Thus though the constitution makers had not used the word secularism in the explicit fashion, Indian constitution was standing on the firm foundations of secular principles. Indira Gandhi merely added a descriptive word for something, which was already ingrained in the constitution. The spokesmen of Hindu Right taking advantage of the fact that the word was added during the much-dreaded 'emergency' are trying to throw mud on the very concept of secularism, which is anathema to their political interests.

Hindu Right Wing

The rise of Hindu right wing, RSS combine, with BJP as its political wing and Vishwa Hindu Parishad as the wing operating directly in the name of religion and roping in Mahants and Sadhus, came up to challenge the basic notions of Indian constitution form 1980s. The process of its rise was very assertive with large sections of affluent middle class supporting it in the face of rising assertion of dalits and women in the society. It managed to externalize the internal goals, by deflecting the whole aggression against minorities, Muslims and than Christians. It went on growing in intensity assuming horrendous proportions after Babri Masjid demolition. The riots of Mumbai, burning of Pastor stains in 1998, coming to power of BJP at center and trying to review the constitution as per the agenda of RSS were the major setbacks to the secular values of the nation. These also halted to progress of the nation in a serious way with adverse effects of globalization being presented as shining India. The Gujarat carnage may be the biggest blot on the plural and democratic values of India and Gujarat by now has become a sort of Hindu Rashtra in one state, where the rights of minorities have received a severe blow, where they have been reduced to second class citizens.

With this the human rights of weaker sections of society, Dalits, Adivasis and women have also taken a severe beating. Hindu right talks of Hindu Rashtra and wants the Indian constitution to be based on the values of Indian holy books. With the global phenomenon of terrorism the demonization of Muslim minority in India is more or less complete and their human rights in severe jeopardy. One realizes that during this phase many a neighboring countries have also faced an onslaught on the prospect of their path to democracy. Wherever the religion based politics, politics deriving its legitimacy from religious identity came to the fore the trampling on human rights was very much there. This politics tough will be talking of one or other religion, the women's rights of that community and the rights of weaker sections belonging to that community have taken a backseat.

Human Rights

Concept of human rights begins with the rise of democracies. The feudal societies had a neat division between rights and duties. The Landlords, kings had the right on tribute and free labor, while the peasants and deprived sections had the apportionment of duties for them. Duty to give tax, duty to serve the landlords, kings. Men had the right over the women, while women had the duties towards their husbands, fathers or sons. The concept of Liberty, Equality and Fraternity (community) brought in the era of formal equality between all the citizens. Even the concept of citizenship begins with democratic society and accompanying social transformation.

With the rise of religion based nationalism, the assertion of Taliban in Afghnistan, Zia ul Haq in Pakistan and Hindutrva in India the notion of rights is being sidetracked and major emphasis is on the duties. One had witnessed similar processes in US with the rise of Christian fundamentalism, and in Germany with the rise of race based politics of Fascism. Under the pressure of this politics gender and caste/class hierarchy is asserted in the newer language. Since the society began as unequal one, some of the sections like dalits and women began with a big disadvantage. Social subjugation and gender subjugation were the starting point. The constitution makers kept the provision of affirmative, protective clauses for these so that centuries old disadvantages are done way with and there is a march from formal equality to substantive equality. With the rise of Hindutva in India the opposition to reservation is mainly to retain the social hierarchies. The Hindutva is also opposed to equality in a subtle way.

Women and Hindu Right

The coming to power of these groups affects the rights of women as well. It can very well be gleaned from the interview given by Mridula Sinba, the chief of BJP Mahila morcha. She spelt it out very clearly.

In an interview to Savvy, April 1994, she states that (1) a woman should not work outside the home unless her family is financially very deprived. (2) I gave dowry and received dowry. (3) I oppose women's liberation, as it is another name for 'loose morals'. (4) We oppose equal rights for both sexes. (5) There is nothing wrong with domestic violence against women: very often it is women's fault. We advice women to try and adjust, as her not adjustment creates the problem. (6) Women's future lies in perpetuating the present, because no where else are women worshipped as we are in India. (7) For us women's liberation means liberation from atrocities. It does not mean they should be relieved of their duties as wives and mothers. One of the past presidents of Mahila Morcha Vijaya Raje Scindia, led a group of women in protest march against 'anti-sati' legislation, asserting that, 'It is the fundamental right of Hindu women to commit *sati* (burning of woman on the funeral pyre of her husband), as it is for preservation of our past glory and culture'. Nearly 20,000 '*kar sevikas*' helped the '*kar sevaks*' who went to demolish the *masjid*, by cooking and cleaning for them. During demolition of the masjid Uma Bharati and Sadhavi Rithamhara exhorted their male 'brethren' to participate in demolition.

Wherever Hindu right wing group are dominant, they will try to impose a dress code on women, will oppose the Valentine day and try to create problem if some Hindu girl maries a Muslim boy.

Dalits and Hindutva

BJP has couched its views and attitudes towards dalits in a very clever way. It will not criticize dalits, but when faced with their movements, demands and cultural upsurge it will start beating the drum of abolishing reservations and upholding merit. This was perfected as an art when Mandal commission recommendations were implemented and later when BSP began a verbal tirade against the symbolism projected by RSS combine. To counter Mandal, it did not want to be visible in opposing it. So it did not support the upper caste Hindu students self

Table

Showing the differences between Hindu Rahtra and Secular Democratic India

Hindu Rashtra	*Secular Democratic India*
This concept began as the goal of RSS and Hindu Mahasabha, which were not part of the freedom struggle.	This concept evolved as a part of the freedom struggle led by the Indian National Congress. Revolutionaries like Bhagat Singh, and of the streams led by Babasaheb Ambedkar stood for this.
Supporters of this concept in the earlier period were Brahmins, Banias, Jamindars and now the this gets support from uppercaste and upper-middle class Hindu elite	Supporters: Vast mass of poor peasants, workers, dalits, and sections of Industrialists
Concept crystallised by ideologues of Hindutva: Savarkar, Golwalkar etc.	Concept enshrined in Indian constituition which was formed by constituent assembly; fairly representative of Indian people.
This nationalism is based on Race, religion and hatred of 'others' on the grounds of race or religion.	Based on recognition of pluralism and geopolitical diversities

(Contd.)

(Contd. Table)

Hindu Rashtra	*Secular Democratic India*
Inherent special status to elite	Based on formal equality of all.
Strengthens 'status quo' based on caste, gender and Class	Provision of liberal space to struggle for the rights of the oppressed.
In this Society to be guided by Hindu clergy (Mahants, Acharyas)	Social life to evolve through mutual interaction of people and communities.
Impose monolithic values and culture on society.	Space for plurality. Respect for diversity.
Franchise to be controlled as per the dictates of the elite, the 'self appointed' leaders of 'Hindu society' i.e. by the leaders of the Sangh Parivar	Universal franchise. Everybody has the voting power. All equal in the eyes of law, irrespective of caste, class and gender.

(Contd.)

(Contd. Table)

Hindu Rashtra	*Secular Democratic India*
Brahminical norms , elite Sanskritised values to be the 'official', 'mainstream' laws.	Indian Constituition to guide social and political life
Everybody has to accept 'Hindu' (Brahminical culture)	Communities free to pursue their own culture
Concept close to Mussolini's Italy, Hitler's Germany, Khoemeini's Iran and Taliban's Afghanistan	Aspires to be a Democracy Values of Liberty, Equality and Fraternity for all. Nurtures liberal space.
Hindu elite and co-opted 'other' elite will dominate and dictate terms	Possibility of everybody constituting the political process

(Contd.)

immolation etc., but to side track the issue it began its Rath Yatra and later withdrew its support from the V.P. Singh government leading to its fall (1990). Similarly when faced with Mayawati's Periyar Mela-anti-upper caste pronouncements its 'political face' Vajpayee, attacked the proposed extension of reservations to non-Hindu dalits and by demanding a review of reservation policy.

While dalit reformers have always stood for opposing the Manusmriti, Dr. Ambedkar burnt it; but the ideologues of Hindutva have always upheld it. They have devised the clever ideology of integral Humanism, which argues that every society is a balanced Integral whole and any change of equations will put it in crisis. The argument is to uphold the caste equations as they prevail. The scriptures and practices of Brahminical Hindu religion do ask for Shudra Dharma, Holy duty of dalits, to serve the upper castes, Stree dharma, to serve the lord and master: husband or the male relative controlling her life.

Minorities

Indian constitution being secular gives right to freedom of conscience and religion and it is also duty bound to preserve the composite culture of the country. Article 15 ensures that there is no discrimination on the grounds of religion. Article 29(1) gives the right to preserve language, script and culture. Article 30 (1) gives the right to establish and run educational and other institutions; while article 30 (2) ensures that there should be no discrimination against minority institutions. Also article 25 gives the Freedom of conscience, free profession, propagation and practice of one's religion.

Rights of Minorities under the Constitution of India:

Article 29(1): "Any section of the citizens residing in the territory of India or any part thereof having a distinct language, script or culture of its own, shall have the right to conserve the same."

Article 29(1): "No citizen shall be denied admission into any educational institution maintained by the State or receiving aid out of the State funds on grounds only of religion, race, caste, language or any of them."

Article 30(1): "All minorities whether based on religion or language, shall have the right to establish and administer educational institutions of their choice."

These provisions ensure that minorities are able to lead their lives in full security. Most of these are endorsed by United Nations commissions, to which India is a signatory. Irrespective of this the communalization of state apparatus and direct assault of RSS affiliates has resulted in a situation where the minorities are slipping rapidly into the status of second class citizens. While this is the overt plight of Muslims/Christians in Gujarat, other states are gradually slipping into such a situation.

Conclusion:

Secularism is an inalienable part of democracy. The modern transformation to democracy essentially stands for the abolition of structural hierarchy of caste and gender and its replacement by formal equality. The democratic state in turn gives a liberal space which can be the ground for transforming the formal equality towards substantive equality.

The Religious right wing abolishes secular values, in the garb of 'minority problem' and its core agenda is to bring back the feudal caste and gender based structural hierarchies. While the minorities get the boot in the apparent way with the attack on secular values, the core victims of this are the deprived sections of society, whose rights get suppressed. In current times it is an attempt to abolish the liberal democratic space by rousing the hysteria of religious sentiments and use this suppression of democratic values to perpetuate the pre modern status quo of caste and gender hierarchy. Human rights are essentially a concept which can go along only with democracy, which in turn can only be secular. So in Indian context the opposition to secularism is basically an attack on the human rights of workers, women, dalits and minorities, with religious minorities bearing a direct brunt of violence, intimidation and also being relegated to being second class citizens.

References

Asghar Ali Engineer, 1996 "Some thoughts on pluralist model of Nation Building",

Minorities in India, Conference papers, Rajiv Gandhi Institute For contemporary Studies (RGISS)

Ashwini K Ray, 2000 "Constitution Reform", EPW March 18,

Fali S. Nariman, 2000 The Constitution of a review", Asian Age May 2,3,and 4, 2000.

Imtiaz Ahamd, 1996 'Indian Minorities', Minorities in India, RGISS

Iqbal A. Ansari, 1996 Readings on Minorities: Perspectives and Documants, Institute of Objective Studies, New Delhi

Rudolf Heredia; 1995 Secularism and Secularization, Towards Secular India, Vol. 1, No. 3,

S. P. Sathe; 1996 Secularism and Supreme Court of India, The Lawyers Collective, August

Satish Saberwal, 2000"Constitutional Ideas and Political Practices", EPW March 11,2000

Shiver Larry; Conception of secularization in empirical research in Sociological Perspectives, Pelican 1971, Eds. Thompson and Tunstall.

Subhash Kashyap, 1995 Indian Constitution, National Book Trust Delhi

Suhas Palashikar, 2000"Why We Must oppose Review of Constitution" EPW April

Upendra Baxi ,2000 "Kar Seva Of Indian Constitution", EPW March 11,

Upendra Baxi, 1995 The struggle for redefinition of Secularism in India, in Heredia and Mathais (Secularism and Liberation) Indian Social Institute.

4

India : Nation in the Making

For India the major achievement of the century has been the Freedom struggle and the accompanying social transition. For his contribution to this major transition, Gandhi was recognised as Father of the Nation. At the turn of the century when India is moving to the new millennium, a political tendency has come up whose practitioners deny the epithet of Father of the Nation to Mahatma Gandhi. Also few decades ago one of the followers of this ideology, which is based on hatred of others' religion, killed him accusing him of 'appeasement' of minorities. Also Gandhi's ideology of 'Religion as a personal matter', and secularism are being denigrated to no end. To understand the precise role of Gandhi, leader of one of the biggest mass movements of twentieth century, we need to have a peep into the process of transition of India from the colonial–feudal society to the current one based on the formal principle of Liberty, Equality and Fraternity. We need to understand the contribution of this man in the major transition of the century.

Colonial set Up: Before the advent of the British, large part of India was under the sway of the Mughal Empire. The administration was based on small kings, noble lords, zamindars and the like. The arrival of the East India Company began a different process, whereby power of more and more kingdoms was taken over by the East India Company, and after the failure of 1857 revolt India came to be the direct colony of Britain. The primary goal of the British was to search for markets for the products of their industries and also plunder of raw materials for their industries.

British went on to set up new agrarian commercial and industrial ventures in India. In these, Indians first acted as their subordinates but in the process they came to learn the modern technology giving rise to a new class of bankers, merchants, industrialists, plantation owners and brokers. In 1835 English was introduced as a medium of instruction and Macaulay, the initiator of this move went on to declare that the main aim of this policy was to create in India, a class of men, who would be Indians only in appearance, but English in taste opinions and interests. But things don't happen so simplistically. There was a deeper dialectic hidden in this. The introduction of a newer production process and common language in due course facilitated the exchange of ideas and newer common urges emerged, which led Indians towards the newer phenomenon of 'nationalism'.

Social and political Changes: Initially this nationalism was not against the British but *en-rapport* with the Raj. This also initiated the process of different reform movements, the new associations and unions of economic, social and political nature on the Western pattern. Despite the flaws of the British education policy, one can say that it was designed primarily to produce the administrators for the British rule. At the same time it helped in laying the foundation of modern Indian

Nationalism. The educated elite who were recruited as clerks or so, in due course were dissatisfied with the clerical jobs and aspired for administrative offices, and the intelligentsia started demanding widening franchise, simultaneous holding of examinations in India of Indian Civil Service, and Indianisation of services etc.

Meanwhile participation of Indians in modern enterprises in lower rungs of administration and modern business went up tremendously. It also unleashed the process of change in villages from where landless and poor peasants started coming to cities looking for newer employment. These new economic and social processes, and improved communication, in a way, laid the foundation of Indian Nationalism. The positive and negative factors of alien rule e.g. New Learning, Imperial unity, Western liberalism, (free) press, modern system of communications, along with racial arrogance (of British), economic exploitation of India, weaknesses of Judiciary, and assertion of cultural superiority of English filled the Indian mind with a new spirit of national consciousness. The British rule and its processes were always pregnant with contradictory processes. Modern means of communication introduced by the British like the postal system, railways and free press played a crucial role in creating political consciousness and in promoting nationalism. One of the positive things was that English newspapers in India believed in freedom of expression, and were engaged in criticism of the official policies and this also helped in developing an Indian outlook.

After the 1857 mutiny, the arrogance of the British bureaucracy reached its peak; they treated Indian subjects with contempt, inciting a deep feeling of hatred towards them. The bureaucracy practiced the principle of divide et emporia (divide and rule), playing off Hindus against Muslim, princes against common people and educated people against the rest.

Nationalism in India: Political Battleground: The British in India were in alliance with the landlords, and the princes, who were given autonomy by the British to rule their states. With the emergence of newer social classes industrialists, modern businessmen, bureaucrats, modern professionals and intelligentsia, a new type of national spirit started getting crystallized. This found its initial expression in the formation of various local associations, which in times to come, culminated in the formation of the India National Congress. Initially, those groups had a strong religious zeal and caste solidarity, which later gave way to secular ideals. Some of these organisations were The Bombay Association, Madras Native Association, Poona Sarvajanik Sabha, Madras Mahajan Sabha etc. From here many individual members started thinking of a national association. The major national conference of these groups was held in Calcutta in 1883, calling itself as the first step towards a national parliament. And this was the precursor of the Congress in the real sense. The objective of this political enterprise was to lay the foundation of secular and democratic movement, inspired by Indian Nationalism. Their major demands pertained to adult franchise, holding of Civil Services exams in India, and more facilities for industrial growth of the country. Remarkably majority of regional associations were represented in the Congress. The demands of Congress pertained to the newly emerging sections of the society consequent to the growth of industries and other administrative changes. These demands were opposed to the interests of the feudal lords, and section of the clergy whose interest was more tied up with the zamindars. And these interests, their opposition to change came to be articulated in communal politics, Muslim as well as Hindu, which in due course became a political force to reckon with due to the implicit encouragement to these from the British rulers, in consonance with their policy of divide and rule. More of this we will pursue in the next section. But roughly the communal politics resorted to the use of 'religion' to safeguard the interests of *zamindars; Brahmins* and *banias* in the society and the British patronage came in handy for them substituting for the mass support.

The Major Streams: Indian freedom came about due to multiplicity of factors. The foremost amongst these, and in a way embodying the struggle for Indian nationalism, has been the Indian National Congress. The tallest person who represented this nationalism was Mahatma Gandhi, who in his own life time became a legend due to his towering contribution to the freedom struggle and was the one to innovate the methods of struggle against the mightiest of the empires. The struggles unleashed by Gandhi and the Indian National Congress (INC) were prolonged and popular. It successfully exploited the constitutional space. It used it effectively in combination with non- constitutional struggle to over throw the British rule. This movement was based on a democratic, civil libertarian and secular vision of the Indian State. Over a period of time Congress came to become a broad platform in which on one side of spectrum were socialists and on the other side of spectrum were conservative pro-Hindu elements. But over all it was dominated by the politics of secular nationalism. Its main focus was on industrialisation, land reforms and secular democracy. But as even the other shades of conservative elements were part of this broad platform none of these could be implemented in full. It went on to popularise the ideas of democratic institutions in India, for introduction of representative government, based on elections which in turn were to be based on adult franchise.

The Communal Reaction: This was in contrast to the communal organisations. Later agrarian reforms also became part of Congress agenda (contrasting with the agenda of Muslim League (ML) or Hindu Mahasabha (HM) that were opposed to such reforms). To top it all and as a logical accompaniment of this none of these policies were to be based on the religious consideration (again contrasted with ML and HM, whose primary consideration was the community based on religion). The major draw back of this movement was relegating of the class and caste issues to a secondary position, secondary to the anti-imperialist struggle.

The Secular Vision: Despite the partition of India and the accompanying communal holocaust it did succeed in enshrining secularism in constitution of free India. This drew into its fold different sections of society - emerging industrialists, modern businessman, section of emerging middle class and vast mass of peasants. Succeeding the phase of petition politics, Gandhi's arrival on the scene transformed it into a big mass movement and different agitation's were launched, culminating in the independence from the clutches of British. Supplementing this mass movement were other movements, which were eroding the social base of colonial rule. These were, the anti-landlord agitation's, for the rights of untouchables and other efforts of Dr. Ambedkar, which weakened the material base of colonial rule. On similar ground were the workers movements, led by, to begin with Narayan Meghaji Lokhande, Com. Singarvelu, and later on by, Communist party. These movements also shook the very roots of British Empire. The revolutionaries like Bhagat Singh (Hindustan Socialist Republicans Army), Chandrashekhar Azad; Ashfaqulla, Surya Sen and others also contributed to freedom by challenging the hegemony of the British. Role of Netaji Subhash Chandra Bose's army in freedom struggle also cannot be under rated. On the other side of the fence was the British might, aided by the Muslim and Hindu Communalists whose main 'role' in history of independent struggle was to provide reliable allies to the British rule. Whose main 'contribution' to the struggle had been to ridicule and oppose it at all stages.

Nation in the making and Father of the Nation: It need not be elaborated in detail that Gandhi was at the center of nationalist movement and he galvanized the movement in a big way. He adopted unique and novel ways to ensure that vast masses of peasantry and other people became a part of it. It was towards this end that one should see the importance of his methods. He was quick enough to perceive the state of society: deeply in the grip of religion of orthodox variety. To ensure that the people are to come out from this orthodox paralysis he gave a 'unique interpretation to religion, emphasizing more on the humanistic aspects of religion which could transcend the boundaries of a single religion, and in the process he got overwhelming response from the people. His dispute with the practitioners of communal politics (Muslim League, Hindu Mahasabha & RSS) can be located precisely at this spot. These communalists were themselves mostly 'non religious', like Jinnah and Savarkar, but they were using religion for narrow ends of consolidating their communities against the other. They perceived serious threat from Gandhi's deep-set religious humanism. It is for this reason that both Hindu and Muslim communalists spewed poison on him, (holding him responsible for the 'mess' which in a way was the outcome of communal politics itself), it is precisely for this reason that one votary of Hindu communal politics murdered him and in the process won overt and covert kudos from the supporters of the politics of religion based nationalism.

It is clear that the present Industrial India has emerged from the struggle for the freedom from the clutches of British colonialists. During the process the new industries and the new social and political values and structures evolved which gave modernity to the society and it is because of this that India was termed as a 'Nation in the making'. Also since Gandhi was presiding over this process he is called 'The Father of the nation'. Incidentally both these notions are rejected by those whose politics is based on the 'hatred of others' religion' i.e. those claiming to be 'Religious nationalists.

Gandhi's contribution in uniting all the people of India, irrespective of region, religion, caste and gender, in the single thread of Indianness has no parallel. He did unleash and lead the biggest ever mass movement in the World, the freedom movment of India.

5

Social Roots of Partition Process

The partition tragedy has been a multifaceted phenomenon in which lot of factors played their role. Unmindful of that, various formulations are popularized to suit the political interests of vested interests. One of the most common causes for partition, propounded by the RSS and its progeny (Sangh Parivar, SP), has been that it was Gandhi's appeasement of Muslims, which emboldened them to demand Pakistan. Also, Jinnah has been given the 'distinction' of the man who broke up India by some of the scholars. A new theory comes from Dr. Murli Manohar Joshi. According to him Communist Party of India resolution on linguistic and religious nationalism provided Muslim League with the logic of the much-needed 'Two Nation theory'. While RSS chief Mr. Sudarshan states that as the division of India has been done into Muslim Pakistan and Hindu India, so to complete the partition process Muslims should be packed off to Pakistan and Hindus from Pakistan should be brought back.

Partition tragedy needs to be related to the complex social roots and the goals of imperial powers in the region. With the control of India by British, to plunder its raw materials and to create the market for their industrial goods, railways, telegraphs and modern education were introduced. Due to this came up group of Industrialists, educated civil servants, professionals, modern businessmen and workers. These groups started forming various citywide and region wide associations, the culmination of which took place in the formation of Indian National Congress (INC). This organization started putting forward the demands related to more provisions for industrialists to set up their industries here, bigger role in local administration, better facilities for education and land ceiling. Rising assertion of newly emerging classes put the Feudal lords and Kings of princely states, belonging to both religions, to unease, and they came together to form United India Patriotic Association (UIPA) just a couple of years after the formation of INC. This association condemned the INC demands and saw this as an indication of disloyalty to the British crown. They resolved to cultivate the loyalty of local population for the Queen of England. Incidentally it was the same decade in which communal riots began. Over a period of time mainly due to the British policy of divide and rule this association gave way to the formation of religion-based bodies like Muslim League (ML) and Hindu Mahasabha (HM). Remarkably the leadership of these organizations was coming from the same sections that formed the UIPA.

Later on RSS also joined in as another outfit for the 'building of Hindu Nation', it had predominant support base from Brahmin and traditional Bania communities. Most remarkably these both outfits (ML on one side and HM+RSS on the other) spewing venom against each other shared the common premise of Nationalism in the name of religion. The only difference being that HM+RSS said it is a Hindu Nation so people of other faiths have to remain subordinate to Hindus if they do not accept Hindu culture, while ML asserted that since Muslims are separate Nation and they should have a separate country for themselves. They were critical of National movement led by INC, and most significantly they shared the same class base to a great extent (Kings, Feudal Lords)

With INC's movement becoming mass movement, people from different communities irrespective of their religion started joining it. This movement was the movement for India Nation in the making. For this nationalism the Nationalism propounded by ML and HM+RSS was like a fly in the ointment but this fly was given life and blood by the British policies in a very subtle and overt ways. While Muslim League was overtly recognized and acted as 'the representative of Muslims', unmindful of the fact that majority of Muslims were with the INC. The majority Muslims stalwarts, Maulana Abul Kalam Azad, Khan Abdul Gaffar Khan being the most well known amongst them, the Ulemas of Barelvi and Deoband School, all supported this Nationalism. The Hindu Nationalists though they were not 'officially' recognized as the representatives of Hindus, they were merrily operating through the INC itself. The foundation of Two Nation theory emerged parallel amongst Hindu Nationalists and Islamist Nationalist. Savarkar articulated it most powerfully in his 'Post Andaman' book, 'Who is a Hindu', while Chowdhary Rahmat Ali conceptualized Pakistan (Punjab, Afghans, Kashmir, Sind) around 1930s.

The negotiations for the single united country were bound to fail with these diverse pulls, pressures and machinations. In the wake of Nehru committee (1927), Muslim League kept certain demands, which though accepted initially, had to be backtracked due to the pressure of Hindutva elements. Again in 1937 elections first the request for joint alliance with ML was rejected and later the request to accommodate it in the ministry was rejected by Nehru on the ground that he was keen on land reforms and alliance with feudal elements of ML will make it impossible to achieve the same. Similarly after accepting the Cabinet mission plan, which called for a federation of states, Nehru practically backed out on the ground that for a proper development of a strong center is a must. This was like the last straw on the camel's back after which Jinnah became adamant on his demand for a separate homeland for Muslims.

It is worth noting that the popular support for ML or HM as reflected in the election results shows that both these parties had a very narrow base, and both these had abysmal performance at the hustings. The passing of Pakistan resolution in Lahore in 1940 was met with a march of thousands of Ansari Muslims to oppose it. As ML used the religious symbolism it succeeded in raising a bogey of demand for Pakistan, due to the emotional appeal associated with the propaganda laced in religious idiom. So it gave the impression as if all Muslims are in support of the Pakistan. The Two Nation theory was repeatedly proclaimed from the sessions of ML and HM, In 1937 Hindu Mahasabha Session a resolution was passed stating that Hindus and Muslims are two separate Nations. While a year later Bhai Paramanand in his Presidential address stated that "Mr. Jinnah argues that there are two nations in the country. If Mr. Jinnah is right, and I believe that he is right then the Congress theory of building a common Nationality falls to the ground. This situation has two solutions, one is the partition of the country into two and the other is to allow to grow the Muslim state within the Hindu state."

We can see here that the failure of negotiations had more then what meets the eye. The goals and perceptions of different actors in this play were different. Jinnah under the mistaken notion that ML represents all the Muslims and following the communal vision of politics like its counterpart HM+RSS, assumed that 'Hindu' INC will subjugate the interests of Muslims once the British left. Mahatma Gandhi kept working for peace all through, at all occasions but here Nehru and Patel's wish to have a strong center finally broke the possibility of negotiations and compromise. Nehru wanted a strong center so that the development could be done in a planned manner and landlordism could be abolished, while Patel wanted a strong center for an overall strong state. It was a tragedy, which played with lives of millions and its ghost continues to haunt us till the day. The result of the partition was a truncated Pakistan, which further broke down into Bangla Desh and Pakistan, just to prove that religion cannot be the basis of Nation states, and India, did inherit the mantle of struggle for independence, the values emerging from the biggest mass movement of twentieth century, the values of Liberty, Equality, and Fraternity. It came up as the true representative of the aspirations of the participants of the freedom struggle for whom their Indian ness bound them in a single thread. For them religion was not the primary identity. For them a composite Indian Nationalism rising above the other varieties of narrow nationalism (Race, Language, Religion) was the primary principle of society and country. It is precisely these values, which came to be enshrined in our constitution.

At this point to say that the two Nation theory got boost from the CPI resolution is nothing but travesty of truth. We have seen the genesis of Two Nation Theory and its sustenance by ML and HM+RSS had been going on for decades before CPI resolution came up. About Sudarshan's statement the less said the better. It is no surprise that this patriarch of Hindu Rashtra politics can never understand as to what Indian Nationalism is. His ideology and organization was never a part of Indian National movement barring few exceptions. The concept of secular democracy is Greek and Latin to the followers of Hindutva ideology. Could the concept of Secularism and Indian Nationhood come up and survive without the crucial contribution of all the communities to the process of Indian Nation building? India and Indian secularism survive because most of the people of India choose to be Indians first by rejecting the narrow Nationalism based on Religion, be it Muslim Nationalism or Hindu Nationalism.

6

Jaswant, Jinnah and Ghost of India's Partition

Jaswant Singh's latest book on Jinnah (August 2009) has rekindled the debate 'who did it' of partition. The storm created by this work can be gauzed from the fact that BJP, the party for which Jaswant Singh has been working from last three decades expelled him from the party. The basic point Singh is making is that Jinnah was a secular person, he has been wrongfully demonized in India, that Nehru and Patel rather than Jinnah were responsible for partition of India because of which there was gory violence and that Muslims are being treated as aliens in India.

To take the last point first. One concedes that Muslims have and are being treated as aliens in India. One of the major political parties which has targeted Muslims and because of which they have been excluded from social and economic space is BJP, itself. The alienation of Muslims is due to the aggressive politics pursued mainly by BJP. The question is what has Mr.

Jaswant Singh been doing when BJP has been asserting the concept of Hindu nation, has been part of processes which have relegated Muslims to the status of second class citizens? One is not arguing that the maltreatment of Muslims is only due to BJP, the major factor has been the subtle penetration of RSS ideology in the social and political arena of Indian life. While Jaswant Singh does not come from the RSS shakhas, he has been part of the party, which is the political vehicle of RSS. In this case his 'alienation of Muslims' look like crocodile tears!

As far as Jinnah being secular is concerned, it is ironical that a party, which Jinnah headed with 'brilliance', had the name Muslim League! If that does not clarify the communal evaluation of a person what else will. Jinnah despite his exposure to the Western culture, despite his being part of the Indian National Congress for initial part of his life, did become the 'sole spokesman' of interests of Muslims, i.e. Muslim elite, in due course of time. One agrees that the individual attributes of the Qaed-e-Azam of Pakistan were remarkable, but that does not make him secular. Secularism essentially stands for relegating religious identity to private realm to one's life, while Jinnah chose to accede to lead Muslim League, where the religious identity was the base of the national identity.

There were people like Maulana Abul Kalam Azad, Khan Abdul Gaffar Khan, Rafi Ahmad Kidwai and others who chose to be part of National movement for composite Indian nation. Majority of poor Muslims continued to support and follow Mahatma Gandhi and national movement. There were even Muslim religious leaders, and seminaries like those of Barelvi and Deoband, which stood for composite Indian Nationalism, despite the fact that Muslim League a product of the politics of Muslim Landlords and Nawabs and later joined in by section of educated Muslims kept talking of interests of 'Muslims' and kept labeling Congress as Hindu party, despite its secular policy of Indian Nationalism.

The language of Interests of Muslims, leading to the notion of 'Muslims are a separate nation' was quiet akin and parallel to the concept of Hindu nation propagated by Savarkar-RSS, of India being a Hindu rashtra. Do all Muslims have similar interests about as asserted by Jinnah? What was the similarity between the interests of Ashraf and Arjal Muslims? What was the similarity of interests between the interests of rich landlord, businessmen Muslims and the poor artisan Muslims? Savarkar and RSS talked of the interests of Hindus, which layers of Hindus were these? Essentially the same layers which as Muslims were the beneficiaries of Muslim Leagues' articulation.

Jinnah's enticing 11th August 1947 'secular speech' notwithstanding, the whole Muslim League predominantly consisted of those communal elements, who did want to convert Pakistan into a Muslims Nation, which they did in due course. And it was the same Muslim League under Jinnah's leadership, which called for a separate state for Muslims, Pakistan, in 1940 Lahore resolution. Just because Jinnah was a non-practicing Muslim and a Westernized person does not make him secular. One's association in politics should determine this label.

As far as role in the partition of the country is concerned, most of the debate is generally focused at superficial level, Muslim League, Nehru-Patel. Most of the debate is in the language of Heroes and villains, the deeper processes which gave rise to the political streams, which believed in religion based nation state, the role of British in creating such a situation is missing in the debate. While in Pakistan a large section will blame the intransigence of 'Hindu Congress' for partition, in India, Muslim League, Jinnah are blamed for the same. The source of 'Hate politics' in India, the RSS ideology, holds Gandhi also as a major culprit. According to the RSS-Hindu Mahasabha thinking expressed in so many ways, most clearly in the speech and action of Nathuram Godse, Gandhi is to blame for partition as he followed the policy of Muslim appeasement leading to their becoming assertive and going on to demand Pakistan. In most of the communal discourse, a large part of which has become part of social common sense in both the countries, the role of British in leading to the divisive path, and class character of communal organizations, which believed in the Religion based nation state, is missing altogether.

After the coming into being of Indian National Congress in 1885, from the rising classes of Industrialist-Businessmen, educated sections and workers, the old declining classes of Landlords and Kings came together (1888) to form United India Patriotic Association. It is in this organization that the future founders of Muslim League and Hindu Mahasabha were working shoulder to shoulder, e.g. Raja of Kashi and Nawab of Dhaka. British played their cards very well and in pursuance with the imperial policy of divide et empera (divide and rule) recognized Muslim League as the representative of Muslims in 1906. That time it was predominantly formed by Muslim elite, who themselves were contemptuous of low caste Muslims; Arzals and Azlafs. Similarly Hindu Mahasabha, which was founded in 1915 had Hindu elite who were for Hindu Nation and average Hindus and low castes had no place in their scheme of things.

There is a lot of deeper parallelism in the agenda and language of both these communal streams. These were not only predominantly male dominated organizations, they talked only of identity issues, while at the same time the process of social transformation of caste and gender was going on these communal streams emphasized on Muslim (elite) Hindu (elite) interests. That's why they kept aloof from the national movement which aimed to bring in people of all religions, regions, castes and gender into a single stream of Indian ness. Jinnah's focus on Constitutional methods and deep opposition to participation of masses was quite similar to Hindu Mahasabha and RSS policy of keeping aloof from freedom movement. It is from the Hindu stream, Savarakar that the concept of Hindu nation and its politics, Hindutva emerged, and later picked up by RSS. There was not much difference in many a formulation, which came from these two stables. As a matter of fact Savarkar goes on to quote approvingly Jinnah's statement that there are two Nations in India, Hindus and Muslims. And then says that since this is a Hindu nation predominantly, Muslim nation has to remain subordinate to the same. The deeper agenda of communal streams was same, the only difference was Muslim League called for parity and Hindu Mahasabha-RSS wanted subordination of Muslim nation.

While Hindu Communalism got fragmented between Hindu Mahasabha, RSS and some part of it entered Congress also, Muslim communalism remained a formidable force and later on a section of the Muslim educated classes came to support the same.

It is in this background that the logistics of partition has to be seen. For Muslim League and Hindu Mahasabha-RSS it was a control over nation, for National movement-Congress, it was to get freedom, to come out of the shackles of feudal system and to lay the foundation of Industrial society on democratic basis. It is because of this that Nehru refused to accommodate Muslim League demand of take them in UP ministry in 1937, despite the defeat of Muslim League. Nehru's argument was that since they want to go for land reforms etc., how they can have a landlord representative sitting in the cabinet. Also Nehru refused to believe that Muslim League is a representative of all Muslim, the same way he opposed the formulation that Hindu Mahasabha-RSS are representatives of Hindus. Cabinet Mission plan, to which Congress and Muslim League both had assented, suggested a federal structure with all powers to provinces and have only defense, communication, currency and external affairs with the Central Government. During the course Nehru and Patel both realized that such a weak center will not be able to undertake the programs for country, programs for centralized planning for industrialization and related progress.

Superficially Nehru and Patel can be held responsible for what happened, but that's like looking at the tip of iceberg. The deeper seeds of divisiveness, the protection to landlord elements was the British policy. It is in pursuance with this, that the Muslim League and Hindu Mahsabha were never the subject of British wrath, while the leaders of national movement had to make the British jails as their second home.

For Advani and Jaswant Singh the deeper fascination for Jinnah has some logic. Jinnah pursued two nation theory and succeeded in forming a Muslim nation. They have the wish to have a Hindu nation, so a subtle admiration as to how Jinnah could achieve his goal and so is a great hero for those pursuing religion based politics. At ideological level they are on the same wave length, religion based nation state as Jinnah was. They also visualize that by exonerating Jinnah from the blame of partition they are cornering Nehru and Congress, which at one level serves the BJP agenda. And here lies the problem. Since Nehru and Patel are inalienable as for as the trajectory of practical politics is concerned, Patel also comes in to the gambit of blame which cannot be tolerated by large section of BJP followers. Another reason is through RSS shakhas the blame of partition is put on Jinnah's head and on the follies of Gandhi and Nehru. So how can Jinnah be resurrected without annoying the RSS module of indoctrination? Here lies the dilemma of RSS controlled Rajnath Singhs, and so the expulsion of Jaswant Singh for writing all this. Advani could save his skin despite his 'secular Jinnah speech' because of electoral exigencies, as with sickness of Vajpayee, it was difficult to fill the gap by anybody else.

History has strange lessons to teach. Today lot of powerful opinions are being voiced, but most of them are based on one or the other superficial observation e.g. Jinnah's earlier period when he was part of Congress or his 11th August speech in the Parliament. Similar type of historiography is also used for the communal historiography where kings are glorified or demonized according their religion. The deeper issues related to the workers, peasants and other average people are missing in this discourse. Same is the problem with the presentation of recent history, where the roots of communal streams (Muslim League, Hindu Mahsabha, and RSS) from the feudal lords and feudal values (Birth based hierarchy of caste and gender) is undermined and deliberately overlooked. This attitude also revels in creating heroes and villains; one streams' hero being another streams villain. No wonder Bollywood is so successful in using this formula. And as Bollywood is not bothered about the deeper issues of broad layers of society so are many of the worthy commentators for whom this wavelength is something easily understood and deliberated upon, as to who is the guilty and who is not of the partition process!

7

Partition Puzzle: Role of British Policy

Jaswant Singh in his recent book on Jinnah has praised the secular nature of Jinnah and has held Nehru-Patel responsible for Partition of India. Many people from Pakistan are praising Jaswant Singh's book to the sky, while here in India there is a mixed reaction. Most strong one came from BJP President Rajnath Singh who hinted that any praise of Jinnah, will be met with strict action. The problem with such formulation, Jinnah was secular, Nehru-Patel were responsible for partition, is that it is an extremely superficial analysis and does not look at the complex multilayered phenomenon of partition tragedy. It totally by passes the role of British rulers and the different interests of diverse classes during freedom movement. The response to the book is either at emotive level, our leader versus your leader, or how dare you speak against our icon!

In the midst of the whole debate, the British get away with the cake. As such they not only took all the measures, implemented all policies which were divisive but also accepted all the demands of communalists which led to partition. In the process they ensured that even after they leave the interests of imperial powers, UK-USA, in the Middle East remain safe and secure. This ensured that they continue to dominate the area and retain their military and political base in the region. While the mini battle, Jinnah versus Nehru-Patel is on, the role of the major culprits of partition, the Colonial powers of yesteryears and the imperialist power of today is generally not being brought under scrutiny.

If we look at the British polices, right from the beginning there were germs of divide and rule. They saw Indian society as divided along religious lines, underplaying the fact that the real divisions were not along religious lines but along class and caste lines. Shaken by the massive revolt of 1857, their subtle policies of 'divide and rule' started becoming more overt and articulate. In 1858 Lord Elphinstone, Governor of Bombay Province, in his communication to The East India Company's executives wrote, "Divide et Impera' (Divide and Rule) was old Roman motto and it should be ours." In return Charles Wood, Secretary of State for India wrote that, "The antagonism of Indian races was an element of strength to the British India. Therefore 'a dissociating spirit' should be kept up, for if India was to unite against us, how long could we maintain ourselves."

Both these quotes amply indicate towards shape of policies in times to come. As a foundation of these polices, 'doctoring of mass consciousness' along religious lines began through specially sponsored History books. The two major ones' in this direction were Six Volume 'History of India as told by her Historians' by Elliot and Dawson and 'History of India' by James Mill, who periodized the Indian History into Hindu Period, Muslim Period and British period. This periodization gave the impression that history's period is determined by the religion of the king.

Needless to say that the medieval administration of Kings was never based along religious lines; their court officials and chain of Landlords were belonging to both the religions. These British sponsored accounts of History argued that Muslim Rulers had enslaved India and now British have come to end the misrule of Muslim rulers. Such an account became a convenient tool in the hands of Hindu communalists, Hindu Mahsabha and RSS, to play their part of divisive politics amongst masses. The Muslim League turned it around to say that Muslim rulers were glorious and great.

This communalization of minds was the fertile soil on which the communalists could plant their narrow agenda of Muslim Nation and Hindu Nation. Another British Historian Sir T.W. Holderness in his book 'Peoples and Problems of India' mooted the idea that Hindus and Muslims regard themselves as separate nations. This book came out in 1923 and in the same year Savarkar came out with his book, 'Hindutva or Who is a Hindu'?, where the same formulation was presented in a different way.

At concrete level on the political chessboard Lord Curzon, the then Viceroy of India, partitioned Bengal with communal motivation and this was probably the first concrete experiment in communalizing the politics at big level. Curzon went on to declare that this is an attempt to invest in the Mussalmans of Eastern Bengal. Just a couple of years later the delegation of Muslim Landlords and Nawabs was received by Viceroy, where he declared these Muslim elite to be the representatives of Muslim community. The delegation went to ask for separate electorate for Muslims, and these separate electorates introduced later acted as the trigger to polarize the nation along religious lines. Many a members of this delegation were also part of United India Patriotic Association, an organization of Hindu and Muslim landlords and Kings which had come up in the wake of formation of Indian National Congress. Indian National Congress was critical of British and in response, this association pledged to enhance the loyalty of the people to the British crown.

Thus Viceroy Minto subtly encouraged Muslim communalism, and later the same delegation members went on to form Muslim League. Lady Minto in her communication takes pride in what the Lord had organized. She commented that what has happened, the receiving of delegation etc. will pull back sixty million people from joining the ranks of seditious opposition, meaning the rising national movement.

MacDonald's Communal Award of 1932 was the next step, which enhanced the communal divides. Interestingly in 1939 Congress firmly told the British that they will not join the war efforts until they are guaranteed freedom in return. And lo and behold in 1940 Jinnah comes with the demand for Pakistan at Lahore Muslim League convention. Can such things be coincidental? Demand of Pakistan may have been a bargaining counter but its timing is interesting.

No doubt the Cabinet mission plan could have prevented partition, but it is debatable whether it would not have sown the fissiparous tendencies amongst the princely states and the states where Muslim League was in majority. The other necessity which made British to partition India, related to their strategic needs in the area. At the end of WWII, the global power equations changed. USA and USSR both emerged as major powers. US had posted its representative in India from 1942. With British deciding to leave India, freedom was imperative. The British calculation at this time was that an Undivided India with leadership of Congress will not let Britain continue with its military bases in the area. With USSR coming up in a big way, Mao Tse Tung rising in China and section of

Congress leadership impressed by socialism, UK-USA were sure that India will not side with them in their global designs of countering USSR militarily and in continuing their oil plunder in middle east. Here comes the Radcliff Line, which runs in the areas adjacent to Iraq, Afghanistan and Sinkiang. British diplomats had the job cut out for them, to make Jinnah accept moth eaten Pakistan and to make Congress leadership to accept the partition.

Somehow the plans of imperialists were immaculate. And in times to come the Pakistan where Mr. Jinnah wanted to have religious freedom, was converted into a land ruled by Mullahs, Army and American Ambassador. It was the same Pakistan which was supported to the hilt on the Kashmir issue; the idea was that US strategic interests are safe with this arrangement. It is a matter of great relief that Pakistan is struggling to come out from the vice like grip of Army, but can it shed its client state type status vis a vis US, is the million dollar question. The people of Pakistan have been big victim of Imperialist designs all through while Pakistan military has been having all the green pastures for itself.

In partitioning India, colonialists reaped rich harvest at the cost of the people of the subcontinent, millions dead, a single entity India, divided into Pakistan, India and Bangla Desh. These countries keep on spending a major part of their budgets in investing in armaments and fattening of their armed forces, something which could have been meaningfully invested for the growth and development of the region. We need to wake up from the blame game and see the real culprit.

8

Nehru: Foundations of Modern India

The contemporary discussion on the follies of India's secularism, Industrial policy and foreign policy, lead many a critics to infer that Nehru is the person responsible for today's problems, communalism and 'pseudo secularism', and for his other policies. Nehru also happens to be criticized most severely by RSS combine for his 'appeasement of Muslims' and for laying the foundations of the policies leading to pseudo secularism. Also many an intellectuals believe that Nehru's secularism was opposed to the one by Gandhi, it was against religion and so the problems faced by us today. There are umpteen critics, questioning his industrial and foreign policy.

As such Nehru probably was able to grasp the reality of Indian society and the problems faced by the state very accurately, when he said to Andre Marloux that the biggest problem he faces is that secular Indian state is riddled with a society in the grip of religion. Though a rationalist, he did not dismiss religion like the communist regime in Russia, which had put a ban on the Churches. He did realize the importance of religion in society, "India is supposed to be religious country above everything else... (And yet) I have frequently condemned (religion) and wished to make a clean sweep of it. Almost always it seemed to stand for blind belief and reaction, dogma and bigotry, superstition and exploitation. And yet I know well that there was something else in, it, and something that supplied a deeper inner craving of human being."

His deeper commitment to democracy and secularism guided his policies in the difficult terrain of Indian society. The first major problem he handled was the pressure to renovate Somanth temple by the state, he put his foot down and said state is not going to spend money for such purposes. At the same time, Gandhi said the similar thing in a different language when he said that Hindus are capable enough to raise funds to build a temple of theirs. Then came the reqest of President Rajendra Prasad to inaugurate the same as the President of India. Nehru was to affirm that he can do no such thing in his capacity as a President.

While such issues gave an insight into his mind there are other places where he creatively applied his wisdom to prevent the future conflagration of potential problems. When some miscreants installed the Ram Lalla idols in the Babri mosque he told Govindvallabh Pant, the then UP Chief Minister, to get them removed immediately. Since lower down the communal elements posed too many obstacles, the idols remained in the mosque. How that was made a pretext to communalize the society is a painful chapter of Independent India.

The other major initiative he took was to form the National Integration Council, to ensure that the religious divides do not come in the way of the growth and prosperity of the country. It is another matter that this council is not taken seriously and has not been able to do enough to promote these values despite such serious challenges to the integration of the nation, posed by the communal elements. Interestingly so far every Central Government has constituted it, barring the BJP led NDA, which deliberately did not constitute it.

Many other issues which required the demarcation of the state versus society's intervention came up. The issue of Kumbh Mela and managing the huge gathering, the Amarnath Yatra, the Hajj subsidy were all tricky problems. In case of Kumbh melas and the Amaranth pilgrimage the idea was that state will look after those arrangements which affect the health, law and order leaving the other matters to the organizers of the religious events. Hajj issue has been misrepresented. The point was that so many pilgrims are going to Mecca and after the stoppage of sea liners and the monopoly of national airline, Air India, given the full responsibility to transport the pilgrim, a subsidy was thought of for the airlines. As the matters stand, every pilgrim has to shell out a substantial amount, and if this monopoly of Air India is done away with this amount is sufficient to cover the travel costs. As this issue is regularly used to buttress the argument of appeasement, we have to remind ourselves that even the NDA govt carried on with this subsidy. Also a large section of Muslims wants that this subsidy be done away with and the maters be left to the social organizations who can get the travel planned with the amount of money, currently being spent by the pilgrims.

So where did Nehru go wrong? The broader picture shows that the land reforms and the grip of clergy, Maulanas and Gurus remained strong in the social affairs. The religion rather than remaining private matter was gradually pushed forward, first in the social space and than in the political space. RSS combine is very hostile to Nehru because he was a rationalist, and firm believer in secularism. Some other streams are critical of him on various grounds. Surely he was no messiah, his direction was correct and limitations in that direction infinite. Despite this Nehru implemented polices which were innovative and original in Indian context. Despite being impressed by the Soviet model he never talked of banning temples or mosques. The charge of minority appeasement also does not hold. Indian constitution, the outcome of India's freedom movement did incorporate that there should be affirmative action for the minorities and there should be recognition of the problems of minorities at all the levels.

He was aware that though Congress is a secular party some communal opportunist elements have made their entry into the same for the sake of power. His observations of that time are applicable today as well. Also after his death the leadership at times did slip and made blunders. Visits to the temples in public glare was started, Shah Bano case and Ramshilanyas were goofed up, many a political leadership slept when violence was taking place or mosques were being demolished and some of them actively colluded with the communal forces.

Nehru has his own quota of shortcomings and faults, but as far as his secular policies were concerned the major criticism can be that those down below blocked his policies getting actualized. Some of these were/are in the party and the others in the bureaucracy.

Jawaharlal Nehru has also been under criticism from different quarters all through for forcing India into Socialist Russia's camp and taking up 'Socialist model of development' through the Public sector industries. Their argument came up once again in the backdrop of Left's pressure not to sign the nuclear deal with U.S (2007). One of the inherent arguments of critics of left and others is that not signing it will keep us away from the deeper friendship of U.S., the land of wealth and prosperity, whose alliance will benefit us a lot.

In the complex scenario, which our world is, to support or oppose a political line is not easy enough. Also the left while opposing the nuclear deal has an attitude towards nuclear power, energy itself, which is not acceptable to most peace workers. While one will like that the left takes a stand which is totally against the nuclear energy and weapons, this is not the case. The major built in argument in their current stance in opposing the nuclear deal with U.S., is that this will push us in the camp of America, as its satellite ally and that will be the doom of India's foreign policy, which has been that of non alignment. There is a criticism that in the name of non-alignment India was tilted towards the Soviet block of yesteryears. Some also pose the question, is it possible in today's post 'Soviet regime' era to remain non-aligned, not to toe the singular pole of global power, America?

Critics of Nehru's foreign policy undermine the fact that India's foreign policy was aimed at minimizing the domination of imperial powers in the World in general and India in particular. Though U.S. and USSR both were the superpowers, there was some difference in their attitude. While opposing the concept of global poles, one also recognizes that most of the countries which were coming out from the slavery of colonial powers needed to develop their industrial infrastructure. U.S. and U.K. were not for helping these countries with the technological support for this infrastructure while USSR partly helped India in building the foundation of industries, which in turn laid the base for the major industrial growth in times to come. The contrast is most visible, when India is compared to its major neighbor Pakistan, which allied with America, and the difference in the in the trajectory of two nations is there for all to see.

Pakistan, happy with the short cut of supply of industrial goods, as a US ally, free market, no license permit raj, a free economy to begin with landed up as a puppet economy in due course. India seeing that the industrialists here cannot set up the base of industrial growth on their own opted for the mixed economy, public sector, many of which were supported by the USSR, for heavy industries and private sector for the rest. The at this point of time. Industrialists did want the state to set up infrastructure industries. Here centralized planning and its accompaniments, which later became frozen and were unable to change with times and led to the demise of Soviet socialist economies.

India's charting independent path with the help of others, more particularly with USSR, in setting up the infrastructure, helped it stand on its feet, while most of the countries which became independent at that time and opted for pro U.S. policies eventually marched towards banana republics, without the core, the base for their social and economic systems.

Parallel to this economic path, India took the road of non alignment. The major opposition to the non alignment policy came from the BJP and its predecessor Bharatiya Jansangh, who has always advocated thick relations with U.S. Politically their ideologue Golwalkar had listed communists as a threat to Hindu nation. So far the policies of RSS-BJP had always been in parallel to those of US. In late 1940s America was following MaCarthism and hunting communists. Around that time in the aftermath of Gandhi murder, Golwalkar was writing to the Sardar Patel that RSS workers should be released from jails and in turn they will help the government to contain communists. And today when U.S. is leading the global anti Muslim tirade, RSS is the lead organization spreading anti Muslim venom here in India.

USSR had no problems with the this non alignment course in foreign policy so it not only endorsed it but also kept giving core support to India for its indigenous growth. US annoyed with India's not accepting US patronage branded India's policies and non alignment in general as the decoy for being pro USSR. India did keep supporting the national liberation struggles in Vietnam and many other nations to the annoyance of US. Today with the changed of World scenario, US is keen that India does not form another block away from U.S., that's why its tilt towards India, away from its nurturing of Pakistan till date.

The basic dilemma which countries like India faced was weather to have 'ready made goods' or to produce the same the hard way. US wanted India to go on this ready made path, while India defied it and pursued independent path. The same got reflected in the foreign policy and attempt to stay clear of US-USSR blocks. It's another matter that USSR for its own strategic reasons was supportive of the non alignment.

This had reflection in India's policy vis a vis Israel-Palestine. Israel, the hub of US interests, hand in glove with Western powers, dominated the region, led to the exile of lakhs of Palestinians and installed an authoritarian state. Palestinians has been struggling for years to get back their own land. Here the aggressor-victim duel was clear and India did opt to keep away from Israel and kept supporting the cause of Palestine. US designs in the region were prompted by the lust for oil, its policy is hegemonic, it theme, 'Oil is too important to be left to the Arabs'.

In this direction it overthrew the Government of Mossadeq in 1953, installed Raza Shah Pehlvi who in turn brought in superficial westernization not bothering to develop the country's infrastructure. The political rebellion against him was given a religious turn and so came in Ayatollah Khomeini. And with this began another chapter in World history. US projected it as signaling the rise of Islam as the 'new threat' to freedom and democracy and this slogan has been serving it in all its aggressions in the Middle East.

While condemning the foreign policy charted out by the builder of Modern India, Nehru, these ideologues conveniently forget that it is important for the World as a whole to promote democratization amongst nations and democratization within nations. The attempt to keep India out of the stifling patronage of US is of paramount importance to ensure the building of democracy amongst nations, away from the hegemony of global bully. The current hegemonic, bullying policies of US, which are the major cause of violence in the world, aggression on Afghanistan and Iraq was preceded by promotion of terrorist outfits, Al Qaeda and its clones, to fight Soviet occupation of Afghanistan. These need to be understood in their proper perspective. We do have to keep the goal that the world marches towards peace and harmony amongst nations and amongst people.

In the contemporary scenario it is easy and also fashionable enough to criticize Nehru's economic-foreign policy. It is difficult to see today that it is precisely these policies of public sector and non alignment which resulted in India charting the course of democracy and economic growth. One is not saying that what has been achieved is satisfactory. The point is this was the comparatively better option, which did help us go some distance in the direction of industrialization-education in the given circumstances. World is essentially global, how we strike a balance between external support and internal growth is a million rupee question. Blindly submitting to the wishes of super power number one, may land us up in the direction of many a banana republics or lead to the fate which our neighbor is seeing due to embracing Uncle Sam.

Time that we build the non aligned movement again, time that we promote regional alliances, time that we see the vision of Nehru in its perspective of indigenous growth and global democracy away from the domination of one or the other superpower.

Despite his multiple failings Nehru essentially charted the path of secularism, industrialization and foerighn policy which helped it to stand on its feet. It is these polices which have given inherent strength to Indian democracy.

9

Hinduism and Hindutva

Currently the term Hindutva is very much in vogue. Despite it being a political category, it is loosely used as sysnonym of Hinduism. This has been deliberately propagated. Both these terms have very specific meaning.

Today's social common sense believes Hinduism to be the religion of all the people in India except those who are specifically Muslims, or Christians. It will be interesting to note that contrary to the popular belief the terms Hindu and Hinduism originated much later and were used by British administrators. They believed that "the essence of India existed in a number of key Hindu classical scriptures such as Vedas, the codes of Manu and the *shastras* that often prescribe hierarchical ideas"...a conclusion "supported and elaborated by Brahmins"[1] British not only absorbed this understanding, but also they put an official seal on it "by applying a legal system based on Brahminic norms to all non-Muslim castes and outcastes, and created an entirely new Brahmin legitimacy. They further validated Brahmin authority by employing, almost exclusively, Brahmins as their clerks and assistants".[2] This fabrication through repetition of "India as unitary Hindu society has obscured the reality of a segmented society, with Brahmins and other upper castes exercising a monopoly of power, fabricated Hinduism is found everywhere".[3]

This historical process whereby Brahminism gained ascendancy has variously been formulated by different sociologists. To give an example Arun Bose[4] writes, "The ideological and a fortiori social, political and economic development of Indian society was arrested at a primitive nomadic stage by the despotic power of ruthless caste of Brahmin priests who fabricated more successfully than any other priestly caste ever known, myths and legends to deceive, oppress and exploit the remaining castes, particularly the Sudra caste. By draconian punishments, reinforced by legends about creation and the cycle of rebirths through which strict conformity with caste taboos was rewarded and infringements penalized, they were able to enforce total and resigned submission to their omnipotent power."

Initially the term Hindu began with regional tones. The term was coined by Arabs and others, who pronounced 'S' as 'H', and to denote the people living on this side of Sindhu (Indus) they called them Hindu. It is only much later that this term was bestowed with a religious meaning. Nehru[5] pointed out that "Hinduism as a faith is vague, amorphous, many sided, all things to all men. It is hardly possible to define it, or indeed to say definitely whether it is a religion or not, in the usual sense of the word, in its present form, and even in the past, it embraces many beliefs and practices, from the highest to the lowest, often opposed to or contradicting each other."

Formulating it more sharply to bring to focus the caste factor, Hinnells and Sharp[6] concede that "A Hindu is a Hindu not because he accepts doctrines and philosophies but because he is a member of "caste", thus implying that Hinduism is a social order and not a religion. Romila Thapar[7] in her analysis posits that, "The new Hinduism which is being currently propagated by the Sanghs, Parishads and Samajs is an attempt to restructure the indigenous religions as a monolithic uniform religion, rather paralleling some of the features of Semitic religions. This seems to be a fundamental departure from the essentials of what may be called the indigenous `Hindu' religions. Its form is not only in many ways alien to the earlier culture of India but equally disturbing is the uniformity which it seeks to impose on the variety of "Hindu' religions".

Hindu sects are multiple and diverse with many founders, and these sects have survived over a period of centuries. At times scholars used the word for a group of different indigenous religions, which could vary in their belief system from animism to atheism, which are looked at with suspicion by today's votaries of Hinduism. Thapar goes on to say, "Hinduism as defined in contemporary parlance is a collation of beliefs, rites and practices consciously selected from those of the past, interpreted in contemporary idiom in last couple of centuries and the selection conditioned by historical circumstances. In a strict sense, a reference to 'Hinduism' would require a more precise definition of the particular variety referred to Brahminism, Brahmo-Samaj, Arya Samaj, Shaiva Siddhanta, Bhakti, Tantricism or whatever."

The major religious categories, which existed earlier, were Brahminism and Shramanism. Shramans were those who were often in opposition to Brahminism, these are the groups which had belief structures away from Vedas and Dharmashastras. Their teachings transcended castes and communities, and in contrast to Brahminism, which categorized religious practice by caste, Shramanic religions opposed this in order to universalize their religious teachings. Bhakti tradition emphasized selfless action projected as the need to act in accordance with one's moral duties. This shift of emphasis, away from Brhaminical rites and sacrificial rituals provided the root, in later time, for a number of cults like *Shaiva, Vaishnava* and many others. It also provided the rough outlines of much that is viewed as traditional 'Hinduism'. Lot of variations occurred in this tradition. Much later Kabir and Nanak brought in Sufi ideas in their teachings. Shakta sect and Tantric rituals also gained wide popularity. These are now played down as being anathema to the current version of Hinduism, i.e. Brahminical Hinduism.

The religious practices of untouchables and Adivasis have a lot of rituals, which involve offerings, and libations of meat and alcohol. Also these groups could not afford the costly donations required for Brahminical *yagnas*. Gradually *dharma* (religious duty) became central to religion, regarded as sacred, which had to be performed in accordance with one's *varna, jati* and sect and which differed according to each of these. Thapar(7) goes on to add, "Hindu' missionary organization, taking their cue from Christian missionaries are active among the adivasis, untouchables and economically backward communities, converting them to 'Hinduism' as defined by upper caste movements of the last two centuries... That this 'conversion' does little or nothing to change their status as adivasis, untouchables and so on and that they continue to be looked down upon by upper caste 'Hindus' is of course of little consequence". Jainism and Buddhism were major amongst Shramanic tradition. These religions were persecuted in many parts of the country. The pre-modern Hinduism was not a monolithic religion, as being projected by the Sangh Parivar, but was a juxtaposition of multiple religious sects.

Thapar calls the Hinduism, currently being propagated by Sangh Parivar as 'Syndicated Hinduism'. This projection is made by the social base of the Sangh Parivar, a powerful urban middle class with a reach to rural rich who find it useful to bring into politics, a uniform, monolithic Hinduism created to serve its new requirement. The Hinduism, which more or less has won the social space and draws mainly from Brahminical texts, and also draws from *Dharmashastras*. The attempt of this exercise is to present a modern reformed religion. The net result is a repackaged Brahminism. The Hindu communities settled abroad, look for a parallel to Christianity, as their religion. This is to overcome the sense of inferiority and cultural insecurity, which they experience in their life. Thapar goes on to say, "Syndicated Hinduism claims to be re-establishing the Hinduism of pre-modern times; in fact it is only establishing itself and in the process distorting the historical and cultural dimensions of indigenous religions and divesting them of the nuances and variety which was a major source of their enrichment."

To put the understanding in a linear way: "The Hindu religion as it is described today is said to have its roots in the Vedas. In any case, whatever we call the religion of these nomadic clans, it was not the religion that is today known as Hinduism. This (Hinduism in its current version) began to be formulated only in the period of Maghadha-Mauryan State, Buddhism and Jainism (as well as the materialist Charvak tradition) were equally old-Hinduism as we know it, was in other words, only one of the many consolidations within a diverse sub-continental cultural tradition, and attained social and political hegemony only during the sixth to tenth century A.D., often after violent confrontations with Buddhism and Jainism".[8]

As per Gail Omvedt this Brahminic Hinduism adopted and identified with the authority of the Vedas and Brahmans. Material base of this system was the caste structure of the society. Its co-optive power was qualified to the extent that dissidents had to accept their place in the caste hierarchy. The masses of people did not have the identity of 'Hindu'. Multiple local gods and traditions existed side by side forming the base of popular culture. Later, only during colonial period this identity of 'Hindu' was constructed for all the inhabitants of this land except those who were followers of Islam or Christianity. This construction was thrown up by English scholarship and by Indian elite. Gail posits that, "In the nineteenth century, people like Lokmanya Tilak adopted the 'Aryan theory of Race', claimed a white racial stock for upper caste Indians and accepted Vedas as their core literature. Tilak was also the first to try and unite a large section of the masses around Brahminical leadership with celebration of Ganesh festival." One gets a clear idea that Sangh Parivar has succeeded in perpetuating a perception amongst Hindus to forge a communal solidarity through elective projections of the past, and this does involve a deliberate reformulation of history. Emergence of nation-state does bring in a homogenization of religion. In case of India this evolution of "national religion and Hinduism has mainly been defined in opposition to the Muslim 'other'".

Hindutva: Ideological Foundations

The construction of Hindutva is to be seen in the backdrop of emergence of Hinduism as a homogenous religion. The concept of Brahminical Hinduism, projected as Hinduism was at the root of multiple religious revivalist movements. Its political translation began mainly with Bal Gangadhar Tilak, who initiated the Ganapati Festival to wean away the popular participation of lower castes people in Muharram festival. Some sociologists[9] have called such ideological maneuvers as "manipulative reinterpretation of cultural material" and "invention of tradition". Later Tilak went on to organize a festival in honour of Shivaji, who broke the Moghul hold on western India and opened the way for rampage of Maratha armies through much of India. A strong anti-Muslim slant was brought into the function.

Anti-Muslim sentiments were consistently used to project a political methodology of consolidating the Hindus. Starting from Bankimchandra Chatterjee, various other Hindu national ideologues had whipped the fear psychosis with Muslims as the ones' threatening the survival of Hindus. All these fabrications were manufactured and propagated by the ascendant, nascent, amorphous Hindu nationalist forces. The combination of 'Syndicated Hinduism' with nationalism was brewed by Vinayak Damodar Savarkar who can be called the first exponent of the doctrine of Hindutva. The mix of Brahminical Hinduism with nationalism reflecting the interests of upper castes and part of upper class was defined and later refined on the exclusionist principles, which are so basic to the Brahminism. Savarkar's initial anti-British struggles were very impressive. After assuming the role of the proponent of Hindutva his major energies were channelized in strengthening the politics of hate, formation of communal Hindu Mahasabha and helping RSS from distance.

Savarkar's work 'Hindutva: Who is Hindu' (1923) became and remains the basic text defining this political concept. With the simultaneous rise of Muslim communalism: Muslim nationalism, in due course most of the Hindu consolidations took place by showing the fear of Muslims. This nationalism consolidated itself on the ground of the threatening other, but this threatening other was not the British imperialist colonizers whose rule the country was suffering but was the 'Muslim'. As an aside we should note here that Savarkar's anti-British struggles and anti-British activities totally ceased after his release by the British, and from then on all his guns were to be targeted against the Muslims, presented in most threatening way ,by him. Savarkar argued (later on this became the ideological base of most of the Hindutva organizations) "the Aryans who settled in India at the dawn of history already formed a nation, now embodied in the Hindus.... Hindus are bound together not only by the tie of the love they bear to a common fatherland and by the common blood that courses through their veins and keeps our hearts throbbing and our affection warm but also by the tie of the common homage we pay to our great civilization, our Hindu culture."[10] Thus Hindutva according to him rests on three pillars: geographical unity, racial features and common culture." He further went on to elaborate the criterion for who is Hindu? According to him all those who regard this land as their fatherland and holy-land are the only ones who are Hindu and thereby the people to whom this land belongs. This led to the automatic interpretation that the Christians and the Muslims, whose holy places are in Jerusalem and Mecca are not on par with the 'Hindus' who own this country, initiating the theorizing of the 'doubting of patriotism of Muslim's'.

Savarkar writes, "...but besides culture the tie of common holy-land has at times proved stronger than the claims of a motherland. Look at Mohammedans: Mecca to them is a sterner reality than Delhi or Agra." This development of the concept of Hindutva comes in succession on the construction of Brahminism as Hinduism and this Brahminical Hinduism then forming the base for Hindutva politics. Savarkar began to articulate the ideology of Hindu elite (zamindars, Brahmins, kings) by integrating Brahminical Hinduism with nationalism, calling it Hindutva which further showed the way for building the Hindu Rashtra. His key sentence was `Hinduise all politics and militarise all Hindudom".

Savarkar's politics was polar opposite of Gandhian politics. Gandhi - the representative of Indian Nationalism was branded as conciliator and appeaser of Muslims. Savarkar propounded that struggle for supremacy would begin after British left and that the Christians and Muslims were the real enemies who could be defeated only by "Hindutva". His key sentence was "Hinduise all politics and militarise Hindudom". He maintained that this land belonged to Hindus and so by implication Muslims with Hold Land in Mecca and Christians with Holy land in Jerusalem cannot have equal status to 'Hindus'. This concept was later to be made more explicit by Golwalkar, who despite adoring Hitler, was 'generous' and 'kind' enough to these 'aliens' by granting them the status of second class citizens. With this began the concept of Hindu Raj - the precursor of the present Sangh Parivar goal - the Hindu Rashtra. The final crystallization of Hindutva occurred with foundation of Rashtriya Swayamsevak Sangh (RSS) which became the Father organization for plethora of organizations, which were to take birth after a period of consolidation of the core swayamsevaks (volunteers).

Hindutva: Growth

The early simmerings of Hindutva can be seen in the opposition to the secular Congress movement of 19th century. The Jamindar (landlord) moneylenders, Brahmin and Banias spearheaded the reaction to secular politics. This support base constantly stood by the Hindutva politics all through. Later some industrialists did successfully ride on two boats of supporting secular Gandhian movement and also supporting Hindutva movement. But mostly the modern industrialists stood by the secular movement led by Gandhi. The Rajas (Hindu kings of Princely States) also by and large stood by the politics of RSS. The march of industrialization process changed the social composition and brought in newer layers into society. Though BJP and its predecessor the Jan Sangh began with small electoral support, this support was fairly consistent. It was the urban middle classes, sections of upper castes. Let us have a brief look at the changes in social composition, which have occurred during last 50 years of the republic. The proportion of urban population has gone up by 20-25 per cent. They also constitute

Hinduism	*Hindutva*
1. A collation of multiple traditions traditions: Brahminism Shramanism-Charvak, Tantra, Kabir, Tukaram.	1. Politics of Hindu elite, Drawing from Brahminical Hinduism.
2. Brahminism: Caste system, the dominant ethos	2. Brew of Brahminical Hinduism and Nationalism
3. Brahminism projected as Hinduism initially in 6-10 century, then in early 19th century, Brahminical Hinduism projected to be Synonymous with Hinduism.	3. Aims at Hindu Rashtra based on Brahminical Hinduism
4. (Shramanic traditions: Constant rebellion: attempt to escape the clutches of Brahminism: conversion to Buddhism (early times And now after the lead given by Ambedkar). Vivekananda said: Why amongst the poor are so many Mohammedans..., not due to Escape the tyranny of the Zamindar and the priests.	4. Led initially by Brahmins: Banias: even now dominant Leadership from upper castes.
5. 'Dharma' is a mix of Humanism and caste based religious duties.	5. Political expression through Sangh Parivar now, earlier Hindu Mahasabha and RSS.

(Contd.)

(Contd.Table)

Hinduism	*Hindutva*
6. Semitisation process being spear-headed by SP Holy deity: Ram, Holy Book: Gita, clergy: Shankaracharyas etc.	6. A mix of fundamentalism and Fascism (see table)
7. Its proponents claim it to be tolerant and catholic. cf: earlier it's attitude to shudras cf: Now it's attitude to Muslims	7. VHP brings in the stink of fundamentalism in the essentially fascist politics of RSS, BJP and Bajarangdal.

the ones' which derived maximum benefit of modern education and the facilities thrown up by the industrialization process. They do have a sort of dominant presence in the society. The cultural, social and political aspirations of this sector are the ground, on which has risen the edifice of Sangh Parivar.

References

1. Heynes Douglas and Gyan Prakash eds 1991, Contesting power: Resistance and Everyday Racial Relations in South Asia : Delhi, OUP, p. 6.
2. Arthur Bonner, Democracy in India: A hollow shell, The American University Press, Washington, 1994, p. 40.
3. Ibid, p. 41.
4. Arun Bose, India's Social Crisis, Delhi : OUP, p. 56.
5. Jawaharlal Nehru, The Discovery of India, John Day, 1946, p. 66.
6. Hinndles, John and Eric Sharpe (eds) Hinduism, New Caste, Oriental Press, 1972, p. 128.
7. Romila Thapar, 'Syndicated Moksha?' Seminar, 1987, pp. 14-22.
8. Gail Omvedt, Dalit Visions (Tract for the times - 8), Orient Longman, 1995, pp.7-12.
9. Jaffrelot Christopher, 1993, 'Hindu Nationalism : Strategies in ideology building' *Economic and Political Weekly,* March 20, 93, 517-24.
10. V.D. Savarkar, Hindutva, p.108, Nagpur, 1923, p. 94.

10

Freedom Movement, Savarkar and RSS

The rise of dominant assertion of RSS in the political sphere has been accompanied by its claim of being most patriotic organization, its claim that it has contributed to the nation building and has contributed in the freedom movement. It has also been trying to act as an aggressive judge, classifying people as patriots or otherwise. More so it has propagated that minorities are not patriotic and have not contributed to freedom movement. At the same time, Vinayak Damodar Savarkar, the major Hindutva ideologue, has been adorned as Veer, (Brave), swatantryaveer (brave freedom fighter), his statues have been raised at places, roads have been named after him in different cities. During the BJP led NDA (1998-2004) his portrait was put up in the central hall of parliament. This government also named the Port Blair airport in his name. The word of mouth propaganda has been eulogizing him as the real 'Father of the Nation'.

With the change of regime at the Center (2004), the new petroleum minister Mani Shankar Aiyer replaced his plaque at Andaman's with that of Mahatma Gandhi. This again became a matter of controversy, the BJP-Sena alliance tried to capitalize on this for the elections, in Maharashtra where Savarkar has been projected as a great revolutionary and efforts have been made to show that he was the guiding figure for all the great Freedom fighters apart from being a progressive person of sorts. Even Congress, whose minister, Aiyer had taken the bold step of catching the bull by horns, shivered and said that Aiyer's views are his personal. The Maharashtra Congress going by the electoral compulsions said that Savarkar was a freedom fighter and is a respectable person because of that. One also recalls the committee which cleared that Savarkar's portrait be unveiled in the hall of parliament, had some Communists leaders in it who did not protest against this proposal and the Andaman prison, where he was kept before he got himself released after giving a humiliating apology, has been named after his name. Those opposing Savarkars' being given these honors have been insulted. Similarly Atal Bihari Vajpayee, the BJPs' mask also claimed that he participated in the freedom movement. Where does the truth lie?

Freedom Movement

India's freedom was the greatest mass movement ever, anytime and anyplace in the World. It assumed the mass character after the efforts of Gandhi from 1920, before which it had more of an elite character. This movement primarily aimed at throwing away the British rule, the phenomenon, which were parallel to this were multiple, and they were affecting total social equations and life pattern of society. All this was taking place in the backdrop of process of industrialization, and the introduction of modern education. These twin processes resulted in the emergence of new business industrial class, educated middle class and working class. These twin processes also resulted in the change of social hierarchy of caste and gender. Women and dalits began to have access to education as well as were participating in the social and political movements as equal beings. This whole process of change was captured in the phrase, India as the Nation in the making. The streams belonging to Indian National Congress, majority of sections of left and dalits leaders at most of the times articulated the need for democratic values, the values of liberty, equality and fraternity, which were the slogan of India's struggle for independence.

In contrast to the emerging classes and the concept of India as a nation in the making, those associated with declining classes, landlords, kings and associated clergy stuck to the pre modern values of birth based inequality of caste and gender. They believed in the early formation of Muslim Nation (8th Century) or Hindu nation (since times immemorial) in contrast to the concept of India as a nation in the making. The political streams coming from this section were Muslim league, Hindu Mahasabha and RSS amongst others. These groups never participated in the freedom movement. The major reason being that freedom movement aimed at democratic values, while these groups hold on the birth based inequality. Here it should be clear that Hindus and Muslims belonging to the rising ideology and 'nation in the making' participated in the freedom movement, while the one's who belonged to the declining classes remained aloof from the freedom movement and indirectly contributed to the implementation of British policy of divide and rule. While most Hindus participated in the movement for freedom, the followers of Hindu Mahsabha and RSS kept aloof. While most of the Muslims participated in this movement, the followers of Muslim League did not do so. Incidentally the Maulanas of Barelvi and Deoband did associate with the struggle for independence of India.

Savarkar and Freedom movement

Savarkar has been the founder of Hindutva ideology, the base of Hindu right wing feudal values. One needs to look at the trajectory of his life to understand this transition from anti-British revolutionary to the ideologue of Hindutva. Savarkar initially was an anti British revolutionary. Later his life underwent major transition during his confinement in Andamans. He was a changed man after the period of his jail life. He was an anti-British revolutionary prior to his deportment to Andaman's but later he never associated with any thing even remotely sounding as anti-British.

He had gone to study law in London and for his anti-British stance he was denied the barrister-ship. In England Savarkar formed 'Free Indian Society' committed to overthrowing British rule in India. That time he rejected the British proposal to give the undertaking not to participate in politics. His group had learnt the art of bomb making from a Russian revolutionary in Paris. One member of the group killed a top-ranking official in India office (London) and was sentenced to death. For involvement in this and for another charges on him in Indian courts, Savarkar was arrested, sentenced and was to undergo life imprisonment. He was deported from England. The ship carrying him stopped at Marseilles, where he jumped into the sea and swam to the shore to claim asylum on French soil. He was captured back and was transported to Andamans for life imprisonment.

The conditions in Andman jail were very painful. The political prisoners were tortured badly. He could not bear the torture like most other inmates of the prison. It seems that conditions of jail life broke his spirits. Incidentally from 1920 Indian National Congress was asking for his unconditional release, but due to reasons best known to him Savarkar preferred to give a written undertaking to get released from the jail, "I hereby acknowledge that I had a fair trial and just sentence. I heartily abhor methods of violence resorted to in days gone by and I feel myself duty bound to uphold law and constitution (British, added) to the best of my powers and am willing to make the 'reform' a success in so far as I may be allowed to do so in future" (from facsimile of Savarkar's letter to British authorities, Frontline, April 7, 1995. Pg. 94). The reforms he is referring to here are the Montague Chelmsford proposals of 1919, which did not satisfy the nationalist movement's demands.

In response to this, as a trade off, the British Government released him under the condition that he will stay in Ratnagiri district in Bombay province and will seek permission of the government to leave the district. Also that he will not engage in any public or private political activities without the consent of the government. The period of conditions lasted till 1937, when the Congress ministry was sworn in. Subsequent to this he assumed the office of the President of Hindu Mahasabha. This aspect of his total surrender is totally hidden by the Hindutva forces; they confer on him the epithet of 'Veer (brave) Savarkar'.

Why did British government release him? How is it that after his release the track of his politics totally changed and he came to adorn the mantle of ideologue Hindu Rashtra? How is it that later he never undertook any anti British agitation? How is it that he never joined and supported the major movements of those times like Quit India movement? How is it that instead of being the part of freedom struggle, he chose to help the British in recruiting Indians for their army? One can have ones' own inferences but his compromise with British hides lot of messages about the nature of his politics from then on. He did emerge as the undisputed leader of Hindu Mahasabha In most of the times, post-1937, and his politics was the polar opposite of National movement led by Gandhi and 'no support to Congress move' was his basic dictum. This can be best exemplified in the 1942 Quit India movement, when Gandhi gave the call for the people to leave the government jobs. Instead Savarkar issued the edict

"I issue this definite instruction to all Hindu Sanghathanists in general holding any post or position of vantage in the government services, should stick to them and continue to perform their regular duties". (quoted in A G Noorani Frontline, Dec. 1, 1995). Also working committee had passed a resolution on August 31, 1942 asking all Mahasabhaites to remain at their jobs. Savarkar does have the 'honor' of brewing Brahminical Hinduism with nationalism, and he was the first exponent of the doctrine of Hindutva. Savarkar's initial anti-British struggles were very impressive but after assuming the role of the proponent of Hindutva his major energies were channelised in strengthening the politics of hate, formation of communal Hindu Mahasabha and helping RSS from distance.

As an aside we should note here that Savarkar's anti-British struggles and anti-British activities totally ceased after his release by the British, and from then on all his guns were to be targeted against the Muslims. Savarkar argued (later on this became the ideological base of most of the Hindutva organizations) - "the Aryans who settled in India at the dawn of history already formed a nation, now embodied in the Hindus...Hindus are bound together not only by the tie of the love they bear to a common fatherland and by the common blood that courses through their veins and keeps our hearts throbbing and our affection warm but also by the tie of the common homage we pay to our great civilization, our Hindu culture." (Hindutva, Page108)

Thus Hindutva according to him rests on three pillars: geographical unity, racial features and common culture. He further went on to elaborate the criterion for who is Hindu? According to him all those who regard this land as their fatherland and holy-land are the only ones who are Hindu and thereby the people to whom this land belongs. This led to the automatic interpretation that the Christians and the Muslims, whose holy places are in Jerusalem and Mecca, are not on par with the 'Hindus' who 'own' this country. Initiating the theorizing of the 'doubting of patriotism of Muslim's', Savarkar states -"but besides culture the tie of common. Savarkar's politics was rival to Gandhian politics. Gandhi - the representative of Indian Nationalism- was branded by Savarkar as conciliator and appeaser of Muslims. Savarkar propounded that struggle for supremacy would begin after British left and that the Christians and Muslims were the real enemies who could be defeated only by "Hindutva". He maintained that this land belonged to Hindus and so by implication Muslims with Holy Land in Mecca and Christians with Holy land in Jerusalem cannot have equal status to 'Hindus'. It is also worth remembering, that murderer of Gandhi, Godse was his ardent follower. Savarkar himself was the co-accused in Gandhi murder, but was let off for lack of the corroborative evidence and as Godse took the whole responsibility of this murder totally on his own self.

Now it is being claimed by his followers, that surrendering to British and seeking their pardon, was a clever strategy on the part of Savarkar. Many anonymous things are being attributed to Savarkar. It is aimed at the Hindutva followers want to twist and turn the interpretation of events and his writings to blindly eulogize him. That he wrote anti British articles after his release is a pure figment of his imagination and a 'Savarkar mythology' is being created to replace the exact history, which is available through his writings and authentically published works and documents from impeccable sources. One point being made is that he knew India is going to get Independence any way so why waste energies in fighting against

British. We see that as the political process unfolded, the Pakistan resolution itself was passed in 1940 and the chances of avoiding partition were very much on the horizon till the 1942's Cripps mission's recommendations were doubted by a section of Congress leadership. Most of the political movements, which are committed to transparency, do keep agitating for their goals till they are achieved as shown by the leaders like Gandhi and Nehru. Some of his followers also claim that the apology to British was just an eye wash. These people forget that every statement has a political impact and that's how Bhagat Singh reprimanded his father when he wanted to plead and to British to release his son.

Rashtriya Swayamsevak Sangh

Coming to RSS, the RSS Combine (RC) claims to have contributed substantially in the process of 'nation building' and freedom struggle. History textbooks introduced in schools wherever BJP governments have come to power delve at great length about the contribution of their ideologues in National movement claiming that Dr. Hedgewar was himself imprisoned during the freedom struggle. Fact of the matter is that Hedgewar himself joined the *Satyagraha* movement only briefly and was imprisoned for a short while, but overall the struggles leading to national independence are non-events for RSS. (Civil-disobedience (1940-1941), Quit India struggle (1942), Azad Hind Fauj, 1945-46 upsurges around INA trials and the Bombay Naval Mutiny.)

RSS as an organization was never a part of Anti-British movement. Its founder Dr. K.B.Hedgewar, had been first sentenced to jail before he founded RSS, in the wake of Khilafat movement. This was on the charges of giving provocative speech. The second and last time he was sentenced to jail during the 1930 call of Gandhi to the people to break the laws. Hedgewar told the RSS that we will not participate in this movement as

RSS but those who want to participate in their personal capacity they can do so. He himself was jailed during this. His biographer clarifies that his main goal in participating was, "Dr. Sahib had the confidence that with a freedom loving, self sacrificing and reputed group of people inside with him there, he woul discuss the Sangh with them and win them over for its work" (C.P.Bhishikar, Sanghvriksha ke Beej, Dr. Keshav baliram Hadgewar, New Delhi 19994, p 20). The idea was very clear, not to participate in the movement but to get contacts for building the divisive politics of RSS. Hedgewar later dissociated himself from it from 1931 onwards and never again he was part of any National movement.

From then on Dr. Hedgewar's ideological break up with the national movement was complete and he abstained from the freedom movement. This non participation was ideologically formulated by MS Golwalkar, as per whom fighting against British is reactionary and he accused the Congress for reducing the national struggle to 'mere' anti British movement. Golwalkar writes, "Being anti British was equated with patriotism and nationalism, this reactionary view had disastrous effect upon the entire course of the independence struggle, its leaders and the common people" (Golwalkar, Bunch of Thoughts 1939). Obviously, with this ideological formulation the Sangh Parivar did not and could not fight against the British. The RSS equated its nationalism with being against Muslims and hence its constant harps against the national leadership for 'appeasement of Muslims'. "The Hindu Mahasabha and RC kept away even from Naval revolt because they (mutineers) used guns against the British and the Sangh Parivar considered fighting against British as "disastrous" and "reactionary".

Anderson and Damle (Brotherhood in Saffron) point out "Golwalkar believed that the British not be given any excuse to ban the RSS. On April 29, 1943 Golwalkar distributed a circular that 'We discontinue practice included in the governments order on military drill and uniforms to keep our work clearly within bounds of law, as every law abiding institution should'..." (Quoted in A G Noorani, Frontline, Dec. 1, 1995). The description of RSS and freedom struggle is necessarily brief, as one cannot describe a non-phenomenon beyond a point. RSS in nutshell was not only consciously absent as for as freedom movement was concerned, but on the contrary it was acting from the opposite angle by opposing various movements for freedom struggle (especially Quit India movement). Also it was active as a communal body, boosting the impact of Muslim communalism and participating in the process of mutual supplementation of Hindu and Muslim communalism.

Vajpayee and Freedom Movement:

Much is also made of 'participation' of BJP's *mask*, Mr. Atal Bihari Vajpayee, in Quit India movement. This was the time when young Vajpayee was a recruit of RSS. In an article put on the net (this article also appeared in newspapers) "The Sangh is my soul" for the consumption of NRIs and for soliciting their support for Sangh Parivar, he says, "When I wrote '*Hindu Tan Man Hindu Jeevan*' I was a student of class X. Till 1947 I did the RSS work at *shakha* level...*I also participated in the Quit India movement in 1942 and was jailed.* (italics added) I was then studying for my Intermediate examination. I was arrested from my native village Bateshwar in Agra district". This claim of his has been investigated in detail and findings published in Frontline Feb 20, 1998. (Manini Chatterjee and V K Ramchandran.) This investigation nails the lie of his participation in Quit India Movement in 1942.

The controversy around his role in the Bateshwar incident makes it clear that he had nothing whatsoever to do with freedom movement. He had given a confessional statement in the court which helped in his release from the jail for his being just the onlooker and part of the assembly which went on to damage the government property. As pointed out above he was a dedicated and active member of RSS. He did not participate in the movement according to his own confession, (Frontline, Feb. 20, 1998) and for a brief while was part of the crowd, as an onlooker, which went to break the forest law. He could have been prosecuted under section 149 of IPC *but* for his confession, as the approach of the government was very harsh against the protestors. In his confession he wriggles out of active participation. "I along with my brother followed the crowd; I did not cause any damage. I did not render any assistance in demolishing the government buildings". His statement provided an accurate description of the events on which prosecution could build its case very well. Also it named two leaders of the protesters Kakua alias Liladhar and Mahuan, both of whom were tried in the case. As per Liladhar "Atal Bihari's confessional statement was not part of the evidence in the court that led to his sentence, but it did help shape the prosecutions case at the investigative stage. ...... Prosecution's case largely echoes Atal Bihari's statement." This is so far as the 'patriotic' writer of Hindu *Tan Man Hindu Jeevan's* role in the freedom struggle goes.

Freedom Movement: Democratic Values

It should be apparent that only those participated in the freedom movement who stood for democratic values, those who aspired for multicultural, multi-religious plural country. These were the one's who stuck to tricolor, while those for saffron flag or green falg had no role to play in this mass movement, which built the India, which we are. It is a sign of times, the retrograde one's that those who kept aloof, criticized and opposed this movement are today claiming to be the custodians of Nationalism. Their nationalism is not Indian nationalism, theirs' is a sectarian, religion based one, the total anti thesis to what India is!

11

Perceptions and Reality: Social Common Sense

Why has the communal violence been growing, why has been the killing of innocent victims possible? And why does the large visible section of society quietly condone the killing of innocents? These questions have been dogging the minds of social activists. At various levels the issues raised by the communal politics have posed a serious challenge to the democratic values. One of the obstacles to the values of harmony comes from the notions held by the people about the minority community. We have to understand that the 'social common sense' prevalent in the society projects the minorities in negative color. What are these understandings about the minorities? How they came into being? How do they get strengthened? What is their impact? And how does one overcome it were the main questions posed for discussion.

The prevalent notions are encountered through the casual talk with the people, can be gleaned through the media, and are perceptible in different aspects of cultural expressions in the society. The ones' prevalent relate to the history, more so of medieval India, the so called Muslim period of Indian history, related to the ancient Indian history, related to the freedom movement and to the partition tragedy in particular. About the contemporary society there are many related to Muslims marrying more number of times, having twenty children, being aggressive as they eat meat, being conservative, being more unjust to 'their' women and also that all terrorists are Muslims. Many of these pertain to the Christian minorities also, like Christian missionaries are converting forcibly in the adivasi areas. Also that Muslims should be sent to Pakistan and that Christians are foreigners. As the time passes most of these myths about minorities are becoming stronger by the day.

It should be pointed out that the root of history based myths is the communal historiography introduced by the British to pursue their aim of enslaving this country and also their policy of divide and rule. The mass consciousness has been doctored in a way that the minorities are looked at with suspicion. This doctoring of mass consciousness has been achieved by various mechanisms including the role of communal organizations boosting each other in all the ways. The intensity of these varies from place to place in India but its trajectory is the same. It is maximum in Gujarat, followed by Jammu. In different parts of the country these prevail in one or the other form with varying shades of intensity.

It was James Mill who periodized Indian history on grounds of religion, the identities which had begun to become stronger during the British rule. The ancient India being Hindu Rashtra as it was the period of Hindu Kings got further boost from the theory propounded by Golwalkar that Aryans are the original inhabitants of this land. The Kings cannot be the markers of religion neither can the history be periodized as per the religion of Kings. At no point of time was the whole area ruled by the Kings belonging to one religion. Also that Kings kept invading different regions depending on their armed might. Kingdoms cannot be equated to modern nation states. The issue of Somnath temple and Ram Temple destruction are uppermost in the minds of the people. It is not realized that Kings destroyed temples for appropriating wealth and for showing their hegemony over the defeated kingdoms. Also British historiography was keen to present the Muslim rulers in the unfair light, as they had to win over the loyalty of subjects of the country.

That pertains to the Babri Masjid as the British Gazetteer A.F. Beevraidge put the unfounded question mark that there might have been a temple at the site where the mosque is located. There are infinite examples of the Hindu kings destroying Hindu Temples,(Temple Destructions in Ancient India- Richard Eaton), Muslim Kings destroying mosques, like Aurangzeb destroying Golconda mosque when tribute was not paid by Tana Shah for few consecutive years. Hindu kings got the initial mosques made on the Malabar Coast. Tipu sultan went on to repair the temple Shrirangpatanam, which was destroyed by retreating Maratha armies.

The rule of kings was not based on the religion of the courtiers, as Kings selected courtiers from all the religions. The nine Jewels of Akbar, The Muslim generals of Shivaji and Hakim Khan Sur assisting Rana Pratap in his battle against Akbar are too well known.

Similarly conversion to Islam in this country is seen as the act of the kings while in reality Islam spread in India because of the humane teachings of Sufi saints. Surely some individuals and landlords did convert to Islam out of fear or expectation of reward but those are few compared to the Shudras who embraced

Islam in large numbers. Many an Islamic/ Hindu communities imbibed the traditions from both the religions communities, Navayat Muslims of Kerala, Mevs of Rajasthan are example of that. Today source of origin of many of our traditions, food and customs cannot be attributed to any one particular religious source. We have syncretic traditions in all streams of our life. Celebrating diversity is one way of looking at it. As such communities do live with each other constantly interacting and transforming their norms of life. It cannot be related just to religion.

Similarly the freedom movement saw the rise of Hindu and Muslim communalism both. The elite landlord sections were the one's to begin these communal streams which were later joined in by some middle class intellectuals, who provided the ideological elaboration for the communal politics. It was the British goal to have a foothold in South Asia due to which they were keen on partitioning the country and the Muslim and Hindu communal streams played in their hands.

These myths had matching myths from the Muslim communal stable. Both communal streams spread it recklessly. Here in India the RSS has been the major body spreading the venom against minorities, to communalize the sections of society. Initially RSS had Shakhas where through Bouddhik (intellectual) sessions, 'hate minorities' was spread. Later different swayamsevaks trained by RSS, infiltrated in the field of bureaucracy, education and media to keep perpetuating these myths. Especially after the Janata Party came to power and Lal Krishna Advani became the information broadcasting minister he planted the swayamsevaks in key positions in the media establishment due to which the communalization of social space began at a rapid speed.

It is also interesting that the myths about the current life of Muslim community came into being, due to the historical reasons of educational backwardness of section of Muslim community, which in turn was due to the economic deprivation and maltreatment by the state apparatus and the society. This educational backwardness and poor education resulted in the large families while it started being said that it again is due to Islam. The Ghettoization and backwardness led to the fertile ground for the hold of Mullahs, and the policy of state Govt to appease the fundamentalist sections of society led cases like Shah Bano. It went on to build up the anti Muslim biases in a big way. The biases were cleverly mixed up to project that Muslims belong to Pakistan and that they should leave India and go to Pakistan. By this time the media started playing a dangerous role in strengthening the stereotypes. The print media was supplemented by visual media and the picture started becoming much vitiated. After the occurrence of communal violence, one could see that after the violence the intensity of hate due to myths/stereotypes goes up exponentially.

There was a realization that the school books as currently prevalent in the state level boards are having such inherent biases, while the NCERT books which were good, were replaced during the NDA regime. All in all the school books, RSS propaganda through word of mouth and its affiliates and mechanisms developed by it, through media had already prepared a fertile ground for the communalization of the social space, more so the middle classes. With the violence spreading to villages and with the RSS affiliates like VHP reaching the villages the communalization also began to reach the villages.

Today we are standing at a very sensitive stage of social common sense. It has not only spread it has also gripped the sections of society, middle class in great severity and other classes in general. Ghettoisation has added up to the problems and this emotional distance has brought in the physical separation in the form of borders coming up between Hindu and Muslim communities. Most of the urban centers in north India, which have witnessed riots, are having separate dwellings for Hindus and Muslims and it is impossible for a Muslim to get a house in 'Hindu' area. Many a professional also face the problem in the cosmopolitan offices where the communalization has percolated far and wide. Few are the social spaces which have not been influenced by this communalization. Many instances were cited by the participants about what they hear and how it intimidates the minorities.

The ghettoisation and poverty result in poor hygienic conditions which are again affixed to Muslims while its origin is purely social in nature. The rate of literacy amongst Muslims has been low because of the discrimination, because of their coming mostly from Shudra background and lack of affirmative action for them. While it is a social causation it is fixed to their nature as a blot. Victim is presented as the culprit in this case. As far as communal violence goes a new myth has been making rounds that Muslims start the communal violence as they are violent in nature. This is the highest success of the Right wing organizations. The minority is generally cornered and than attacked mostly in a preplanned manner, but it is projected as if minorities, Muslim start the riots. Most of the investigation commissions have pointed that, the riots are engineered by a group affiliated to RSS and many a riots are well planned by communal organizations right in advance like the one of Gujarat. It is interesting that while the inquiry commissions have one type of conclusion the popular notions are totally against that and are getting deeply ingrained in people's minds.

Interestingly food habits and violence have been linked up in the popular psyche and those who are out to demonize the Muslims have gone to the extent of saying that they are violent due to non vegetarian food. This went to the extent that one airline stopped serving non vegetarian food in its flights from

Mumbai to Ahmedabad. Flights. Muslims are looked at with suspicion and there is not much which is happening to counter these in the society. In Anand in Gujarat one boy recounted as to how the dental surgeon, to whom he went for treatment happened to be good despite being a Muslim. In Mumbai a house buyer was told by the real estate agent that the colony is very good as there are no Muslims in the area. More so in Gujarat the polarization has gone to the extent the even the lawyers are being labeled as Hindu or Muslim lawyers. One photo journalist of high professional career could not get a house on the ground that he is a Muslim. One young Muslim boy, a promising and bright young man was questioned in the aftermath of blasts in Varanasi. Such incidents abound.

To add to the whole picture the 9/11 and its projection by US media, and our media picking up the lead from there, the Muslim demonization is close to complete. Cricket match and few Muslims celebrating Pakistan victory is the most important 'proof' of all Muslims being loyal to Pakistan. The Al Qaeda, which as such was propped up by U.S. was projected as the 'representative' of Muslims and every Muslim has been subtly and overtly presented as a terrorist. The Mumbai blasts, in the aftermath of first, the Mumbai riots and than in the aftermath of Gujarat violence, left no doubt in the mind of middle class, which has no time to have critical thinking to see the difference between the acts of terrorists and the Muslim community at large is the point which leads to the myth that all terrorists are Muslims. Now, in a loose manner Muslims are labeled as terrorists, without much compunction. After every stage-managed or maneuvered encounter few Muslim names come in handy as those who had been shot and one more layer of stereotype is added on to the prevailing ones. The atmosphere created due to these is so intense that Muslim youth do feel the intimidation and threat. Clever use has been made by the manufacturers of these stereotypes, they use each and every phenomenon to fit in to their picture of mythification. In this the use of Azan from the mosques is cleverly done, Haj subsidy is brought in and what have you.

Section of 'intellectuals' have been picking up from Koran, the words used by terrorist organizations and demanding that those words should be removed from the Holy book to ensure peace. It is another matter that the interpretation of most of the holy books may have problems with other sections, and that the acts of terror are not due to the reading of those books but due to the political use of those words by the bigger players of the game, like CIA getting the word Jihad popularized as the attack on communists in Afghanistan, and Kafir for the non believer communist armies occupying Afghanistan. Their broadened general use is the logical extension of the same is not a religious phenomenon related to Islam but a political phenomenon. Also these books, Koran, Vedas and Bible all will have some or the other thing not palatable to big sections. They are records of those times. What is needed is to distinguish between religion and politics, and politics in the garb of religion. Islam has come under the chopping block of imperialist and communal forces. Madrasas are being seen as the places where terrorists are bred. Most of the scholarly studies on Madrasa show that poor Muslims who cannot afford modern education are the one's sending their children to Madrassas.

The demonization of this community has started having effect on the psyche of the section of that community. One can see the over bending the back and surrender at places by sections of the community. A section hides behind strengthening the conservative identity while another section is trying to shake off these orthodoxies to come to grips with the modern values and focusing on modern education etc, one section has decided to surrender and do the bidding of communal forces; another section of course is joining the tormentors to save their own skin.

Not to be left behind, the Christian minorities have also been 'taken care of', more so since 1996. It was the time when RSS affiliate Vanvasi Kalyan Ashrams work came to fruition and with this the Christian missionaries were tagged with the image that their primary work is conversions. Amongst various reasons for taking up Christians for attacking one was also partly related to Sonia Gandhi, a Catholic coming to the fore in the political space. Her unexpected mass appeal bowled the opponents over. She was called as 'foreigner' and a sinister campaign was initiated which was picked up by section of Congress itself to break their own party. Today apart from the conversion bogey the threat of a foreigner ruling the country and India coming under the grip of Italian rule is being conjured up in a serious way to section of middle classes. The language press in particular has fanned the myths about minorities in a serious way. The fear amongst the Christians living in the villages is going up. While in cities the parents of all shades of political thinking vie to put their children in the Christian missionary schools, in the small mofussil places, the Christians are projected a foreigners.

The major strategy is to work for manufacturing these myths, stereotypes and keep percolating them on constant basis apart from keep producing new ones on continuous basis. The social space today seems to be largely gripped by the ideas produced in the RSS shakhas and its head office, and it has serious repercussions on the political chessboard of the country. It becomes clear that the myths which form the base of 'Hate Other' and in turn also provide the raison detre for the violence against minorities. Interestingly the violence against minorities in turn goes on deepening the myths, violence also leads to polarization, to ghettoization of minorities, which is emotional to begin with and then becomes physical. The physical aloofness in turn worsens these misunderstandings to no end.

The question is how can we overcome this serious flaw in the social thinking? The secular movement cannot but take it as a task on urgent basis, to have the dissemination of correct picture, through efforts like talks, workshops, films, plays and songs to ensure that the middle class in particular and other social sections in general get over this stifling grip of divisive social common sense.

12

Indian Pluralism: Jai Ho!

India's political and cultural mosaic has been a matter of multiple volumes by social scientists. In a very simple by profound way aspects of this fascinating phenomenon of Indian society also get reflected in most of the expressions of Indian cultural phenomenon, including films. The currently popular Slumdog Millionaire is no exception. The film and the aspects associated with its making display the rich cultural canvass of our society. While the apologetic critics have been talking about the film showcasing India's poverty to the World, the other interesting aspect of the film relates to on screen and behind the screen aspects of the film showing India's plural heritage and its continuation today.

The film bagged three Oscars. And they have a lot of tale to tell. All the three recipients of the Oscars have Muslim names; one of them is a Sikh (Gulzar) who has assumed Muslim name to keep him reminded of the partition carnage of 1947, which he witnessed with great anguish and pain. The second one is a born Muslim, Resul Pokkuty and third one, Alla Rakhha Rahman, was a Hindu Dilip Kumar, who changed to Islam under the influence of a Sufi saint, a Pir. When Resul accepted the award he said it is a Shiv Ratri (Hindu festival of Lord Shiv) gift for him and that he is accepting it for his country, India.

Allah Rakkha Rahman converted to Islam when he came in contact with a Muslim Pir, during the period of sickness of his father. Rahman is not alone in this as in India most of the Muslims converted to Islam due to the humanistic teachings of Sufi Pirs. There is a popular perception that Islam spread in India due to the threat of Muslim Kings, who came with Koran in one hand and sword in the other. The best counter to this was put by none other than Swami Vivekananda, who points out that Islam was embraced by Shudras to escape the tyranny of Landlord-Brahmin combine. Interestingly same Rahman has composed one of the most beautiful tunes on the song, Vande Matram.

There must have been many other reasons for conversions to Islam, apart from this major reason of the caste oppression, but this anyway remained the major one. A good number adopted Islam due to social interaction, like Navayats in Malabar Coast in Kerala and Mewats in Rajasthan region. As such in religious tradition there are many interactive ones'. There have been Bhakti saints who had following amongst Muslims and Hindus both, and there have been Sufi Pirs who had followers amongst Hindus and Muslims in equal measure. The saints like Ram Deo Baba Pir are amongst the most popular one's amongst the poor and low caste, cutting across the religions.

Contrary to the present perceptions that Hindus and Muslims were two hostile communities, there has been a natural amity and harmony amongst the religious communities. This gets reflected in all the aspects of our social lives, be it the arena of literature, music, architecture or any other, one can clearly see the influence of each on other. The culture was hardly dictated by religion alone, within same religion there are many cultures and in most of the cultures in India one can see the influence of different religions. Many a regional aspects of the culture have been thickly intertwined. While for Ustad Bismillah Khan life was unthinkable without the river Ganges and the Kashi Temples, Munshi Premchand could think only of Urdu as the medium of his writing when he began his career as a writer. Rahi Masum Raza can write the script for the most popular Hindi mega serial Mahabharata with effortless brilliance, and the likes of Javed Akhtar can write the best of Bhajans for the Hindi films.

Even amongst kings the enmity was not around religious issues. We see the Hindu kings in the court of Muslim kings, Raja Todarmal and Birbal being the part of Akbar's nine jewels, while Raja Mansing being his commander in chief. Aurangzeb, supposedly the most fanatic Muslim ruler had 33% of his officials from amongst Hindus and one of his important Generals was none other than Raja Jaisingh. Shivaji, the highly revered Maratha King had Maulana Haider Ali as his confidential secretary, Siddi Sambal as his commander and Rutam-e-Jaman as his body guard-spy. He was the one who built the Dargah in honor of slain Muslim King Afzal Khan, whom he had killed for political reasons.

The food habits also got mixed up, beef eating which was prevalent in Vedic times, had become a taboo later, as Cow came to be revered as mother by Hindus. To defer to the sentiments of Hindus, to respect the feeling of their Hindu subjects, many a Muslim Emperors advised against the killing of Cows. It's due to all this that, Dara Shikoh, wrote a book Majma ul Bahrain, elaborating in the book that India is a vast ocean made of two seas, Hinduism and Islam. One of the highlights of 1857 rebellion against the East India company rule was the coming together of Hindus and Muslims, at the level of Kings, soldiers and peasants. It was this intercommunity unity which gave a warning signal to the British and they intensified their policy of divide and rule, introducing communal historiography, which even to the day remains as a part of social common sense. It led to those policies which encouraged communal politics in the form of Muslim League and Hindu Mahasabha-RSS.

Indian pluralism has been unique in more sense than one. There has been a heavy interaction of religious communities, at the level of power (Kings-Landlords), at the level of culture (Music, literature, customs, food, attire) and at the level of religion (Bhakti and Sufi traditions) It is the rise of communal politics post 1980 that the British initiated project of divisiveness has resurfaced, and has tried to narrow down all the politics at identity level and made the religious identities firm and deep. The fundamentalists of both religions are now looking down at the mixed traditions and pluralism, saying they are against 'our' religion. Slumdog Millionaire while portraying the social reality, the impact of communal violence on society also highlights the deeper and most worthy interactive traditions.

Tragically from last two decades the voices opposing the syncretism and plural cultural and life in India have become stronger, opposing Gazal concerts, destroying paintings, opposing those celebrating festivals like Valentine day, opposing inter-religious marriages and what have you. Hope we are at the end of the phase during which the communal politics created a hostile atmosphere against the plural ethos of our society.

13

Anatomy of Sangh Parivar

The arrest of Sadhvi Pragya Singh Thakur in the context of Malegaon blasts of September 29, 2008 has been an important step in the investigation of bomb blasts which have been blowing the social peace and communal amity. Along with her the arrest of army officers, retired and serving, has unfolded the whole new dimension about investigation of acts of terror. The involvement of Bhonsala Military School has also come under the scanner of investigating agencies.

The Sadhvi has been the member of Akhil Bhartiya Vidyarthi Parishad and Durga Vahini, which are the parts of Sangh Parivar, before she adorned the saffron robe. Sangh parivar is the word coined by the RSS and its progeny for the whole combine, all of them put together. RSS acts as the central controller and its trained volunteers, swayamsevaks, set up and manage different organizations to pursue the goals of RSS.

Sadhvi's connections with BJP/RSS top leadership came to the surface and the BJP leadership in particular, distanced itself from her, initially. The ideological and political association was attempted to be played down to a mere acquaintance. Disowning the member of its outfits, after they do the crime is nothing new for Sangh organizations. The first such disowning was done when RSS prachark Nathuram Godse murdered the father of the nation, Mahatma Gandhi. Since RSS was not keeping records of its members etc. Nathuram claimed in the court that he had nothing to do with RSS, despite the fact that he was a trained RSS volunteer (swayamsevak). In an interview given to 'The Times of India' (25 Jan 98), his brother Gopal Godse, who was also an accomplice in the murder, elaborated the apparent reasons for hiding their affiliation with RSS. "Technically and theoretically he (Nathuram) was a member (of RSS), but he stopped workings for it later. His statement in the court that he had left the RSS was to protect the RSS workers who would be imprisoned following the murder, on the understanding that they (RSS workers) would benefit from his dissociating himself..."

The second major disassociation has been that from Rajendra Pal, alias, Dara Singh who murdered Pastor Graham Steward Stains. His case in the courts was fought by BJP ex Minister Dilip Singh Judeo's brother. Dara Singh himself was an active worker of VHP, Bajrang Dal and other Sangh organizations. All this was denied shamelessly by RSS combine. And now come the one related to the Sadhvi.

After initial quiet on the issue, now the Hindutva parties (BJP, Shiv Sena) are raising the army of lawyers to fight the case for her. Now their plea is that every accused has a right to be defended. So far they have kept quiet when the lawyers of the accused in the acts of terror have been beaten up and many lawyers associations have resolved not to fight the cases of accused in cases of acts of terror.

It was also stated by BJP spokesperson that there is no evidence, proof of involvement of the Sadhvi. The technicalities of this proof in this case apart one will like to know how many times, in how many cases of arrest of 'alleged Muslim terrorists' this question is raised. Their being a Muslim is a good enough proof of being a terrorist in this scheme of things propagated by RSS combine, and even the encounters, fake most of them, are welcomed by a section of these.

Then there was the argument that since Sadhvi is a follower of 'cultural nationalism', she can't be a terrorist! Here the partisan attitude of those involved in this politics is clear. What they are referring to by cultural nationalism is Hindu nationalism. As such cultural nationalism has been promoted by the practitioners of politics in the name of religion. Be it Muslim terrorists taught in the US promoted Madrassas in Pakistan in yesteryears or the fundamentalists, doing politics in the name of any religion. In case of Hindutva, this cultural nationalism is the opposite of democratic nationalism, where diversity and equality of all is the foundation of the political ethos.

In case of RSS, cultural nationalism is based on the some religious texts and the culture of elite Hindus, which gives priority to the Brahminical values, the values of caste and gender based inequality. Democratic nationalism has its focus on respecting and approving all cultures and religions, while in RSS scheme of cultural nationalism the Brahminical culture is the base of political nationalism. So what label does one put to the acts of Godse and Dara Singh? Both of them were steeped in the Cultural nationalism propagated by RSS combine. The formula that terrorism done by Muslims is anti national and the acts done by the ilk of Sadhvi are nationalism defies all the logic. Any act of violation of the Indian law is anti national, there can't be separate set of laws for those indulging in violence and heinous crimes in the name of religion.

After initial hesitation, it started being said that she was pained by the terrorism committed by Muslims, so this revenge terrorism was meant to protect the Hindu society, and so subtle justification and approval for this variety of crime as being the answer to the terrorism done by Muslims. Some commentators are openly glorifying this and some others are quietly going by this logic. One can say that the Bajrang Dal and Sadhvi's ilk is not into terrorism because of so called Islamic terrorism, it is in this more due to the indoctrination which they have received through RSS indoctrination module. This indoctrination reduces all the political-social issues to the religious ones.

RSS indoctrination is carried out through its Shakha Baudhiks (Branch intellectual sessions) and camps. It says that this is nation belongs to Hindus alone. Here, the Muslims and Christians are foreigners, and that the secular people are trying to say that this country belongs to all the people, which is wrong. We need to ensure that these threats to Hindu nation are dealt with properly.

RSS type indoctrination has also created the myth that all terrorists are Muslim, deliberately overlooking that terrorists come from all the religious communities, but not due to religious reasons. The reasons behind terrorism are social, economic and political. Be it LTTE, Khalistanis, ULFA, Irish Republican army all have indulged in terrorism, the reasons being anything but religious. In RSS scheme of things all the acts of terror have been projected to be due to Islam and Muslims. So the two modules merge and create the mind set of Sadhvi or Bajrang Dal members who have died while making bombs in Nanded and Kanpur or members of Hindu Jagran Samiti who planted bombs in Thane near Mumbai.

The current involvement of army officers, Bhonsla Military School and the members of different wings of Sangh privar should not be a surprise if one sees the structure and functioning of RSS. RSS founded to oppose democracy and to work for Hindu nation has been working, indoctrinating and creating more and more organizations to fulfill it objective of Hindu nation, which in essence means to restore the feudal hierarchical values of caste and gender in Indian context, to work for status quo around the modern version of Brahminical system. Its trained swayamsevaks, have been on one hand directly entering the political formations, Bhatiay Janata Party, Akhil Bhartiya Vidyarhti Parishad, Vanvasi Kalyan Ashrma, Vishwa Hindu Parishad, Hindu Munnani, Bajrang Dal, Samajik Samrasta Manch on one hand, creating subordinate organizations amongst women, Rashtra Seviak Samiti, Durga Vahini etc on the other hand. Vast layers of Saints, the likes Asaram Bapu or Sri Sri Ravishakar, or Narnedra Maharaj are ideologically on same wave length as RSS and through their work they lay the ground for the politics of RSS to flourish in different sections of society.

Its second strategy has been that of infiltration in the different wings of state machinery, police, bureaucracy, Judiciary. On yet another layer its recruits have been working in the field of education and media by the mechanism of infiltration. Its hold vicious grip on society cannot just be assessed by the electoral strength of BJP. That's why Atal Bihari Vajpayee, the then Prime Minister, in Staten Island could assert that first he is the swayam sevak of RSS and then the prime minister. That's why in 1977, when the Bharatiya Jansangh, previous avatar of BJP, who were part of Janata Party, were told to severe their links with RSS, they preferred to break the Janata party rather then severing their affiliation with RSS. Its strength comes from the earlier silent, by now violent, infiltration in all spheres of social and political activities. Its wing amongst retired military officers ensures that people like Retired army Officer Upadhyay is probably the part of the Malegaon and other such blasts.

Bhonsala military school has been managed by RSS in more ways than one, so not only it may be a place for hatching the conspiracies for blasts, but also for turning out recruits who can aid and assist this Sangh combine while serving in the army. Surprise is not that Bhonsla military school's connection with this politics is coming to surface, surprise is not that Upadhyay and Purohits' links are coming to surface so late; surprise is that how they hid it so long and so well?

Various components of RSS family sometimes have some differences also, but these are sorted out by the patriarch RSS, through subtle control and ideological mechanisms so that their cohesion with the goal to destroy democracy, through all the means, including using democratic platforms for the same, remains intact. Sadhvi is involved in the blasts or not, army officers or involved in these acts or not should hopefully come out despite their ideological plants scattered all over. What it has brought to our notice is the dangers of this multi headed hydra, which is working in the democratic system with a goal to abolish democracy itself and bring in Hindu nation, another name of fascist formation, abusing the Hindu religion, the religion persons like Gandhi!

In RSS scheme of things the organizational affiliation comes second, the primary thing which they instill is the ideological subordination. Most of those involved in these acts will not have any remorse for what they did, as like the Al Qaeda variety, they are indoctrinated to believe that it is nationalism (Hindu in this case, in Al Qaeda variety it is Islamic nation of course) so what you are doing while instigating anti minority violence or while planting the bombs is for the service of your religion!

While superficially at loggerheads the ideological wavelength of RSS indoctrination is similar to the one used in

Pakistani Madrassas for training Al Qaeda. Here the religion is different paradigms are same. To deal with such ideologies leading to acts of terror, what is also needed is to combat their ideological foundations.

14

Electoral Parties and Secular Values

In our democracy committed to secular values how do we choose whom to vote for. What are the secular credentials of different political parties in the electoral arena? The lead party of ruling coalition, Congress is no clean body as its hands are also full of blood of Sikhs in the 1984. Large numbers of communal riots have taken place during Congress regimes. BJP is the ally of organizations which spew poison against minorities and its role in Babri demolition, Gujarat carnage and many other riots is very obvious. Not to be left behind now the left, CPM in particular, with its role in Nadigram massacre in toe, has made many of the radical elements to equate it with BJP and its communal agenda. At minor level Samajavadi Party, has stood by minorities but there are occasions when it has compromised and let the communal organizations make merry. Mayawati of BSP is on record to have campaigned for Narendra Modi and put the blame of Gujarat carnage on Godhra train burning by Muslims.

How do we weigh these parties on the scale of secularism? Are BJP, Congress and CPM comparable in this regard? One can dismiss BSP as being too opportunist to be considered as secular. Amongst the major one's, we will focus on Congress, Communists and the BJP. A tough situation has been created due to the weak policies of Congress and the arrogance of CPM in Nandigram. Are all these parties in the same league or is there a shade of difference which is worth recognizing in order to save the democratic ethos, which has been weakened due to the happenings of the current times.

Congress began as a secular party with the inclusion of people of all religions, and their continued association with this party during freedom movement. At the same time many a communalists formed the part of its leadership, Lala Lajpat Rai, Madan Mohan Malaviya and Dr. Moonje. Even the founder of RSS, K.B. Hedgewar was associated with it till 1934. At medium and grass root level many a Hindu communalists in particular remained and are part of this party. It is this which made Nehru to warn that Congress should be cautious of those members who sound secular but are communal in the real sense. At the level of policies Congress took quite a principled secular path till the demise of Pundit Nehru, after which it was compromised regularly. The problem became apparent with Indira Gandhi's election speeches in, Rajiv Gandhi's 'when a big tree falls'; Shah Bano, shilaynyas, and Narsimha Raos' afternoon siesta when the Babri was being razed to the ground. Many a riots took place during its regime when the ruling Government either acted as the silent witness or colluded with the rioters.

While evaluating this it has to be kept in mind that the riots take place due to three major factors, the instigator and conductor, which according the inquiry commissions, (Jagmohan Reddy, Justice Madon, Vithayathil, Shrikrishna and Venugopal)mostly has been some organization which is a offshoot of RSS.

The second factor is those who are supposed to control it, the political leadership. In this case the Congress when in power has been weak and ineffectual at places and actively colluding at other. Mostly it has been lacking the political will to control it effectively. The third force is the police and bureaucracy, which has been regularly communalized and been the force providing the umbrella to the rioters or has been the active participant in the execution of the pogroms. Communalism is not the program of Congress, its basic program remains Secularism, but its execution of those values has been lacking in will power.

Left and CPM, has come in this arena of discussion after Nandigram, when in order to execute the global economic agenda, they used their cadres to settle the point by 'paying its opponents back in the same coin.' Its program remains essentially secular, while the proactive will to counter the communal issues is not visible at all, be it the plight of minorities or the worsening hate against minorities in the states ruled by the left parties. The communism prevalent in the minds has not been tackled at all.

BJP is the political child of RSS, which has the agenda of Hindu nation. Irrespective of its temporary mask of Gandhian Socialism, it does lapse in to the 'Hate minorities' mind set at the drop of the hat. It has the patriarch RSS and associates; VHP, Bajrang Dal, Vanvasi Kalyan Ashram, Bajrang Dal etc, who have been communalizing the mind set, which is the base of communal violence. This RSS combine has been actively initiating situations which bring in violence. It has led many a carnages and with the help of certain elements of Congress and the helpful state machinery, has been polarizing the communities along religious lines. The scholars of communal violence have made the observation that in the aftermath of most of the communal violence, RSS combine becomes stronger in the areas, where the violence has taken place. Communalism, in overt and covert language is its political vehicle towards the Hindu nation. Its communalism is programmatic.

In our semi secularized society, where the values of liberty equality and fraternity are not fully rooted, where the transformation of the caste and gender equations are not fully achieved, one can classify the secular formations, individuals in to four broad categories on the scale of secularism. The first category exists as a rarified group This category belongs to the party/individual who proactively strives to bring in caste and gender equality in a substantive way. Here land reforms are the key and the endeavor to bring in the unity between communities is the hall mark of this group. Some dalit formations, gender right groups, groups working for communal harmony fall here. A synthesis of values of Bhagat Singh, Gandhi and Ambedkar can best describe this group, which today is not in a very good state of its health.

The formations like Left are genuinely secular but they have ignored the proactive measures to pursue this. Congress is mired by too many power seekers to be able to stand firmly to oppose the communal elements and lands up being the accomplice, in part or in full, of the phenomenon. BJP is the aggressive, intimidating opponent of democracy and secularism, whatever its expression. Its biggest 'achievement' is that some of the political workers compare it with other electoral formations. That's the bankruptcy of our times and cleverness of this party. It is effectively using the electoral space to do away with democratic values in due course. It is the Indian face of fascism.

The anti Sikh violence was a sort of single go phenomenon, which had more to do with the ethno-regional factors. The Nadigram carnage is more of economic massacre, while the BJP led pogroms are targeted at the minorities as minorities, to consolidate RSS political hegemony. To be sure none of the violence can be condoned. The subtleties of these differences point out that while we do not have the real good choice for electoral arena, we will have to keep putting the civic pressure for bringing in better and better political policies through the grass root campaigns. All the same to compare BJP with other electoral formations will be undermining the threat of the agenda of RSS, which seeks to abolish democratic space and build a society in the image of 'glorious' Hindu past.

One can very well say, today in electoral arena we do not have a choice between Good better and the best. We are riddled with bad, worse, worst and BJP!

15

Bharatiya Janata Party: Future Trajectory

BJP has emerged as the major political party from 1990s. Though it has ruled as a part of NDA (National Democratic Alliance) its imprint on the Government policies has been very strong. The allies have been content themselves to playing a junior partner and barring keeping out the core Hindutva agenda, Ram Temple, abolition of article 370 (Related to autonomy of (Kashmir) and Uniform civil code, they have let the BJP agenda prevail in most of the social fields and in the political governance of the country.

Power in the Center:

From a small north Indian-Hindu Political party, its transformation as a major player began with its Ram Temple campaign. This campaign became stronger after the affirmative action in the form of Mandal Commission implementation. This was a move on the part of VP Singh Govt. to implement an affirmative action for the weaker sections of society in the form of reservation in the govt. jobs. BJP essentially has support base amongst the urban upper classes/castes and does represent their interests in preference to the longings and aspirations of weaker social groups. The campaign was accompanied by a subtle anti minority slant and culminated in the demolition of Babri Mosques, one of the biggest shame for the Nation. This was followed by intense communal riots in different parts of the country. This led to the consolidation of its base and the rise in its electoral power. By a gradual intensification of its electoral support it came in the position to be the largest political party despite polling a miserly 23% of votes in the last Lok Sabha (Parliament elections).

Political Ideology:

BJP-RSS relationship is crucial to understand the politics of BJP. It is really the RSS which through various mechanisms, ideological and organizational, controls the second largest party, BJP, in the country.

While RSS has always been calling itself as the cultural organization, by now its mask is off and the society at large knows that it is a political organization which is very shrewdly and cleverly been training swayamsevaks (volunteers) who in turn have formed various organizations to control the politics at all the levels. These organizations formed by it range from Rashtra Sevika Samiti in 1936 to Akhil Bhartiya Vidyarthi Parishad, Bhartiya Jansangh, Vishwa Hindu Parishad to Vanvasi Kalyan Ashram etc. These organizations in turn have formed other subordinate organizations. What is common in these is that they are all formed by trained RSS swayamsevaks (ideological control) and that the core figures of these organizations meet often under RSS control, to coordinate their strategy. Their aim and job is to carry on the work of RSS, i.e. to push the country in to becoming Hindu Rashtra. Notably all the major characters from its stable from Nathuram Godse, Vajpayee, Advni, Narendra Modi etc. have been the RSS pracharaks at various points of time.

As far as BJP is concerned it is the new avatar of Bhartiya Jansangh which was formed in 1951 jointly with Shyama Prasad Mukerjee of Hindu Mahasabha. RSS that time felt the need for a political organization in the aftermath of murder of Mahatma Gandhi. This had led to its ban on RSS by the Government of India, with Sardr Patel as the Home minister. For the formation of Bhartiya Jansangh RSS loaned three of is prominent Pracharaks, Atal Bihari Vajpayee, Deendayal Upadhyay and Lal Krishna Advani. After Mookerji's death RSS tightened its grip on Jana Sangha.

Later at Sindi (Wardha, Maharahtra) in 1954 from March 9 to March 16 a political training camp was organized for 300 pracharaks. The camp was aimed to train national RSS leadership for running the affairs of the country through Jana Sangh. RSS sarsangh chalak (supreme dictator) M.S. Golwalkar in his speech (March 16) elaborated his vision for Jana Sangh, "If we say that we are part of the organization and accept its discipline then selectiveness has no place in life. Do what is told. If told to play kabaddi, play kabaddi; told to hold meeting then meeting...For instance some of our friends were told to go and work for politics that does not mean that they have great interest or inspiration for it... If they are told to withdraw from politics then also there is no objection. Their discretion is just not required." [Golwalkar, M. S., *Shri Guruji Samagar Darshan*, Volume III, Bhartiya Vichar Sadhna, Nagpur , 1978, p. 32.] Essentially the swayamsevaks deputed to work for BJP are expected to dance to the tunes of RSS and are there merely working to fulfill the agenda of the controlling organization, the RSS.

After emergency, Bharatiya Janshangh also became part of Janata Party, put together by Jaypraksh Narayan. This coalition was torn apart when the issue of duel membership came up. The socialist members of Janata party raised the issue that there cant be double membership, meaning there by that those who are members of Janata party can't have affiliation to RSS. The Jansangh component of Janata party broke way as they said their loyalty to RSS is above the membership of Janata party. Their basic goal was out in the open, they were mere players, while RSS is the real controller.

Later the same component resurfaced as Bharatiya Janta Party. They pretended to have Gandhian Socialism as their goal. It was a mere ploy for them so they dumped it soon enough to latch on to the chariot of Lord Ram; exploiting whose name they gradually increased their electoral clout. Especially after their coming to power one could see that they are not only subservient to RSS organizationally and ideologically but even in the matters of small detail like when Jaswant Singh was to become finance minister, RSS got it changed and Yashwant Sinha was made finance minister.

When Atal Bihari Vajpayee was Prime Minister, in his speech in Staten Island US, he reaffirmed his primary loyalty to RSS. Advani has been a regular visitor to RSS office in Jhahndewalan Estate and Nagpur RSS head office. It is well know how RSS, was unhappy with his 'Secular Jinnah' speech and so he had to resign from the President-ship of BJP. We also know that the core organizing secretaries of BJP at different levels are RSS nominees and RSS has a special top-level secretary looking after/supervising the BJP affairs.

The BJP, its leadership not only obeys the RSS orders, it has internalized the RSS agenda and its job is to devise different strategies and moves to ensure that RSS agenda of Hindu nation becomes strong. When in power BJP makes ground for infiltration of its siblings (other RSS progeny) in different wings of the state apparatus, social work, education and other possible conduits for transforming the state and society in the image of

RSS. It is not for nothing that at election time all RSS volunteers and the workers of its progeny all come in full force to campaign for BJP.

BJP is political wing of RSS, the core organization, which controls different political and quasi political formations like Vishwa Hindu Parishad, Bajrang Dal, Vanvasi Kalyan Ahsram and the like. Most of these organizations are the ideological affiliates of BJP. It is these organizations which spread hate against minorities on a regular basis. These organizations also have branches in different countries including US from where they collect funds from the NRI Indians on the pretext of social work. Most of this fund goes in spreading the Hindutva ideology, which bases overtly on spreading hate against Muslims and Christians in particular. Hindutva basically stands for a Hindu Nation, where the modern democratic decencies are done away with and the pre-modern social relationships are imposed in the modern garb. This ideology treats Muslims and Christians as aliens and questions their patriotism. In effect this ideology reduces them to second class citizens.

Masterminding Hate

The intimidation of the minorities has reached worst proportions during last two decades. BJP along with its associates have regularly demonized the minoeiries. This lays the basis of the violence against them, which in turn ghettoizes them. The ghastly expression of this came in the form of Post Babri demolition riots, burning of Pastort Graham Stains and later the Gujrat carnage. This is doing incalculable harm to Indian society and Indian Nation. The bondings between communities which came up during freedom struggle and got themselves sustained in first three decades of republic are being torn aprt and atmosphere of fear and mistrust is being forged due to the Hindutva ideology of this organisation.

To buttress its divsive impact on the soiety its Govt. has changed the earlier text books in schools, especially in the discipline of History. The previous attempt was to rationalize history, BJP Govt has communlaized history and its impact amongs the growing children will be immense and is fraught with serious disaster. The central rule of this party is the one which promotes the state units to be aggressive against the weaker sections of society. Despite its claims the communal divides are growing and this is leading to the weakening of the Nation as a whole. The earlier direction which Nation had, seems to have been hijacked in an adverse direction.

After exploding the nucler devise it has also changed the security scene in the worst direction and relations with Pakistan have been mercurial ever changing depending on the political calculations. Its aspiration to change the democratic constitution was manifested when it appointed a constitution review commission. Fortuantley due to popular pressure the commission also could not advise the desired tampering.

Its worst was displayed during the Gujarat riots. The local BJP unit led by Narendra Modi played a very devious role in bringing about this tragedy and in sustaining the same. The state responsibility in the rehabilitation work during the riots and post riot relief was conspicuous by its absence. Even the deliverance of justice to the riot victims is totally missing and some of them have to go out from Gujarat in order to seek the semblance of justice. The Gujarat unit of BJP is duely backed up by the central BJP led coalition in these acts of violation of democratic and constitutional norms of our country. It also supported the efforts of its affiliate Vanvasi Kalyan Ashram in spreading the hate against Christians in particular in remote places, the effect of which came in the form of burning of Pastor Stains, attacks on Nuns and missionaries in remote villages and also in getting the destitute Adivasis in their participation in the Gujarat violence as the foot soldiers of Hindutva politics in launching assault on the minorities.

Economic Policies:

Lately through advertisement blitzkring it has put forward the slogan of 'India Shining' and it is being attributed to the economic policies of the BJP. The major economic initiatives in the present dierection were undertaken by the Rajiv Gandhi earlier and in more fuller form by Manmohan Singh in Narasimha Rao regime. These polices aimed to remove all the state controls on the economy which were earler pused to build India's economic infrastructe as it came out from the colonial rule. To provide the heavy industry and infrastructure the state through public sector had to intervene. It was on this base that the private industrialist could build up the industrial network. The educational policies laid during this phase laid the foundation for the growth of software industry and India's ability to produce the software professionals in large number as the leading Nation in the world.

BJP during that phase of Industrial progress was operating as Bharatiya Janshang and was totally opposed to the public sector, when it was playing major role in country's development. It was a party which also opposed all the social welfare measures undertaken by the Govt. while calling for the development of Nuclear weapon as far back as in early fifties. During later phase BJS mainly concentrated on the demonisation of minorities, Muslims in particular.

In the present phase of industrial development, its afflaite Swadeshi Jagran Manch came up in a big way to oppose the new industirla policies. In a way it was a superficial effort to keep a section of its support base of small industirlaits in its flock. They were not serious about it very clear from their conduct during last five years or so of the BJP rule. During this phase BJP not only undertook those policies, it pursued them with utter recklessness, and the Swadeshi Jagran Manch kept total quiet forgetting its earlir noises against the new industrial policies.

The two major hallmarks of BJP's implementation of economic policies were totatlly doing away with social welfare measures, in the area of education and health. India's vast number of poor is dependent on thse two state sponsored measures, these being the only source of their access to health and education. Since this is not a section from where BJP seeks its electoral base it has been totally unconcerned about this serious flaw in the policies of the state Govt. The other major factor has been to pursue the policies in a way in which the urban affluent benefit at the cost of urban poor and the rural masses in genral.

Its claims about economic achievements are from the world of make believe. The economic indices of growth have been presented to show them in a manner where they project themselves as the achievers. The real facts show something else. The farmers have been in acute distress and the number of farmers committed suicides, frustrated by the policies of the govt. The Per-acre yield has been declining. The cheap credit has not been extended to the farmers. The manufacturing sector has been on the decline, But the average annual growth of manufacturing has been substantially *lower* in the five years of BJP rule than in the previous three-year period. The average growth rate of manufacturing was 9.4% in 1995-98, and only 5.2% in 1998-2003. Growth fell *sharply* in almost all the leading 2-digit industry groups... Much of this growth has been both jobless and energyless, as cost-cutting measures and efficient practices in industry have been largely responsible. However, increased corporate earnings are not being translated into new investments. There is an almost total absence of investment demand in the economy. It is also due to the fact that there is much unused capacity, as much as 20%, in industry. (Fact Sheet on Econmic policies-Jairus Banaji, Arvind, 2004)

No where to Future

With vast resources of Central Govt. BJP took up the biggest wastage of state resources for the promotion of its own self. A media campaign 'India Shining' was launchded as a prelude to the elections. It is estimated that over 700 crores of public money has been squandered on the image build up exercise for the ruling party. Apart from the economic waste it is most immoral act undertaken by this political vehicle of RSS. It will create its own economic implications and the scarce public resources have been wasted in a very blatant way.

It is true that on economc front the core policies may not be different between various political parties in the electoral fray. But the implemtnation of the same also determines a lot. The BJP tilt towards affluent sections is resulting in the major imbalance in the social arena.

The resounding defeat of BJP in the 2009 elections, decline in number of seats and decline in voting percentage prompted various BJP insiders and sympathizers to do some introspection. Where did the party go wrong? In his piece in Times of India 4th June 2009, Swapan Dasgupta feels that BJP has got too much identified with Hindutva, which is no more appealing to large section of Hindus so it needs to come out of this image for a makeover. Sudheendra Kulkarni (Tehelka 13th June 2009), looks at the defeat as close Advani aide and also as an insider and points out that Advani was not sufficiently backed up by RSS and BJP. He also says that BJP's implementation of Hindutva looked to be anti minorities and that its links with RSS need to be given a second look.

Kulkarni projects as if Hindutva is all inclusive, Hindu identity is core of Indian Nationalism, and Cultural nationalism is not meant for Hindus alone. One can infer that Kulkarni basically stands by the core RSS concepts of Hindutva, Cultural Nationalism and Integral humanism and finds BJP practices faulty in this direction. One can point out that since Kulkarni is an insider, associated with BJP from the times of Advani's Rath nay, blood yatra, and is close to the top echelons of BJP and that he had all the time to point out to BJP leadership as to how their practice is deviating from the genuine Hindutva. One is not sure whether this has been done inside the party forums, any way lets keep that aside.

Concepts and ideologies are not made in the thin air. They reflect the needs of social groups. These terms couched in the language of religion were devised by ideologues of declining sections of Hindu society, the landlords and Brahmins from early nineteen twenties onwards. The term Hindutva in particular came into being as the politics of Hindu Mahasabha and RSS. It stood for politics of Hindus, for the building of Hindu Rashtra. This word was coined by Savarkar in 1920s and was meant to be an alternate notion of politics to the one being articulated by national movement led by Gandhi. Similar concept of nationalism, based on the values of liberty, equality and fraternity were also articulated by Ambedkar, while the third major stream during freedom movement, Bhagat Singh and Communists, dreamt of a Socialist society, based on the notions of substantive equality and state regulating the social relations to ensure this equality.

It must be pointed out that the concept of Hindutva aims at Hindu nation, in parallel to the concept of Muslim nation being propounded by Muslim League, and in opposition to the concept of democratic secular nation, the concept for which national movement was working. This Indian nationalism is all inclusive, inclusive of all religions, castes and both genders. The concepts of Hindu and Muslim nations are exclusive concepts. The second point is that the Gandhi-Ambedkar Nationalism was based on the equality of caste and gender while Hindutva and the ideology of Muslim nationalism were continuum of the feudal values, the harping on caste and gender hierarchy. In the same direction later Deen Dayal Upadhyay the ideologue of RSS-BJP very cleverly put up the concept of Integral Humanism. This concept argues that as any organism is well balanced due to the division of work between different parts of the body, similarly different social groups perform different well defined tasks to provide the equilibrium for the proper social functioning. This in a way talks of status quo in the caste and gender relation prevalent in society.

Similarly Cultural nationalism as propounded by RSS and adopted by BJP stands for the elite Brahminical culture as the synonym for Indian ness. All in all this is precisely what RSS defines and BJP practiced so far. There cannot be equal place of dalits, women and non Hindus in this scheme of things. Swapan Dasgupta feels BJP has to drop Hindutva, to provide an alternative based on good governance, non dynasty politics etc. Kulkarni's reading of Hindutva and integral humanism is from the world of make-believe, totally off the mark. The simple question is why were these practitioners of Hindutva, cultural nationalism aloof from National movement? It is this National movement which laid the basis of India and achieved India's independence. These streams which take the cover of glorious traditions focus only on those traditions that are elitist. In Indian context the concepts Hindu nationalism and Muslim Nationalism derive their legitimacy from Brahminical and Ashrafs (Muslim elite) stream respectively. Why can't RSS-BJP talk that primarily they are loyal to the values of Liberty,

Equality and Fraternity and dump all those concepts built around religious identity? It is because these religion based concepts are the best cover for oppression of women, dalits and non Hindus. And in turn these concepts also demonize, intimidate and commit violence against minorities, trying to reduce them to second class citizens.

BJP could come to power only because of harping on identity of Lord Ram. BJP does hold Ram is the symbol of India's identity. This is one of the expressions of their cultural nationalism. The question arises why only Lord Ram is the symbol of India, why not Shambuk, or Bali or Sita. In nutshell their cultural nationalism picks up those characters which suit the interests, agenda of Hindu elite. Surely had Ram temple agitation not taken up, Babri mosque not demolished and Mumbai and Gujarat violence not instigated, BJP would have been on the margin of Indian politics. Its very raison detre is due to the fact that it is a progeny of RSS, to the fact that it is related to VHP, Bajrang Dal etc., whose vagaries it keeps defending most of the time. It is thoroughly exclusionist and that's why it justifies Gujarat violence, Kandhamal, rejects Sachar committee etc. It is not a mere coincidence; it is the core of BJP politics. It is not that the concept of Hindutva is inclusionary and practice is faulty, the very concept of Hindutva is exclusionary, in theory and practices both.

Can BJP throw away Hindutva, aim of building Hindu Nation around *glorious* Hindu traditions of Manu Smriti etc? The question is misplaced as BJP is nobody to decide that. BJP is merely a political arm of RSS; it is RSS which has to decide that. Can RSS cut its own legitimacy off by renouncing Hindutva? The question does not arise. RSS essentially is aimed around these goals. Kulkarni's confusions and his welcome concern about poor, minorities and dalits are misplaced as those are not the concerns of RSS, they have never been and can never be the concerns of BJP and company at any point of time. Hindutva or integral humanism is cleverly worded disguise to undermine the concept of democracy. Last two decades had been a nightmare where the values opposed to Indian nationhood asserted themselves aggressively, bringing immense miseries. One hopes with the trend of decline of BJP, those striving for democratic struggles, struggles for equality and rights of dalits, women, adivasis, workers and minorities will come to occupy the main social space and protect the nation from the damages done by the politics in the garb of religious identity.

16

Cow's Urine as Medicine: Faith's Leap into Blind Alleys

Recently the BJP ruled Uttarakhand Government (Feb 2008) has announced that it will procure cow's urine, on the pattern similar to the procurement of milk by dairies, refine it and sell it to Ayurvedic pharmacies. Other BJP ruled Governments are also working on similar lines.

Cow has been having a central place in the political symbolism of RSS combine. The place of this symbolism may be only next to Lord Ram. On these premises, so far cow has been projected as mother. In its major campaign against minorities' right since 1950s, BJP predecessor Bharatiya Jansangh, had undertaken a nationwide, *Desh Dharm ka nata Hai Gau Hamari mata hai* (Cow is related to us through our religion and nation as mother) and also *Janm Janm Ka Nata hai Gau hamari Mata hai* (Cow is our mother in our every birth). Since Muslims, one does not know why Christians were not targeted for it, are not prohibited from eating beef and since many a butcher belong to Kasai (butchers) occupation, this fact has been used to demonize the Muslim community. We worship cows, they eat, they butcher cows! This has been used to rouse the sentiments of majority community time and over again.

With Uma Bharati becoming the chief minister of Madhya Pradesh (2005) for a brief while, she introduced cow based economy, funds for Goshalas (cow sheds) were given from Government treasury, and her official residence became the first such Goshala. Cow based economy aimed at promoting cow products as the core of economy. The present effort now transcends the earlier efforts as faith is being transformed into blind faith. The Government's move to collect urine, to procure it, refine it and sell it as a medicine defies all the logic of science and medicine. It is converting the political symbolism into health related prescription which is fraught with dangers.

As such urine is a product excreted through kidneys and contains the waste metabolites. It can also contain the bacteria, bovine tuberculosis for example, and other harmful germs and metabolic products. The biochemical studies of urine have clearly shown its composition. There are some who claim magic healing powers of drinking one's own urine, called Shivambhu, the most famous consumer of the same was Morarji Desai. Some claim that it contains antibodies which act against the harmful diseases affecting our body, but analytically and biochemically it has not been proven so far. Physiologically kidneys do not let the antibodies pass out of the body as the molecular weight of antibodies is much more than the pore of the kidney membrane. Of course when kidney is damaged, these antibodies can pass out, not when the cow is healthy.

Murali Manohar Joshi, who as MHRD minister initiated the introduction of faith based disciplines like Astrology, Paurohuitya (Ritualism) also diverted some of the funds for doing cow research. One CSIR lab went to the extent of obtaining a patent on a pharmaceutical composition contating cow urine distillate and an antibiotic. Another CSIR lab, in collaboration with a NGO undertook a study to see the effectiveness of cow urine in cancer treatment. Our own ayurveda does not mention any medicinal use of cow urine. Ayurveda as such has lot of valuable empirical observations which can be deepened by rooting them on firmer rational grounds but that is shrouded in mystery and faith and any questioning of it meets angry protesters, who claim their faith is under threat. Baba Ramdeo does claim that his 'Ramdeosim' is scientific but forgets that the basic premise of science is peer review, facing the questions and a constant transcendence of inadequacies in our knowledge system. The faith based enterprise of Ramdeo is too individualistic, too much dipped in faith and has too little to offer on rational grounds. Same is the method of cow medicine, too much faith, and that too of blind variety, too much assertion and zero scientific research. One will like to explore the veterinary sciences to see if there is something drastically right in cow's excreta in contrast to the excreta of bullock or buffalo or a dog for that matter. Also one does recall the claims of the section that cow dung has purifying effect. Impurity brought in by the shudras touching of water was undone by mixing cow dung with the water touched by a dalit.

The basic difference between medical sciences, empiricism, and grandma's medicine needs to be understood before state Government investing and promoting cow excreta, urine, for human consumption and application. Mercifully one has not heard so far of such efforts to promote cow dung. The present effort by the BJP government is an extension of RSS combine's cow politics. It is totally against the understanding of modern medical sciences and also has no mention in the traditional wisdom gained over a period of time. In a way it is the translation of RSS combine's political understanding in to the arena of application to human society. In some Islamic countries, on similar lines, state sponsored research to undertake the study on *djinns* (ghosts) to solve the energy problem. As per mythology *djinns* are supposed to be infinite source of energy so why bother about oil and electricity when these blessed beings can solve our problems for good. Surely these will also prevent the wars which are taking place in the globe for controlling the energy reserves. And not on a very different track, Christian right is asserting creation science to oppose the theory of evolution.

These efforts have no rational and scientific basis, something which our constitution ordains us to follow in the public domain. Social auditing of efforts, which affect human health are mandatory, control by bodies sanctioning the drugs and other medicinal means are an absolute must for public safety, all the claims of politics notwithstanding.

As such enough of politics has been woven around cow. Just a few years ago, one of the eminent historians of Ancient India, Prof. D. N. Jha, came out with a book on the dietary habits in ancient India, which showed that beef was one of the major items consumed in Ancient India. The move to project Cow as holy animal, mother, was a response to the non violence propounded by Lord Gautam Buddha. With the rise of agricultural society the cattle wealth was to be preserved. As people started embracing Buddhism, the aggressive reaction of Brahmanism came up at theological, social and political level. Cow was projected as the symbol of rising Brahmanism, as a counter to the non-violence of Buddha, and has remained so through centuries. Many a Mughal kings in deference to these sentiments, to respect the feeling of the section of society, advised against cow slaughter. Babar in his will writes to his son Humayun to avoid the slaughter of cows.

In Hindutva politics also there are many streams. While Savarkar called cow as a useful animal, the other sections ignited the emotions against Muslims around cow. Irrespective of that many a poor Hindus and Adivasi did consume beef. Incidentally it is amongst the cheapest source of protein for the poor. Many a surveys showed that a vast number of Indian communities consume beef. RSS combine's propaganda went on to assert that Muslims are violent and one of the reasons is that they consume beef. This is so much against the pyschosoiological understanding of the human mind and the violence. While one knows that beef is a staple diet in major parts of the World, one also knows and modern psychological theories demonstrate that violence does not emerge from diet but from social and political situations. Beef can surely build muscle power in conjunction with proper exercises, but violence is located in the mind.

Undoubtedly one should respect those regarding cow as their mother. RSS combines' many followers devote their lives organizing fodder and other supports for Gaushalas. Some of them, the upholders of Cow as mother, non violence, go to the extent of justifying violence against dalits on the ground that they were skinning a dead cow as happened in the killings of dalits in Gohana. This cow urine in the pharmacy shops defies all the logic and faith and is directly a threat to health of people of the society. Faith can take such dangerous turns is to be seen to be believed!

17

Ram Sethu: Man Made or Natural

Different agitations are on to oppose Sethusamudram project linking Gulf of Mannar with Palk straight. Dharam Sansad (religious Parliament, a VHP initiative) has been mobilized around 'faith', on the ground that this project will destroy Ramar Sethu, the one which was built by Vanar Sena (Army of Monkeys) to help Ram cross over to Lanka to rescue Sita. The project was supported by most of the political parties in the past including NDA alliance Government. When complete, it will cut short the long journey of the ships from east coast to the west coast, and vice versa. Like Panama Canal it has been conceived to promote the transport, employment and to improve trade. Half way now, it has been facing two oppositions. The one is from the environmentalists, who are worried about the destruction of flora and fauna and the dangers of silting in the canal. These are the arguments which need to be taken seriously.

The other ground, the one based on faith need to be dealt with at another ground. RSS and its affiliates are promoting a view that building this Sethusamudram will involve the destruction of Ramar Sethu which will be detrimental to our faith. The story goes that Ravan, the King of Lanka had abducted Sita to avenge the insult meted out to his sister Shurpnakha, whose proposal for marrying her was turned down by the Lord Ram. Assisted by his loyal devotee Hanuman, the Lord mobilized monkeys and built this bridge. It is claimed that this bridge is a marvel of engineering achievements of the Indian engineers of that time. The assertion is that it shows the acme of technological achievements of this land, and that there are other noteworthy achievements like the advances in aeronautical technologies like aero planes, missiles to name the few.

How do we understand these claims, how do we comprehend this peep in to the past? How do we distinguish fact from fiction, history from mythology? To reconcile history, science and mythology are the complex questions in our public life. To begin with history of events has some definitive characteristics, though their interpretations do vary with the political ideologies. But what about mythology? Here these accounts have been put forward as the fictional accounts of the past. Some of these accounts have been associated with faith. Faith to some extent is natural and sometimes it is being manufactured and asserted for political goals.

As far as Lord Ram's story goes there are several versions of Ramayana, (Many Ramayanas, Richman, OUP). Some of these are very popular like Valmiki Ramayana and Tulasidas Ramcharitmanas. Surely the most popular one currently is the one from *Maharashi* Ramanand Sagar's mega serial which captivated the nation for couple of years. There are other versions, which have been undermined and attacked mostly for political reasons. Sahmat exhibition on different versions of Lord Ram's story was attacked few years ago. Some politically motivated people could not bear one of the versions presented in this exhibition. It showed that according to Jataka version of Ram Katha, in post Brahminical Buddhist Dashrath Jataka Sita is both a sister and wife of Ram. As per this version Dashrath is King not of Ayodhya but of Varanasi. The marriage of sister and brother is part of the tradition of glorious Kshtriya clans who wanted to maintain their caste and clan purity. This Jataka tale shows Ram to be the follower of Buddha. Similarly Jain versions of Ramayana project Ram as the propagator of anti-Brahminical Jain values, especially as a follower of non-violence. What do both Buddhist and Jain version have in common is that in these Ravana is not shown as a villain but a great soul dedicated to quest of knowledge and is a spiritual soul, with majestic commands over passions, a sage and a responsible ruler. Popular and prevalent 'Women's Ramayan Songs (of Telugu Brahmin Women), put together by Rangnyakmma, keep the women's concern as the central theme and present alternate perspective. These songs present Sita as finally victorious over Ram and in these Surpanakha succeeds in taking revenge over Ram.

Many people dispute that the Lanka mentioned in Ramayana is not the current Sri Lanka. Since mythology does not require any proof it can be modulated and constructed in a faith for political purposes. Recently in the Shabri Kumbh held in Dangs in Gujarat, the mythology was modulated in the service of politics. It was said, and that too with great amount of precision, that a particular hillock, which was earlier called Chamak Dongar, which adivasis used to worship as Shivar Deo (protector of crops), was the precise place where Shabri had offered berries to Lord Ram. It was rechristened and a Shabri temple was built on the spot. Nearby, a river six kilometers away, Purna was named as the one where Guru Matang rishi use to take bath. On the mountain on the stone there were three marks which are being presented as the marks where Laxman had sharpened his arrows.

This Ramar Sethu has been shown to be the pre human structure, called tombol, a sand deposition due to natural process. The Geological Survey of India ruled out its being the manmade (or monkey made), construction. Same way the inference from NASA satellite pictures is that it is due to sedimentation of clay and lime stone. It is tombol in NASA language, connecting one land with another, and that it is from times when human habitation is doubtful.

It is easy to construct a flyover to the future but difficult to prevent the formation of mythological bridges of the past. Mythology can easily be constructed and planted in the peoples psyche as it is driven by political goals and rides on the horse of emotion. Reason and logic have no place in this scheme of things. One knows that some Mullahs, having faith in the infinite power of *djinns* advocated their rulers to invest in the research for making more *djinns* so that power crisis can be solved. Also with the resurgence of fundamentalism one is hearing that Creation science is back in the race to compete with the theories of evolution. The question is, should we misuse faith, faith which can be an assuaging balm, for building political agendas?

18

Loving to Hate

Lately (2002) Valentine day, 14th February every year has been marked by the acts of intolerance, violence by the 'Moral Police' of Shiv Sena, Vishwa Hindu Parishad and ABVP. In Lucknow some boys and girls who had met to celebrate the day were beaten up. Similar and related violence including the attacks on shops selling Valentine and other mementoes were also reported. On the eve of the Valentine day and on the day itself one is watching in utter disgust the action of this moral police (MP) in vandalizing the events of the day. Valentine day has come to be synonymous with the exchange of messages of love all over the world. To keep company with 'our' own MP similar groups in Saudi Arabia are also on the rampage. Many a functions planned for this day had to be cancelled and many others just did not dare to plan any function in the light of experience of vandalism of previous years.

The ground on which these MP are operating holds no water. It is being said that such an open expression of love is 'un-Indian', this celebration is not in keeping with Indian culture, multinationals are promoting 'nude revolution' etc. Real reasons for this intolerant behavior have to be looked for in their overall agenda to curtail liberalism, pluralism and to constrain the democratic ethos of the country.

The circumstances under which this day came to become a memorable one, are very interesting and have a deep message. Valentine Day has an ancient legacy. It seems that the early Christian Church had at least two saints bearing this name. As per one story Roman emperor Claudius II forbade young men to marry in the year 200's A.D., as he had strong military ambitions and he thought that single men made better soldiers (As 'our own' RSS believes that single men make better Pracharaks (Propagators) for Hindu Rashtra, and accordingly one can not be a RSS pracharak if one not a 'bachelor boy'). A priest by the name Valentine protested and disobeyed the orders of the King by solemnizing the marriage of young couple's. According to another legend, Valentine was an early Christian who was very affectionate to young children. He refused to worship Roman Gods and on that count was imprisoned. Children missed his affection and love and tossed the notes containing love messages across the prison bars. According to many a stories he was executed on 14th February. This day in due course came to be celebrated in his memory, as a tribute to his courage in defying the inhuman orders of the ruling kings, people started sending greetings and messages of love to their loved one's. The origin of the customs is slightly shrouded due to its being very ancient. Also these customs started taking local hue in different countries wherever this day began to be celebrated.

So why is the Hindutva brigade opposed to Valentine day, which is symbolic of love? Is it because the multinationals are involved in the card trade? We do remember the enthusiasm of Shiv Sena-BJP combine few years ago to dump the Enron in the Arabian sea as an electoral promise, but after coming to power they not only ratified the same but approved the further stage of the project as well! The BJP led coalition at center has been surrendering to one Multinational after the other in quick succession. So aversion to multinational corporations is not the real reason. Is it because this day smacks of immorality and our 'moral brigade' cannot tolerate this exchange of symbols of love, which is obnoxious according to them? We do recall here that one of their ilk; B.L. Sharma had termed the rape of nuns as an act of Patriotism! So what are these scales of morality? As far the event being an un-Indian one, let's just give a thought to the process of evolution of the customs, traditions and culture. With the world being reduced to a global village there is a percolation of different festivals and events across the globe. We have seen that even in Indian context in medieval times there was a thick intermingling of cultures and people of the society imbibed the one's coming from different parts of the continent. People belonging to different religions overcame the boundaries to celebrate each other's festivals and customs. The average people of the society, those who do not have vested interests celebrate diversity and enjoy it thoroughly. Muslims participating in Holi, Hindus participating in Tazia processions are some very few examples from the vast cultural interaction, which was the norm of the times, before the rise and institutionalization of communal politics.

Strangely those practicing politics in the name of religion seem to be averse to this basic human longing of love, friendship and sisterhood/ brotherhood. While asserting that they are open minded and believe in Vasudhaiva Kutumbkam (Whole World is my family), or 'Aa No Bhadra Kratvo yanto Vishwtah!' (Let the noble thoughts come to us from all the universe) for the sake of arguments, these Religious Nationalists are most close-minded and permit the customs and other cultural symbols as per their political convenience. The similarities between 'our' own fundamentalists (RSS progeny and associates) and those across the border and slightly far away are very striking. Taliban regime had imposed similar codes for the people in general and for women in particular. Who will wear what color of dress, what type of dress etc. everything is dictated. The Hindutva bandwagon has been drumming up the 'patriotism' by various dictates. One remembers this brigade's attacks on films (Water, Fire), their attacks on Gazal concerts (Gulam Ali), painting exhibitions (M.F.Husain) from the recent past. BJP's Mr. Rajnath Singh, the Chief Minister of UP, had passed the fatwa, well endorsed by his patriarch organization RSS, which told couples not to go for honeymoon, opposed cutting birthday cakes and burning candles etc.

The Sangh Parivar volunteers in the past have opposed the wearing of jeans by girls. The fanatic MP brigade, belonging to most religions is especially watchful of the 'women's conduct' or whatever can affect that. As the protectors of 'their' women, on whose back the community identity and all the baggage is loaded, are especial target. It is by dictating women that the 'real' traditions are preserved and percolated in this scheme of things. One cannot miss the type of issues, which those playing politics in the name of religion undertake. All the issues they take for ramming the society have to do with emotional cords and spread of hatred against some 'other'. The real issues pertaining to the material lives, human rights of the weaker sections etc. don't mean a thing for these self proclaimed 'super patriots', whose patriotism gets manifested only in burning books, cards, and in intimidating whosoever violates their fatwas. Nothing surprising, again this is in tune with what Mullahs do in some so-called 'Islamic republics'.

All this goes against the democratic and plural ethos of our country. Those working for Hindu Rashtra mercilessly trample on people's choices about various things in their lives. Their wavelength does match with those who are imposing 'Islamic state' in many Middle East countries or even with Mullahs across the border. This moral policing by the followers of Thackeray and Golwalkar derives cheers from the Talibans of yesteryears. They do have company of the Mullahs in Saudi Arabia even today. In this intimidating game where the vandals of these outfits take the law in their hands, the 'sympathetic' BJP govt. smiles in its sleeves with silent approval. In a way incidents like this are a test of our democratic principles, how far we can and will uphold them? How much this MP will dictate our social and political lives remains to be seen. It is at one level not just a question of burning of Valentine cards, the issue has do with the choices of average people, women in particular. Can the people at large have the democratic freedom to live their lives as they please or do they have to take approval from the self appointed guardians of Religion, morality, culture etc. breathing down our neck in our personal, social and political life?

19

Gujarat, Hindutva and Human Rights

The current national scene has been dominated by violence in the name of religion. Communal violence, the biggest violator of Human rights is the festering wound on the body politic of Indian society. The nature of these riots reveals a lot about this phenomenon. First, the number of victims is more from Muslim community and partly from Christian community, second, the loss of property is also more of Muslims and third, police plays a heavily partisan role in favor of the majority community. Initially it used be mainly the poor Muslims who were the major victims, but lately even the middle and upper class Muslims have also been drawn into this vortex.

The post partition riots were followed by a period of comparative calm, in the decade of 50s. This calm was broken in 60s when in 1961 Jabalpur, in 1964 Jamshelpur and Rourkela riots broke out. "Of the bloody pogroms in sixties, the ones at Ranchi, Bihar (1962) and Ahmedabad, Gujarat (1969) stand out as the major events. In seventies the Turkman Gate massacre of 1976 perpetrated by police...., the riots in Moradabad (1980), Nellie, Naogaon, Assam (1983), Bhiwandi (1984) and Meerut (1987) have been the major ones in which more than a thousand lost their lives" (Khalidi, 1995). The Ramjanmabhumi campaign left a big trail of blood in which more than thousand people lost their lives in 1989. The massacres of Bhagalpur, Hydrabad and Aligargh heralded the onset of bloody 80s, which has seen the peak of communal violence.

Advani's rath yatra and post Babri demolition riots were too horrific. The post demolition riots gripped Mumbai, Surat, Bhopal in a major way and many other places in a significant way. With Post carnage Gujarat pogrom the communal violence went to new lows in the violation of human rights. Earlier these riots occurrence is mainly in cities, now the involvement of villages is also there.

Communal Politics

Communal violence is the most superficial manifestation of communal politics. Undoubtedly the Muslim Communal politics, which is a junior partner in the game, has provided enough ammunition to provoke the ongoing march of the chariot of Hindutva. The response of a section of Muslim community to Shah Bano judgment gave the much-needed pretext to the communalists. Also especially since 1990s the ghettoization and its adverse effects on Muslim community had been very serious.

The communal politics, is the anti thesis of democracy. Democracy is based on the concept of liberal space where the concept of Human rights is central to the values and norms of society and polity. In contrast communal politics derives its legitimacy from the identity of religion and here, on the pretext of religious values the concept of rights is totally abolished and substituted by duties, duties to be performed by the weaker sections of society. This politics also assumes that people belonging to one religion have similar interests and these are opposed to the interests of the people belonging to 'other' religions.

After realizing that Ram temple campaign of VHP is getting response from a section of Hindus, BJP decided to make Ram Temple as its political agenda. In a country riddled with the problems of poverty, misery, disease and hunger, Lord Ram's birthplace became the central political issue due to offensive of Sangh Parivar. And all the campaigns, Rath Yatra to Babri Demolition became bloody events. Lord Ram and then the communal violence became the vehicle on which the success of RSS's political progeny BJP depended. Last few years it was loosing electoral appeal and now the events of Godhra-Gujarat has brought it back to the electoral reckoning. The carnage/ genocide has been projected to be the Hindu pride and the process, which is anticipating to fish for votes in the rivers of blood is being planned meticulously.

The major onslaught of this politics manifested through the Babri Masjid demolition and post demolition riots. It also brought to fore the communal party into the fold of power. Lately it was seen that the appeal of this politics was declining, as manifested in the results of elections in the northern states. And that's when Godhra came in handy. And communalists used this pretext for their nefarious designs. What took place was the process of killing and maiming, burning of people and violating the being of women. The central aim of all this is to polarize the society along the lines of religion. That is what the communalists want. Akshardham did come in as an aftermath of the massive anti-minority pogrom and it was not followed by any 'spontaneous Hindu hurt' as Post Godhra events were projected to be.

Godhra:

On 27 February the S-6 bogey of the Sabarmati Express got burnt, with 58 persons being killed. The true facts come out from the Bannerji commission report. The bogey was full of *Ram sevaks* returning from the pilgrimage to Ayodhya where different rituals around the *Ram Shila Puja* were going on. Many news reports pointed to the provocative behaviour of Bajrang Dal volunteers travelling in the train. (Jan Morcha, 25 February 2002). A Muslim tea-stall vendor was humiliated on platform at Godhra station. One Muslim girl was being forcibly taken by the *kar sevaks* but was rescued. The district collector Jayanthi Ravi stated that the tragedy was unplanned. Soon Narendra Modi, the Gujarat Chief Minister, stated that it was a pre-planned act of terrorism and linked it to global terrorism and ISI. He also called a meting of top Gujarat officials late on 27 February and told them that revenge will be taken for Godhra and that they should not try to prevent any local retaliation (*Outlook*, 19 August 2002).

The burnt bodies of the victims were brought to Ahmedabad and the communal temperature was raised by slogan-shouting mobs of VHP and Bajarang Dal workers. It was said that the local Ghanchi Muslims living near the station and Signal Falia had poured the inflammable material from outside and torched the bogey. Later the Forensic Laboratory report came to the conclusion that the coach got burnt from inside, as the amount of inflammable liquid needed could not have been sprinkled from outside. The lower part of the compartment was intact from outside and the maximum damage due to fire took place on the floor of the coach from inside (*The Week*, 7 July 2002) 62 local persons including seven boys were arrested under POTA.

Bannerjee Commission on Godhra train burning

Two-and-a-half years after the tragic incident, Justice U.C. Bannerjee came out with the truth of Godhra. According to the report of this commission, this tragedy was a accident and was not pre-planned one as claimed by Narendra Modi and the RSS combine. During the NDA regime, controlled by the RSS combine, the mandatory commission to inquire into this major accident was not appointed.

Immediately from same day, 27 February, massive rioting – actually a planned genocide of Muslims – began in different cities of Gujarat. Ahmadabad was the major city to be affected. Out of 24 districts of Gujarat, 18 were involved in the violence. Mobs, generally comprising two to three thousand people, sometimes as large as ten thousand, were seen. They were armed with swords, *trishuls* (tridents) and agricultural implements that could kill. 'The manner of arson, hacking and killing was chillingly similar in pattern, all this suggested a well laid out plan behind the attack. It is only trained cadres who can spill out such and organized fashion' (*Communalism Combat*, March 2002, p. 18). The household and business establishments of minorities burnt during the violence were on lists that were with rioters. Even the business establishments which had Hindu-sounding names but had Muslim owners came under the attack.

The majority of business establishments owned by Muslim community were destroyed. Homes and business establishments were burnt using gas cylinders and special powder, which raises the temperature to a great extent. In the loot of business establishments, large sections of the middle classes merrily participated and the looting was coordinated on mobile phones, people came even in their Mitsubishi Lancers to do their bit in the service of the 'Hindu nation' by looting Muslim establishments. In the industrial area of Ahmedabad 43 people including ex-MP Ahsan Jaffery were killed by a mob of over 10000 people and the same evening a mob of over 15000 killed 84 people in the Naroda area. The number of dead in the violence is estimated to be over two thousand. It was not just killings – those who were killed were subjected to extreme torture. Women and children were the especial targets.

Women were humiliated and then burnt. Also under especial attack were places of religious worship, particularly *dargahs*, symbols of syncretic culture. Many holy places were destroyed and roads were built overnight on those sites. At places Hanuman temples came up overnight where the mosques or *dargahs* were located. The *dargah* of the famous Gujarati Sufi saint and poet Wali Gujarati was also not spared. The loss due to burning of business enterprises is estimated to be close to Rs 3800 crores. Hotels, transport businesses, industries and textile shops came under special attack.

The brutality towards children and women was sparked off by the rumour that Hindu women were molested in Godhra. The rumours were found to be totally baseless by numerous investigators. But by the time that the newspapers contradicted the news in small columns, the intended 'aim' was achieved. 'The handiwork of mobs is recorded in chilling detail in women's panel report. The women's testimony is perhaps most devastating and damning accounts of brutality in any riot in independent India. However the inaction of police and administration speaks for itself' (*Times of India*, Editorial, 26 April 2002).

Citizens' Tribunal Report

Godhra, Gujarat and Akhshardham have been the major blots on our democratic ethos in post-independence India. In the din of the tragedies which gripped Gujarat for over a period of ten months, different versions were floating around about who were guilty. The state leadership had one version, while the events themselves were either difficult to decipher or were indicating the cause of the carnage in some other direction. It is at this point that Concerned Citizens' Tribunal was conceived. The most outstanding legal brains of the stature of Justices V.K. Krishna Iyer, P.B. Sawant, Hosbet Suresh and Adv. K.G. Kannabiran; eminent sociologists like Prof. Ghanshyam Shah and Prof. Tanika Sarkar; and social workers like Aruna Roy formed this tribunal.

The task was mammoth and the need for knowing the truth paramount. That is what prompted the tribunal members to examine 2094 oral and written testimonies (both individual and collective) from the victim-survivors and human rights groups involved in relief and rehabilitation. It also examined volumes of relevant material and all this is put together in two volumes – *Crime against Humanity* –(Report of Concerned Citizens Tribunal, Citizens for Justice and Peace, Mumbai 2002) which is in a way a landmark investigation in situations like these, where vested interests not only try to hide the truth but also to distort it.

The findings of the tribunal at one level are close to what many leading human rights activists and scholars suspected. The immaculate method of investigation leaves no doubt about the high merit of the report. Its findings point to the complicity of the state leadership in the whole tragedy. The tribunal in all fairness wanted to hear the version of the state government, central government and many individual ministers. Most of them did not respond, while a few of them did meet the tribunal and opened their hearts. This two-volume report gives interim findings and also recommendations about relief, rehabilitation and punishing the guilty. But the list of those named by the witnesses is so large that it is practically a 'Who's Who' of the Gujarat political and administrative machinery.

The central point of Godhra, which was made the pretext for the riot comes out very clearly in the report. The tribunal concludes that the Godhra incident does not seem to be pre-planned. Neither is there any proof of a 'foreign hand', which was propagated with confidence. The tribunals' tentative conclusion that the fire was lit from inside and not outside will force us to review the whole action-reaction thesis, which was used to give legitimacy to state inaction in the face of one of the most severe riots in independent India.

Why the state political leadership was so eager to jump at make-believe conclusions, and what might have been the deeper design behind the whole carnage becomes slightly clearer after going through the twin volumes. The tribunal also makes it public that witnesses deposing before the tribunal informed it about the meeting called by the chief minister in which instructions were given not to take action against the 'Hindu reaction' to Godhra. This speaks volumes about the real mechanics of the whole tragedy.

Truth behind the Carnage

The Godhra incident was propagated as a planned attack by terrorists. Even before people could realize what was happening, the bodies of the victims were brought to Ahmedabad with great amount of publicity. The report of the railway police debunks the theory that Godhra incident was pre-planned and executed by the hawkers and the residents near Godhra station who are mostly Ghanchi Muslims. On the contrary the report of the Forensic Science Laboratory is clear that the bogey was burnt from the inside, leaving many a question marks about who started the fire. The government had failed to act, it deliberately did not take any precaution in the context of *Ram Sevaks* travelling by the train and raising provocative slogans. The report of Jan Morcha where the *Kar Sevaks* had done mischief at stations on the way was ignored.

During the carnage, from the beginning the complicity of the state government was obvious. The statements of Narendra

Modi were the key igniting factors. His instructions to the top officials to keep aloof from the anticipated retaliation were very significant. Also, trained volunteers led the rampaging mobs and most of them knew no action would be taken against them. Since there was systematic erosion of the rule of law in maintaining state 'neutrality', the anti-minority bias had come to become part of the state policy. Since last more than four years, in the context of uninterrupted BJP rule, the RSS had ensured that Gujarat becomes the laboratory of Hindu Rashtra. While Modi propagated the fiction that the Godhra incident was a pre-planned act by terrorists, his Home Minister Gordhan Zadaphiya saw the hand of 'enemy country' Pakistan in the whole episode. This laid the base for the attack on Muslims, as in the popular mind the link between international terrorism, Pakistan and Muslims is a simple and straightforward one by now.

The VHP-called bandh was fully backed by the BJP and the state. Modi, in tune with his history as a RSS *pracharak*, was keen to see the consolidation of Hindus behind Sangh Parivar. In response to the rising anti-Muslim pogrom he said that there is a reaction to every action, and this statement of his encouraged the rampaging mobs. In addition, despite evidence to the contrary, he kept on repeating that the situation is under control. In the initial period he even went on to claim that the violence had been brought under control within 72 hours. Nobody bought this claim, but his fellow *swayamsevaks* sitting in the Home Ministry in Delhi patted him on his back for his 'efficient' work. All the criticism of his policies was deflected by him by asserting that people are defaming the five crore people of Gujarat.

Many ministers of the Gujarat government personally went to the police control room to ensure that the rioting mob was left free to do what it was doing, to ensure that the mob was not controlled in any way. Many of them led the mobs: 'Gujarat ministers Nitin Patel and Narav Laloo Patel allegedly led violence against women in Kadih and Unja in Mehasana respectively (*Communalism Combat*, March 2002, p. 109). The government's callous attitude towards this is also manifest from the fact that Modi visited the biggest camp, Shah Alam, only when Vajpayee paid a visit to Gujarat, a good two months after the whole tragedy began. Close to a lakh persons living in the camps braved it out without basic minimum necessities. The examination centres of majority community students were shifted away from the minority-dominated areas while such 'care' could not be taken for the students of the minority community who had to appear in the examination in such a traumatized state of mind. The distinction of communities was not spared even in death. The victims of Godhra were to be paid a compensation of Rs 2 lakhs, while the victims of the 'retaliatory violence' were to be paid Rs 1 lakh. After popular protests and media criticism, a uniform amount of Rs 1 lakh was fixed. To get the compensation there was so much running about. The appointment of Justice Shah to investigate the episode also revealed the intentions of the Government Justice Shah has the 'reputation' of delivering an anti-Minority judgement in TADA, Dabgarwad- Laliwala, case, which was later reversed by Supreme court. The apex court questioned the very reasoning of the TADA court in convicting the accused.

The attitude of the government filtered down to the civil service. A former Cabinet Secretary T.S.R Subramanyam (*Indian Express,* 10 April 2002) went on to say, 'There is no civil service left in Gujarat...Over the years civil service has changed from steel frame to non-existent.' This was equally evident in the partisan attitude of police, which not only assisted those conducting the pogroms but also refused to register the FIRs.

Harsh Mander, a civil servant on deputation to Action Aid, was so disgusted after seeing the role of his professional colleagues that he decided to quit the civil service. Also to quit the disgraced service were 20 Muslim officers of ONGC who could tolerate it no longer. P.C. Pandey summarized the attitude of the civil service very well: 'These people also, they somehow get carried away by the overall general sentiment. That's the whole trouble. The police are equally influenced by the overall general sentiments' (*Communalism Combat*, March 2002, p. 115). That the carnage, which has been termed an upsurge of Hindus by the VHP and other RSS affiliates, was not spontaneous is also proved by the fact that cranes, trucks and shovels were used extensively for the whole operation. Also the extensive use of gas cylinders, the lists of Muslim households and business enterprises and the import of trucks of swords and dangerous chemicals also point to the fact of extensive planning which went into preparation of this pogrom.

A section of the media – *Sandesh*, *Gujarat Samachar* and other publication –added fuel to the fire by spreading rumours and by carrying these tragedies as sensational headlines. This supplemented many poisonous leaflets distributed by different wings of Sangh Parivar. The most notorious of this was one distributed by the VHP calling for a boycott of Muslim business establishments and of the Muslim community as a whole. Many of these called for attacking the Muslims in the name of self-defence ('Reply Bricks with stones', *Communalism Combat*, March 2002, p. 136). The training in firearms, distribution of *trishuls* (tridents), which were basically disguised knives, went on unabated before and during the pogrom.

'Deliverance of Justice' in Hindu Rashtra laboratory

Post-riot Gujarat again showed the high-handedness of its administration. Justice Nanavati was appointed to probe the whole episode. Initially Justice Nanavati stated that there was no serious lapse in controlling the communal clashes. He went on to state that there is no evidence against the Bajrang Dal and VHP workers in participating and instigating riots. The Best Bakery core witnesses turned hostile under pressure from the local BJP-VHP workers. Some poor Muslims were made to depose in camera and also in the heavy presence of police officials, forcing them to praise the role of the police in protecting them. The PUCL-Vadodara Shanti Abhiyan boycotted the commission and a delegation led by senior Gujarat journalist and human rights activist Digant Oza submitted a memorandum drawing the attention of NHRC to the gross violation of human rights of minorities in Gujarat and of the need to restrain the Gujarat government in its acts of commission and omission in the violation of basic democratic rights of minority communities.

After the riots the local people put a condition to the Muslims that they would be allowed to return to their homes if they withdrew the FIRs in case they have been filed, or if they gave an undertaking not to file FIRs if they had not yet been filed. The civic groups and citizen's tribunal showed without any doubt the role of the state machinery and police in aiding and abetting the riots. It was a state-sponsored riot. As the state is totally in the grip of the Sangh Parivar, the wall of hatred is sealing the borders between the two communities and the boycott of Muslims in employment and trade is close to total. It is in this situation that police finds it easy to tutor the witnesses. The Best Bakery witnesses turning hostile were a result of all these factors. To begin with there was a simple realization that in such a ghettoized atmosphere it may not be possible to survive while bearing witness against the authorities and the political elements. Besides, more direct threats from different sources are regularly forcing the victims to keep quiet. The Vadodara episode where police has taken the witnesses to depose is the best example of travesty of justice.

The collapse of justice delivery system by now is more than obvious. Of the over 4000 cases filed in 2002, hardly 10 have reached the level of judgement. Most have not even entered trial stage. "Inspite of so much interest taken by Supreme Court there is, to be honest, a complete breakdown of in the justice delivery system in Gujarat. The picture looks very bleak...The FIRs filed were so badly tempered that main accused were not even mentioned...in Ahmedabad, of approximate 1580 people detained in 2002 cases about 1550 were tribals, Dalits and backward class. Upper caste names simly disappeared. To play it safe, saffron forces saw to it that the prosecutors were from VHP." (J.S. Bandookwala, DNA, Jan 5, 2008)

The Supreme Court saved democracy in this adverse scenario. Its observation that Gujarat government has not done its duty in prosecuting the guilty of the riots came as a big slap to Modi, who all through behaved like a rampaging bull. Its judgement to get the cases of Zahira Shiekh heard again with due protection is a landmark. Zahira Sheikh was lured by money and kept changing her statements at the drop of the hat, leading the Supreme Court to sentence her for a jail term.

While the Nanvati-Shah commission appointed by the Government is still on the job, the investigative sting conducted by Tehelka magazine brought out the truth for all of us to see for ourselves. The following summary of its investigation gives the totality of the picture.

Tehelka Expose, Nov 2007

(From the Special issue 3rd November 2007)

The sting investigation conducted by Tehelka magazine showed the guilty of the riots boasting of their crimes on the camera.

* Modi, visited Godhra on 27th and his outburst provided the first sign to Sangh workers that time to corner Muslims has come.

* That very night BJP and Sangh workers met at Ahemdabad, Vadodara and Godhra, and gave the green signal for an all out assault on Muslims across the state.

* A strategy was devised on how to shield the attackers from the law after the ritos. Prominent lawyers were briefed and senior police officers taken into confidence. Workers were told that Modi was squarely behind them.

* The mobilization of under castes, something the Sangh has been engaged in for years, dovetailed into the deep penetration of Hindutva already had amongst the upper castes of Gujarat. Godhra provided the perfect spark to fuse them together.

* From the very beginning the police played a very partisan role, often joining the mobs. Officers who tried to do their duty found their hands tied. The complicity was led by then Ahmedabad Commissioner P.C.Pandey who ensured compliance by a swathe of junior officers.

* Weapons from bombs to trishuls, were manufactured and distributed by workers of RSS combine. They were also smuggled by them from all over the country.

* BJP and Sangh leaders led the bloodthirsty mobs through Ahemdabad's bylanes, Sabarkantha's villages, Vadodara's localities. The police stood guard to the mayhem.

* BJP MLA Mayaben Kodnani drove around Ahmedabad's Naroda locality all day directing the mobs. VHP leaders Atul Vaid and Bharat Teli did the same at Gulbarg Housing society. None of them ever went to jail.

* Fire was the most favoured weapon in rioters hands. That cremation is considered un Islamic fuelled their frenzy to

burn. Petrol and kerosene were lavishly used, as were victims own gas cylinders.

* Babu Bajrangi reveals that he collected 23 revolvers from Hindus in Naroda Patiya. He called Jaideep Patel 11 times and informed Gordhan Zadaphia the then minister of state for home about the death toll.

* Governemnt counsel before Nanvati-Shah Commission, Arvind Pandya, himself worships Modi and describes Justice Shah as 'our man'.

Genocide

The violence in Gujarat showed the extent to which the communal politics can go. Hindutva, the Indian version of Fascism, has been built up around the similar lines. Its is a movment which sustained itself through molecular permeation over a period of time and now is dominating the poltical scene. The ideological constructs against the minorities have laid the ground on which the popular consent and support for anti minority pogrom can be easily whipped up now. The violence this time did fit into the definition of Genocide as laid down by UN. The cleverest part of this pogrom against minorities was that Adivasis and dalits were manipulated to play the foot soldiers of the violence unleashed by Hidnutva forces. The second point was that RSS combine was already gearing up for a massive violence as discernible through the preparations and the systematic work to kill the minorities. In Gujarat it has become a sort of war against the minorities, 'In the undeclared war being waged by the state against minorities, the Government has deployed a wide arsenal of weapons. Amongst these are genocide, sustained demonization by innuendo and falsehood, ghettoisation, and economic bycott...it has succeeded in enduring mass psychology of terror among them most of all by instrument of POTA." (Harsh Mander, the Knockings of Hate Gujarat, 3 years later, Anhad, Delhi 2005)

The team of lawyers was already on hand to defend the culprits. And this time around all the state functionaries, from low to the high were the trained RSS swaymsevaks (volunteers of high rank). Gujarat government's home minister, Gujarat chief minister, the central home minister and the prime minister all came from the same 'Hate University', the RSS shakha (Branch). The popular sentiments were whipped up against a small minority which was known to be more peaceful than in other states.

Violence against women

The communal ideology is founded on the patriarchal notions. Atrocities on 'women of'other community' are reagarded as punishing the other community. The communal violence while very painful for the men from minority community has manifold worse impact on the lives of women. During the violence they are subjected to rape and other sexual assaults. Different women rights groups came together as International Intitiative for Justice in Gujarat and after through investigation came out with a report, Threatened Existence-A Feminist analysis of The Genocide in Gujarat' (Forum Agianst Oppression of Women, Mumbai, 2003). The report points out that the deliberate shaming, especially of girls and women, by raping them publicly or in front of other family members, including children speaks of intentional attempt to subjugate a community by attacking female body. In chapter II, it makes a chilling observation, which was seen in its rudiments in case of Mumbai violence also, "In Gujarat as in Bosnia or Rwanda earlier, the widespread and furious attacks against women of minority community were regarded as legitimate not only by male attackers but also by women of majority community. We heard from testimonies that in some places the rapists were actively supported and even instigated by women of majority community."

Forms of violence against the women were also reflective of the social common sense which by now has become the bae of operative methods. VHP leaflets, openly circulating in Gujarat today, signed by the state general secretary, Chinubhai Patel, promise: "We will cut them and their blood will flow like rivers. We will kill Muslims the way we destroyed Babri mosque". This is followed by a poem

> "The volcano which was inactive...has erupted
> It has burnt the arse of miyas and made them dance nude
> We have untied the penises that were tied till now
> We have widened the tight vaginas of the bibis..."

One of the most spectacular forms of sadism in the recent events had been the way Muslim female and infantile bodies were made to function in the drama of Hindutva terror. There had been earlier anticipations of that. The investigations made by the All India Democratic Women's Association, in 1992-93, especially in Surat and Bhopal, had pointed out several similar features. Women were "tortured, molested, raped, and then burnt to death". Sometimes, their children were killed before their eyes. At the same time, more often than not, such atrocities were whispered about and not always confirmed openly. This time, rape victims as well as their male relatives have no inhibition about reporting rape and sexual torture. (Semiotics of Terror, Tanika Sarkar, EPW, July 13 2002) It is propagated that Muslim women have more children, are more fertile, causing the increase in population which is a threat to Hindus. In the violence what was seen was that women's private parts were mutilated, weapons introduced into them and the abdomen of woman was cut to throw the baby in the fire.

Gujarat vlence once again proved a bit more sternly that while minority men feel humiliated and defeated the minority women, abruptly understood their vulnerability not just in the face of outsider but within their own worlds of familiarity and intimacy. (R. Robnson, Tremors of Violence, p. 124, Sage, 2005)

Post Violence Gujarat

Being ruled by the BJP Govenrment, it did not care at all about the rehabilitation. The efforts were put togethcr by the Muslim trusts who tried to put together with great difficulty. The compensation given to riot victims was meagre and deliberatle harrasment was exercised in disbursenmnent even of the small amounts.

The few state run refugee camps were closed down soon on the pretext that state does not want to run the child production factores. The insinuation was that Muslim produce more children and are a demographich threat to the Hindu nation. The violence resulted in great intimidation of the Minority communitiy. The fear of minority was systermatically cultivated in the psyche of majority community. Today there is a religious clevage in the society with Muslims living in the ghettoes which are poor in hygiene and distant from the main facilities. Many a social facilities, banking, schools, mobile services are denied to them and the large chunk of society is lving in the fear.

Even before the vioelnece, Gujarat was being groomed in to the Laboratory of Hindu Ŗashtra, different towns and villages of Gujarat started putting the boards at various places "welcome to ...village of Hindu Rashtra" now this has gone up in number and extent.

The state of justice was well reflected in the case of Zahira Sheikh's case. The witnesses were harassed and forced to turn hostile and change their statements. There are innumerable cases which are neither investigated nor properly pursued. The justice system also shows lots of holes in the paterrn of justice delivery. The FIR's were not registered, cases were not pursued properly, and the judgments if at all were not upright.

With the victory of Modi (2007) Gujarat has become more or less become Hindu Rashtra factory. The situation of 'Hindu Rashtra in one state prevails; there.

Gujarat: Hindu Rashtra

The status of minorities is the index of state of democracy in a particular state. Today in Gujarat minorities have been relegated to the status of second class citizens. As a matter of fact Gujarat is the 'model' base of Sangh Parivar. It is not for nothing that it was chosen as the laboratory of Hindu Rashtra. The regrouping of social layers in Gujarat has been taking place since last three decades in an intense fashion. Along with urbanization there has been a parallel process in which the rich peasants of Gujarat have achieved an enhanced social status. These *Patidar* caste (cash crop farmers) has been upgraded by a process of religious maneuvering. The polarization of middle class (Brahmin, Bania) and Patidar occurred around 1980, around the issue of reservations for the lower castes. As we have seen above in 1980, Gujarat witnessed an extreme form of caste violence directed against the lower castes. The first major move of hindutva base was to oppose the affirmative action for the Dalits. It got manifested in Anti-Reservation riots during early 80s. It was argued that due to these 'son-in-laws' of the govt. who are good for nothing the children with real merit are suffering in jobs and in admissions in professional colleges. These anti-Dalit riots were the alarm bell of the times to come.

These anti-reservation agitations played a key role in consolidating the base of upper castes and upwardly mobile middle classes. Sangh Parivar stood by to support of these upper caste onslaughts. By using clever strategies Sangh Parivar was also able to give an upwardly mobile channel to a section of Dalits, who were aspiring for a better place within Hindu society. In Gujarat one can clearly see the social functionality of creating the 'other' (Muslim). Here earlier the ultimate object of hate was the Dalit, by a clever maneuver, the Muslim was substituted for that, the Dalit has been unleashed upon the 'other', an atmosphere of terror was created, which helped to maintain a 'status quo' of social hierarchy. Various Yatras and campaigns of VHP gave cohesion to this social base. Sangh Parivars ideological manipulation of the situation played a major role. It operated on two levels.

At ideological level it regarded all those who are not Muslims and Christians as Hindus. This negative definition was given further twist by asserting that Hindus worship Cow, Ram, Vedas, Gita and Acharyas. So in turn all Adivasis and Dalits have to adopt these symbols and ideologies. This was able to give a new identity to large section of subalterns. The large proliferation of different Vanvasi Kalyan Ashrams, Shishu Mandirs and other institutions occupied the cultural space lying vacant due to absence of major reform movements. The major challenge, as Shah (Caste, Hindutva and Hideousness Ghanshyam Shah.- Economic and Political weekly 15-4-2002 p. 1391) rightly points out for the proponents of Hindutva is to build unity among all Hindus without disturbing dominance of the upper castes and class. Hindu Mahasabha had launched the Bharat Hindu Milan Mandir in 1920s and they have been more active in Gujarat since 1970s. Besides undertaking activities to unite various sects and organizing religious festivals, they take up welfare and relief measures for the poor. The main thrust of these organizations is to build unity and harmony among the upper and lower castes.

Similarly RSS has also floated the organization called Samajik Samrasata Munch (SSM) Social Assimilation Platform to attract Ambedkarists and other Dalits for the purpose of developing Hindu unity. Here we again observe two separate strategies, one for Dalits and the other for Adivasis. In both the common factor is that their material problems are not addressed and an assertive cultural identity is brought to the fore. Amongst dalits the new middle class aspired for higher status within the Hindu social fold. Sanskritisation process made them to ape for the imitating the upper caste, to ignore and forget the material plight of their deprived brethren. While the deprived one's amongst them got swept in the cultural whirlpool of Swadhyay, Asaram Bapus, Swaminarayan type sects and Pandurang Shashtris who proliferated in Gujarat duly supported by the affluent middle class. They did bring the traditional Brahminical values in modern garb, laced in sugary syrup. These outfits have spread the idea of Hindutva and the pride in being Hindu based on Hindutva cutting across different communities. Joseph Mcwan (Society Under Siege, Seminar, and May 2002) points out that "enamored by their wealth and power the Ambedkerite dalits turned towards BJP. Those who aligned themselves with RSS also managed to acquire power". The core of RSS project thorough all these mechanisms have been to turn all the castes against Muslims and Christians. Dagger in the velvet cloak was pierced through the material aspirations of Dalits, the ideology of status quo; Hindutva was shoved in a most respectable form.

20

Minorities: Political Dilemmas

1. Introduction:

India's tragic partition (1947) left a deep scar on the South Asian polity. While Pakistan was formed on the basis of Islam, India was formed on secular grounds. That time undivided India had 25% Muslim population. Of this India was left with 11.6% Muslim population, while 13.4 were in Pakistan. Meanwhile a large affluent section of Muslims left for Pakistan. Today Muslims constitute 13.4% of India's population and are 138.18 millions in total population. (2001 Census) The sporadic but regular occurrence of the violence against this community has left it with a feeling of insecurity and has resulted in ghettoization. A large section of this minority was on the lower rungs of socio-economic levels, which went on worsening with time due to the social and political discrimination. This has been put forward by various indices as presented by Gopal Sing Commission in 1982 and by Sachar Committee, 2006. The findings of this committee are very disturbing as this section of India's population has been constantly sliding down.

Muslims have not been able to take advantage of various government schemes one of the reason being that they are mainly small farmers, marginal farmers, agricultural laborers, landless laborers, city based artisans and petty workers. Amongst other reasons one of the main causes for this is the discrimination and indifference on the part of planning and implementation authorities. "Consequently, the limited progress that some sections of Muslims have been able to make in recent years owes almost wholly to their own efforts. Overall the economic conditions of most Indian Muslims are unenviable, to say the least. Most of them eke out a hand-to-mouth existence either by way of self-employment in petty trade or by working in the unorganized sector. They are engaged mostly as construction laborers, rickshaw, taxi and truck drivers, handcart pullers, coolies, barbers, tailors, carpenters, pavement hawkers, or at best as mechanics, fitters, plumbers, electricians or welders." (Report AA, JMI, ISIS, Indian Social Institute 2006)

"As far as education is concerned figures of Sachar Committee suggest that Muslim men and women are less educated than their non-Muslim counterparts. In fact, a large number of Muslims do not even possess basic reading and writing skills. At the national level, the number of literate Muslims is less than non-Muslims. Based on the figures of the 2001 census, only 55 per cent Muslim males are literate as compared to 64.5 per cent non-Muslims, while only one among 41 male graduate as opposed to one among 19 non-Muslims. The condition of the Muslim women is much worse, with only one among a hundred being a graduate." (DNA 4th October 2006)

Their representation in the jobs in the government offices, public sector and private sector is abysmal, more the higher jobs, lower their representation.

Since the decade of 1980s India has seen the unprecedented political phenomenon, the one related to Communalism, i.e.

religious identity based politics. This phenomenon uses the religious identity for political mobilization, which in turn forms their route to coming to political power. The agenda of communal formations is essentially to suppress the human rights of weaker sections of society. It begins by spreading hate against the people of 'other religion', this hate propaganda in turn vitiates the social atmosphere and aids in the precipitation and intensification of communal violence, This violence over a period of time intimidates the minority communities, ghettoizing them.

On the other hand the second biggest minority, the Christians have been facing the violence from 1997. This violence has been gradually stepped up and the worst of it has been seen in Orissa from August 2008. This is happening mostly in Adivasi areas, where the poor sections of society have been deprived of social facilities.

2. Minorities: India Today

Today India is seeing this ghettotisation of Muslim minorities, and an equal intimidation of the Christian minority. Muslim minority has been subjected to repeated communal violence followed by arrest of large number of Muslim youth on the pretext of their being terrorists, while the Christian community has been intimidated due to the attacks on the nuns and priests in remote places and due to the horrific violence, which is gradually becoming more intense. Globally we are witnessing a period of Islamophobia, which has increased the insecurity of the Muslims World over, more so after the events of 9/11 2001, the attack on Afghanistan and Iraq. In South Asia one has witnessed this as a simmering problem right from the decades of 1940s, the partition of India, and migration of Hindus from the then West and East Pakistan. To add the problem the issue of Kashmir over a period of time has come to be seen as a Hindu-Muslim issue while it is the result of ultra nationalism of India and Pakistan and the US design to keep a foothold on this strategically important region through its proxy, Pakistan. The result is aggravation of the anti Muslim sentiments constructed around the memories of partition and the imbroglio which continues in Kashmir. Christian minorities have been living in fear of violence more so in remote places.

3. Genesis of Problem

As such the Hindu Muslim conflict as it is known began during the colonial British rule, when the declining classes of feudal lords resorted to political in the name of religion duly backed up by the British policy of divide and rule. The mis-representation of history and distortion of demographic and other issues went on aggravating the 'hate other' from both the sides, and in India, Muslims were the bigger victims. No sooner had the partition riots subsided the communal violence began in 1961 and went on increasing in intensity over a period of time. By late seventies its threat as an obstacle to realization of democratic principles started becoming obvious.

The politics of Hindu right, intensified its onslaught in the decade of eighties, Rath Yatras (chariot processions) and community mobilization of sections of Hindus around Ramshilas, use of religious platforms for communalization went on through out this decade. The central veering point of this mobilization was the Babri Masjid, which was claimed as the place where lord Ram was born. It was asserted that there was a magnificent temple which was destroyed by Mughal invader Babar. So the idea was to reclaim the birth place of Lord. This intensified into the campaign for demolition of Babri mosque. The demolition led to riots all around, more severely in Mumbai.

From 1987 in particular Vanvasi Kalyan Ashram, an affiliate of RSS (RSS is the father organization, its progeny is controlled by its trained swaymsevaks, the volunteers, like BJP, VHP, Bajrang dal, Vanvasi Kalyan Ashram and the like), became active in the far flung places spreading the hate against Christian missionaries. The charge leveled was that the service of the poor was a mere pretext to covert gullible Adivasis into Christianity. The culmination of this hate propaganda was seen in the burning alive of Pastor Stains and then sustained attacks on the nuns and priests in remote areas.

By 1990 the adverse effects of globalization started affecting the average people and while on one side the relatively affluent sections started emerging, the deprived sections were brought under the influence of identity based politics, which stood on the ground of Hate other. And parallel to this there was a rising impact of identity based politics and the communal mobilization around religious issues shot up drastically.

4. Communal Violence

The two drastic pogroms, the one of 1992-93 (Mumbai) and the one of Gujarat (2002) left a heavy trail of blood and gory tales of violence of unimaginable proportions. Earlier studies had been pointing out that the victims of this violence are predominantly Muslims to the extent of 80%. (Study by Nirmala Niketan, College of Social work, 1993). The Gujarat carnage witnessed the percentage going much adverse to the Muslim minorities.

Table

(a)

Break up of Killed

1969 (Ahmadabad) Incidents 519- Hindus 66 Muslims 558 –Others 49, Total 674

1980 (Assam) 427 87 278 10

Total 375

(Source- Engineer A.A., Communal Riots after Independence, CSSS 2004)

(b)

1990-92	Babri Related	Incidents 4300	Killed 3350
1993-94	Mumbai	2371	1030

(Source-Omar Khalidi, Indian Muslims Since Indcpendence, Vikas, 1996)

(c)

2002 Ahamdabad Killed 292 Injured 440

(Lobo and Das, Communal Violence and Minorities, Rawat, 2006)

The comprehensive religion wise data is no available, also the impact of this on children and women has not been quantified while the overall psychological effect of these pogrom on women and children has been extremely intimidating.

This intensified sustained campaign against minorities did lead to communal polarization and the coming into power of BJP, the RSS offshoot working in the electoral arena, the right wing Hindu political organization. This party regards Hitler as the ideal nationalist and works on similar lines the goal of Hindu Nation. Apart from other offshoots of its political offensive, it has slowly infiltrated in different wings of state machinery, police, bureaucracy, education, media and the like. Through its propaganda it has 'successfully' created the fear in the minds of sections of Hindu majority that Muslims and Christians are out to convert this Hindu majority nation in one where Hindus will be reduced to a minority and that they are being discriminated against, while the Muslim minorities in particular are being appeased for vote bank politics. Lately this propaganda is percolating through school books, television and print media, especially the vernacular press. It is trying to convert Adivisis into Hindu fold and is co-opting the Dalits into its fold. The anti Muslim violence and anti Christian violence, both are the kernel around which RSS politics is built. Of course the characteristics of both these are quite different.

(a) Anti Muslim Violence

The violence in India on communal grounds has been going up in intensity from last more than two decades. As such the rise of sectarian politics during the end of nineteenth century saw a respite for few years after the independence of the country. But it did return in a sporadic manner since 1961, Jabalpur riots. Later Jamshedpur and Rourkela riots broke out. "Of the bloody pogroms in sixties, the ones at Ranchi, Bihar (1962) and Ahmedabad, Gujarat (1969) stand out as the major events. In seventies the Turkman Gate massacre of 1976 perpetrated by police...., the riots in Moradabad (1980), Nellie, Naogaon, Assam (1983), Bhiwandi (1984) and Meerut (1987) have been the major ones in which more than a thousand lost their lives" (Khalidi, 1995). The Ramjanmabhumi campaign left a big trail of blood in which more than thousand people lost their lives in 1989. The massacres of Bhagalpur, Hydrabad and Aligargh heralded the onset of bloody 80s, which has seen the peak of communal violence. Advani's rath yatra (1990) and post Babri demolition riots were one of the worst, the country has suffered so far. The post demolition riots gripped Mumbai, Surat, Bhopal in a major way and many other places in a significant way. From 1960 to 1995 the incidences of riots have been on an upswing. A big proportion of these have been taking place in six states UP, Gujarat, Rajasthan, Bihar, Madhya Pradesh and Andhra. So far these riots' occurrence is mainly in cities, but involvement of villages is also there and has been in the rise but lately even the small towns and villages are also being drawn in the vortex.

The demolition of Babri Mosque in 1992, in a way can be called as a watershed in the political profile of the country. From here on the violence changed qualitatively and its adverse and long term effects started taking the toll of community psyche leading to ghettoization of Muslim minorities and the intense anti minority sentiments amongst a vast section of middle classes and sections of other parts of society.

(b) Anti Christian Violence

The attacks on Christians have begun especially from 1997 onwards. These attacks are being orchestrated by different organizations linked to RSS affiliates and a general hysteria is being created against the Christian Missionaries in particular. During the year (1998-99) many a priests were humiliated (Fr. Christudas being paraded naked in Dumka), one of them being burnt alive along with his two sons aged 11 and 7, many a churches have been damaged in these attacks, Bibles have been burnt and nuns have been raped in interior places. This has occurred in the backdrop of anti-Christian propaganda as per which Christianity is a foreign religion, their missionary activities are a mere ploy for inducing people for conversions to adopt Christianity, their schools and Hospitals are mere tools for the same. The CIA is planning this process and the Pope and Christian agencies, which are out to evangelize the whole country, where by Hindus will become a minority. Most of the inquiries by social activists, National Human Rights Commission, National Minorities Commission have shown that different organizations affiliated to SP are behind these attacks, and the attacks are taking place most in the BJP ruled states Gujarat, in particular. The most dreaded of this rocked Orissa during the period of December 2007 and then from August 2008, killing over 500 Christians, dislocating over a lakh of them and also involving the rape of a nun.

(c) Anti Sikh Violence

The major anti Sikh pogrom took place n 1984, in the aftermath of murder of Indira Gandhi by her Sikh bodyguards. These bodyguards were part of the Khaliastani movement; an extremist Sikh movement which was enraged by Indira Gandhi's sending of army in the holiest of holy Sikh shrines the Golden temple in Amritsar. In this massacre nearly 3000 Sikhs were killed right under the nose of the central government and with the police force looking the other way around. This led to a deep sense of insecurity amongst the Sikhs at large and most of the victims of the violence are yet to receive justice or suitable redressal.

In sum and substance, Muslim community is under-represented in most of the arenas of society barring the jails. One also recalls the report of Gopal Singh committee of 1982 which also had found the poor status of this minority. Gopal Singh committee report kept lying in the deep freeze while the issues like Ram Temple kept hogging the national attention. To add up one can say this community's representation as riot victim is way above its percentage in population. The committee has recommended that an Equal Opportunity Commission should be set up, a national data bank should be started, a nomination procedure should be initiated to ensure their participation in public bodies, in order to promote religious tolerance by a procedure to evaluate text books for appropriate social values, so on and so forth.

It is a matter of conjuncture whether this Govt is really serious about it or is it a mere replay of the earlier broken promises during last several decades. During last several decades while Governments after Governments have been promising to look after the problems of Muslim minorities, nothing much came out. This includes not only the longest reign of Congress party but also of the one's of formations in which BJP was an important component or supporter. Amongst multiple reasons of this neglect of this minority one was the aggressive propaganda of Hindu right that Government is out to 'appease' the Muslims so that they can be used as vote banks. One does not know whether this aggressive anti minority propaganda did contribute to the policies of the government, but one can say for sure that this 'appeasement of minorities' had become a part of 'social common sense' in the face of the worsening situation of Muslims.

What is being called rank communalism is essentially a bit of affirmative action. Surely even the reservations, which were brought in for Dalits have improved their conditions slightly, so now a full fledged opposition to those polices has been unleashed. While in the case of minorities not only the condition is bad as of today, the bigger worry is that it is sliding towards worse very rapidly. We need to distinguish abuse of community identity for politics and the bowing to the institution of religion from the concrete economic steps, social actions to support the weaker sections of society.

References

1. Report AA, JMI, ISIS, Indian Social Institute 2006.
2. DNA 4th October 2007.
3. Lobo and Das, Communal Violence and Minorities, Rawat, 2006.
4. Report on the Socio-Economic Conditions of Muslims in India (Report) by Action Aid (AA), Jahangirabad Media Institute (JMI) & Indian Social Institute (ISI).
5. Study by Nirmala Niketan, College of Social work, 1993.

Bibliography

1. Asghar Ali Engineer, "Some thoughts on pluralist model of Nation Building", Minorities in India, Conference papers, Rajiv Gandhi Institute For contemporary Studies (RGISS), 1996, p. 27.
2. Imtiaz Ahamd, 'Indian Minorities', Minorities in India, RGISS, 1996, p. 27 .
3. Iqbal A. Ansari, Readings on Minorities: Perspectives and Documants, Institute of Objective Studies, New Delhi 1996
4. Vinayak Damoar Savarkar, 'Hindutva, Who is a Hindu?', Nagpur, 1923.
5. M.S.Golwalkar, 'We or Our Nationhood defined', Bharat Publications 1939.

6. Chritophe Jaffrelot, *The Hindu Nationalist Movement and Indian Politics, Viking* 1996.

21

Problems of Minorities and the Laws

The issues related to the minorities have been in the air since quite some time. The two minorities which are in the news are Muslims and Christians. Both have different type of problems and legal issues are also very diverse.

A large section of Indian Muslims comes from the untouchables, shudras, who converted to Islam to escape the tyranny of Brahminical system of Varna, caste. Majority of this section was poor peasants tied to the land. A good chunk was also in petty trade and artisanship. With industrialization process, section of Muslims shifted to the cities to take up employment there. The advantages of modern education did not benefit this section of poor sufficiently and they remained marginalized from the employment in general and in higher echelons of jobs in particular. The efforts of the likes of Sir Syed were restricted more for the Ashraf (elite, upper caste) section of Muslims. With partition the large section of educated elite Muslims left for Pakistan, increasing the ratio of poor and uneducated Muslims in the community.

The Muslim minority faces the twin problem of violence and poverty. Due to being artisans, weavers, some concentration of theirs' took place in some cities where occupation based on their skills were located, Meerut (locks), Moradabad (brassware) Bhiwandi, and Malegaon (textiles). In cities majority Muslims were concentrated in poor localities, with less civic and other amenities. The trade rivalry was to be the first which took the better of the democratic norms and resulted in the violence, beginning from the Jabalpur one. Here the violence was aided by the rivalry of *bidi* (tobacco rolled in leaves) traders. Later the violence of Meerut, Malyana, Bhivandi, and Malegaon came up to show this sore spot of Indian society. Every wave of violence left the Muslims in that area poorer and more marginalized.

The occurrence of regular repeated violence against them has been well documented in various inquiry commission reports (Jagmohan, Vyathathil, Madon, and Shrikrishna). In the communal violence which has taken place between 1961 to 1991, those amongst the riot victims, 80% were Muslims (Muslim population around 12%) This violence and post violence trauma has left the community in a sorry state. On one hand it has aggravated the poverty and on the other it has caused ghettoization, which is the root cause for domination of Mullahs in that community. The insecurity caused by violence leads them to concentrate in few areas and than in these areas the orthodox sections become powerful and dominant. This also results in obstructing the process of social reform and change of social norms related to women in particular. In Mumbai Bhendi bazaar, Jogeshwari, Mumbra are the examples of this. Different cities have seen the emergence of these ghettoes which are derogatorily called as mini Pakistan. The rehabilitation process after the riots is not satisfactory. Gujarat showed the worst of it when the Government refused to initiate any steps to rehabilitate them. At the same time their percentage in employment was low and has been consistently declining.

The losses of minority community, after the violence, just in terms of quantum, are phenomenonal. The Ahmadabad city itself witnessed the massive destruction of property, mainly of Muslims. Tata Consultancy Services surmise the loss of gross value output of goods and services to be about 1250 crores, the loss of trading business about 1000 crores, loss of exports 2000 crores. Many a trading families turned destitute due to the lack of proper rehabilitation and compensation after the riots. The recovery is generally not complete and these families take to economically lower level of occupation.

The families which are victims of this violence, many a times have to be displaced and to rebuild their lives from scratch. The state apathy in their rehabilitation was worst exhibited in the Gujarat violence, which is extreme but in no way the only example of its kind. In most of the riots the rehabilitation process has been half baked, half way and nowhere bringing the victims to their pre riot economic levels. The compensation which is declared for the victims generally does not reach them. In case of Gujarat the prime minister declared that the victims will be given Rs. 50,000 each. The state government modified it to say that the compensation will be given *up to* Rs.50, 000, and finally the victims got compensation which was abysmally low in amount. This has gone on adding to the process of worsening over a period of time.

The educational levels amongst Muslims have remained low due to multiple factors. They have been discriminated against in jobs and other social facilities all through. Most of the scholars on the topic have come out with immaculate statistics on the topic. Omar Khalidi analyzing the National sample survey data, round 43rd, of 1987-88, the later data is worse, shows that there are 53.4% self employed amongst Muslims vis a vis 35.9% amongst Hindus. While 46.7% Hindus are on wages/salaries 28.9% of Muslims are on salaries. (Khalidi, Indian Muslims Since Independence, Vikas, Delhi 1996, p.66) Apart from trade, the places where one can find employment is the jobs in Government, public sector and private enterprises.

Table
Muslims in Public Employment: All Indian Central Services

Service	*Year*	*Total*	*Muslims*	*Percentage*
IAS	1981	3,883	116	2.99
Income Tax I	1981	1,753	50	2.85
Railway Traffic & Account Services Intake during	1971-80	881	27	3.06

Source: Mushirul Hasan, Legacy of a divided nation, p. 282 from Muslim India June 1983, pp. 261-63.

Their representation in jobs also is very low, in 1981, amongst the total of 3883 IAS officers only 116(2.99%) were Muslims (Hasan, 282) same was the pattern in class I jobs in most of the sectors while in lower categories, class II, to IV the situation was marginally better. Data cited by Robinson shows that the percentage of Muslims in police force was roughly 4-5 % in most states, much less than their ratio in population. (Robinson, Rowena; Tremors of Violence, Sage 2005, p. 92).

These data show high rate of self employed amongst the Muslims, the reason being their discrimination in the employment. "Muslims are marginalized from more prestigious domain of regular and salaried employment. Forty six point seven percent Hindus are involved in regular wage/salaried employment in contrast with just 28.9 per cent of Muslims. Muslims are but marginally more represented than Hindus or Christians in the category of casual labor. Later data (Shariff Abusaleh; India Human Development Report: A Profile of Indian States since 1990s, Oxford University Press 1999) also shows that Muslims continue to get their share from artisanship and petty trade as compared to other social groups; in contrast their income is far below the national average and less than that earned by Hindus from this source. NSS data (Rounds 50 and 55 for years 1993 and 1999-2000) reveal the unsettling trend of increasing disparity between Hindus and Muslims during 1990s with respect to the consumption, education, employment and landholdings, though literacy rates of both communities showed gradual improvement.(Hasan2000:248)" (quoted in Robinson, p.67)

Gopal Singh Commission appointed by Government of India in 1980s showed that only 3.41% students in Engineering colleges are Muslims, only 6.77% of them are registered at the employment exchange, in private sector they are 8.16%, borrowers under bank loan schemes-9.41% getting 3.37% of borrowings, poor representation in judiciary(Gopal Singh Commission, Quoted in Puniyani, Communal Politics, Sage 2002, p.145)

The major legal issues pertaining to the Muslim community has been the question of Muslim Personal laws. As per these laws the Muslim men can marry four numbers of times and can divorce by proclaiming talaq three times. Shah

Bano case was the turning point in many ways. The Supreme Court ruling was overturned by the Government to appease the fundamentalist sections of Muslim leadership. As such there is a strong section of Muslim women who want the reforms to take place. Due to the intimidation process of the violence against the minorities the fear complex has set in and the reform process is not easy to get going. An intimidated community becomes ghettoized emotionally also and in such situations reforms are very difficult. One has to recall that the Personal laws in all the religions are different and most of the personal laws are against the interests of women of those religions. All the communities need more and more reform to give gender justice. In case of minorities the problems are always more difficult and in India it is worse off because of the intimidation which they have to face due to spread of communal violence, communal thinking and demonization of minorities. It needs to be recalled here that in Muslim countries where the process of intimidation is not there, these personal laws have been changed in favor of more secular and just laws.

The second aspect of the laws related to Muslim minorities is related to reservations for Muslims in the professional colleges and jobs. The basis of reservation has been social disability which results in a handicap for the progress of the community. Such provisions were given to the dalits and it had a marginal impact in improving their condition. Communal forces are generally against the affirmative action for weaker sections of society. In case of Muslims the opposition is very vehement. The Muslim community does require an affirmative action to ensure that there is some progress in the community but barring few Indian states which are an exception this is not coming through.

The Christian minorities have been facing different type of problems. From 1996 the section of Christian population living in the far off places and Missionaries in particular has been attacked. The Christian have been charged with the accusation that they are converting the poor gullible Adivasis by førce and fraud. On this pretext many a churches have been attacked, Bibles burnt and Missionaries attacked. Pastor Graham Stains working amongst the Leprosy patients was burnt alive by Dara Singh, who was working with Bajrang dal and other Hindutva organizations. In the face of these accusations the Christian community is feeling intimidated and insecure. As such it is interesting to note that while it is being said that Christians are converting, the population of Christians is on the decline, 1971-2.60%, 1981-2.44%, and 1991-2.34% and in 2001-2.30%. Even in the Keonjhar area where Pastor Stains was working there was no significant rise in the Christian population. This marginal decline in the percentage of Christians is due to the better educational and social status of the Christian population.

To legitimize the acts of the attacks on Christians, various state Governments brought in the legislation to prevent the conversions. It is another matter that there is nothing illegal about choosing one's religion. The case of Jayalaltha, TamilNadu is very interesting and shows that anti Christian tirade is just a political move. When BJP led NDA was in power, she brought in a legislation which required that prior permission should be taken before the conversion. When BJP led NDA lost in the general elections and Jayalalitha had to bite the dust in the Lok sabha elections she promptly withdrew this legislation.

Indian constitution grants the right to all of its citizens to practice and propagate one's faith. The sudden coming up of the issue of conversion and 'threat to Hinduism' is a propaganda for the agenda of Hindu right which wants to do away with democracy and bring in a Religion based nation. The rise in the ant minority violence from the decade of 1980s is related to the political processes and does not reflect the clash between relgions or religious communities. In the atmosphere of propaganda against the minorities it has become difficult to protect their constitutional rights and affirmative action for weaker sections is becoming a distant dream.

22

Minority Appeasement

While the opposition to reservation is on its peak, another front has been opened by those opposed to affirmative action of any sort. It may be a common observation by now that the most 'consistent' political and social force opposed to any sort of affirmative action is the communal politics, the politics of RSS affiliates. Surly there are other elite affluent sections who also are diehard opponents of affirmative action and reservation but for communalists, reservation/affirmative action is a red herring. So it was not much of a surprise when Rajnath Singh, the current BJP chief, came down heavily against the 15 point scheme for minorities, which aims at all round upliftment of the minorities, more so the economically deprived sections of minority. Mr Singh, (26th June 2006), went to label the cabinet decision to allocate 15% of the funds for social welfare schemes for minorities as the 'appeasement' of minorities, an oft repeated allegation of this political outfit.

The central cabinet in its meeting on 22nd June approved Dr. Manmohan Singh's new 15 point program for minority welfare, including ways to prevent communal riots. In a comprehensive proposal the prime minister has asked for introduction of ways to enhance the living conditions, and allocation of 15% of funds from welfare budget for minorities. The aim of the proposal is to upgrade the facilities for minority education, modernize madrassa education and to provide scholarships for meritorious students. The program lays emphasis on equitable share in economic activities and employment. It also touches on different facets of lives including the rural housing schemes.

Before we take up the issue whether all this is appeasement or is a much needed measure to ensure that minorities also are able to progress like any other community, it is imperative that we have a brief look at the implementation of National Rural Employment guarantee scheme (NRES) in Gujarat. Reports indicate that Muslim minority is not able to take the benefit of this scheme as the Sarpanchas and concerned officials have been preventing Muslims from registering for this scheme. They are sent back couple of times, after which they get a subtle message and keep away from approaching the authorities.

Currently Rajinder Sachchar committee is in the process of finalizing its report about the status of Muslim minorities in India. What ever one could glean from the parts of report, and from the document prepared by a voluntary organization for presenting to the Sachchar Committee, (National Study on Socio-Economic Condition of Muslims of India, Indian Social Institute, Delhi, May 2006) makes one sit up with deep sense of anguish. The current socio economic status of Muslim minorities in particular, has slipped down in the human development indices. Also their abysmal representation in jobs, the more of them living below poverty line and more of them being illiterate, leaves no doubt in one's mind that without serious affirmative action, this community will go on being deprived more and more. The additional problem of post communal violence ghettotization is adding salt to the wounds, as in the ghettoes the living conditions go down and threatened psyche, fuels the conservative ideology.

Earlier, Gopal Singh Commission report had also brought to our attention a similar fact in the decade of early 1980s. It showed that only 3.41% students in Engineering colleges are Muslims, only 6.77% of them are registered at the employment exchange, in private sector they are 8.16%, borrowers under bank loan schemes-9.41% getting 3.37% of borrowings, poor representation in judiciary. No action was taken based on this report, which has been gathering dust since. Later data (Shariff, India Development Report, OUP 1999) also shows that Muslims continue to get their share from artisanship and petty trade as compared to other social groups; in contrast their income is far below the national average and less than that earned by Hindus from this source. NSS data (Rounds 50 and 55 for years 1993 and 1999-2000) reveal the unsettling trend of increasing disparity between Hindus and Muslims during 1990s with respect to the consumption, education, employment and landholdings, though literacy rates of both communities showed gradual improvement.

While the charges of appeasement abound and have been made part of the social common sense the reality is the contrary. No doubt the earlier governments have appeased the Mullahs and conservative sections of society for electoral purpose; it is also true that the Muslim community has been getting marginalized by the day. Right after partition, the elite Muslims left for Pakistan and majority of the Muslims remaining here were the poorer one's, coming from Shudra background and now living as *ajlafs* with Islamic identity. They were bypassed in the social development process so the percentage of their representation in jobs, bank loans, higher education and other social benefits has been declining constantly. During last two decades when communal politics has been on the rise their situation is worse off, and without a determined effort they can in no way come close to the national averages of social and economic indices. The problem is not that, they are being appeased but that most of the development schemes for minorities have been too few and whatever were there, have not been implemented properly.

Communal outfits, irrespective of which religion they derive their identity from, generally stand for status quo, so any measures which can lead to social transformation are shirked and opposed, some times upfront, sometimes in a subtle way. Since the opposing to reservation for Dalit/OBC will be an electoral hara-kiri, so Mandal is not opposed directly, instead Kamandal (Rath yatra for Babri demolition) is engineered. To oppose the Mandal II, 'Youth for Equality' or some such forum is created. In case of Muslims where talking of reservation, barring at few places, is not a rewarding electoral strategy, the opposition to this can be upfront under the banner of Minority appeasement. As such, communal forces are opposed to minorities' welfare and have been opposing it right since the formation of Congress in 1885. At that time Congress was charged with appeasing Muslims as Congress regarded Muslims as a part of Indian nation. The most ghastly manifestation of this came up when a Hindutva trained volunteer, Nathuram Godse, killed the father of the Indian nation, Mahatma Gandhi on the same charge of Muslim appeasement. And now we have Mr. Rajnath Singh of BJP opposing the welfare measures and labeling these overdue measures as minority appeasement!

23

Communalism and Caste

Communalism is a politics which operates in the name of religion. To be precise it uses religious identity for political mobilization. While it presents itself as a struggle for religion based nationalism, it is essentially a politics to abolish democratic space; to impose the birth based hierarchy of caste and gender, to push back this process of social transformation. It is a politics which is opposed to the liberating concept of Liberty, Equality and Fraternity. It tries to dish out the mantra of harmony while attacking minorities in a blatant way.

This attack on minorities is the external phenomenon. The deeper, core, phenomenon is to crush the concept of social equality. At deeper level this politics aims to restore back the values of Manu smiriti, in a modern language of Integral Humanism. In Indian context its emphasis is on revival of the norms of Manusmriti in a modern form. Integral Humanism argues that as for the proper functioning of human body we require that each part performs its assigned work, so for proper functioning of society each group should perform its assigned duty, i.e. caste equations should be preserved in the contemporary context.

Communalism in India began in the decade of 1880s when the process of industrialization and modern education was resulting in the slow but sure social transformation. It was the period when Jotiba Phule encouraged the dalits to go for Modern education; it was the period when Savitri bai Phule began the process of education for women against heavy odds. At this point of time the declining sections of society, landlords, kings and associated clergy opposed these changes on the ground that these are against our traditions, that these are not sanctioned by our religion.

These forces of conservatism were the ones who were to form the communal organizations in times to come. Due to the British rule the process of secularization was weak and the declining classes and values ran along with the changing values. The declining classes and the associated clergy went on to form Muslim League and Hindu Mahasabha in due course of time and later the ideological consolidation of Hindu communalism took place in the formation of RSS. RSS has Hindutva as its ideology and Hindu Rashtra as its goal.

Hindutva is not a religion but a political ideology based on the Brahminical stream of Hindusim and Hindu rashtra is a concept totally opposed to the values of Democracy, Liberty Equality and fraternity and opposed to secularism. During freedom movement, while Jotiba phule initiated the process of transformation, it got supplements in other states also. Dr. Ambedkar took on the mantle of leadership of this movement and went on to lead the dalits for social equality. While he was doing this work, the communalists, led by Hindu Mahasabha and RSS opposed the movements which he had initiated, sometime vocally and at other times by keeping quiet, by keeping aloof from these significant steps in the direction of dalit aspirations. But today many a times it is propagated by communalists that Hindutva (RSS-Savarkar) and Ambedkar had similar goals, this is a blatant lie.

Ambedkar made all the efforts to struggle against the humiliating treatment given to shudras in Hindu society. His campaigns were to get access to public drinking water (Chavadar Talav, Mahad); Manusmriti Dahan and Kalaram Temple. None of these were supported by the RSS, Hindu Mahasabha. He undertook to burn Manusmriti, while Golwalkar chose to write eulogies for the same book. As per Golwalkar Manu is the first and greatest law-giver of the world, whose code has asked all people all over the world to learn wisdom from traditional Brahmins. Manu had converted the division of labor into Jati, Caste system. As per which the only duty of shudra is to serve Brahmins, who in turn should give him left over food, discarded clothes and utensils. If shudra try to study, their tongue should be chopped off and if they happen to hear the noble 'Vedas', molten lead should be poured into their ears. Purush Sukta states- Brahmins are head, Kshatriya Arms, Vaishayas groin and shudras: the feet.

Movement against un-touchability was never on the agenda of communal forces. In December 1992 Dharam Sansad of VHP passed a resolution stating that- Indian constitution is non-Hindu and should be replaced by a 'Hindu constitution'. Later K. Sudarshan also went to say the same. It is because of this that NDA, BJP led coalition, in 1998 formed the constitution review committee. There was a strong opposition to this idea from the people, all over that the country, because of which it could not work in the direction desired by RSS. For Hindu communalists Manusmriti has provided justice to all, his laws are more important than Constitution of India.

Ambedkar states that Hindus are neither a nation nor are they a society. The reality of social life of Hinduism is caste system because of which there is a lack of dialogue and opportunities in cultural life, and there is no feeling of togetherness. Due to social, economic and educational contradictions the society of Hindus cannot become a nation. After his initial support to the idea of Pakistan on the grounds that Muslims are a separate nation, he realized that formation of Pakistan would increase the possibility of Hindu Raj (RSS's Hindu Rashtra). This realization made him change his opinion saying that 'If Hindu Raj does become a fact; it will no doubt be the greatest calamity of this country. No matter what the Hindus say, Hinduism is a menace to liberty. Hindu Raj must be prevented at any cost.'

When the constituent assembly was formed Dr. Ambedkar was given the responsibility of chairing the drafting committee. At the same time the communal forces said that we do not need a new constitution as we already have the best of it in the form of Manu smiriti.

The slow process of social transformation, which began in late 19th century, became stronger with Independence, and then became more significant from the decade of 1980. The dalit-OBC started coming in the social arena, their presence started becoming significant. The issue of affirmative action became an eyesore to the affluent upper caste. The upper caste struck back in the form of anti-Reservation riots. In Gujarat for example the educated middle classes, mainly the Brahmins, Banias and Patidars sharply reacted to this by starting agitation against the reservation system. The clashes between savarnas and the Dalits in the industrial periphery of Ahmadabad gradually degenerated into caste war that spread to the towns in 18 out of the then 19 districts of Gujarat. In many villages dominated by land owning Patidars in North and central Gujarat Dalit bastis were burnt.

Caste tension resurfaced in 1985 in the second anti-reservation agitation. The BJP leadership drawn mainly from upper caste realized the need to expand their social base to achieve electoral success. They started to co-opt the dalit OBC's in to their gambit by different Yatras and religious symbols and campaigns. Advani's Rath Yatra saw pitched battles between Dalits and Muslims. The process was replicated in different points of time. RSS 'successfully' created rift between the 'Hindu Adivasis' and 'Christian Adivasis' also. In absence of deeper social reforms the modern institutions and values of Liberty, Equality and Fraternity remained weak and at places Hindutva, by default, provided the much-needed identity to the Dalit OBCs. This process saw its heightened expression in the wake of Mandal commission implementation. Mr. Vajpayee formulated this response of RSS-combine to Mandal commission succinctly. He stated that we have brought Kamandal (Religion based issues) in response to Mandal (Symbolizing the aspirations of Dalit-OBCs).

The polarization of middle class (Brahmin, Bania) and rich peasants started taking place from around 1980 all over the country. This took place around the issue of reservations for the lower castes. This is what gave rise to extreme form of caste violence directed against the lower castes. This anti-Dalit riot was the alarm bell of the times to come. These anti-reservation agitations played a key role in consolidating the base of communal politics, upper castes and upwardly mobile middle classes. RSS-combine stood by to support these upper caste onslaughts.

Later by using clever strategies RSS-combine was also able to give an upwardly mobile channel to a section of Dalits, who were aspiring for a better place within Hindu society. Gradually the ire against dalit-OBC was replaced by anger against Muslim-Christians and dalit Adivaisis started being co-opted into this communal politics as foot soldiers of communal politics. Through this political game/social engineering the ultimate object of hate Dalit, was replaced by the Muslim. Due to this co-option dalits could be unleashed upon the 'other' (Muslims), an atmosphere of terror was created, which helped to maintain a 'status quo' of social hierarchy.

Various Yatras and campaigns of VHP gave cohesion to this social base of Communalism. It operated on two levels. At ideological level it regarded all those who are not Muslims and Christians as Hindus. The large proliferation of different Vanvasi Kalyan Ashrams, Shishu Mandirs and other institutions occupied the cultural space lying vacant due to absence of major reform movements. The major challenge, for the proponents of Hindutva has been to build unity among all Hindus without disturbing dominance of the upper castes and class. Hindu Mahasabha had launched the Bharat Hindu Milan Mandir in 1920s. Besides undertaking activities to unite various sects and organizing religious festivals, sometimes they also take up welfare and relief measures for the poor. The main thrust of these organizations is to build unity and 'harmony' among the upper and lower castes.

Similarly RSS has also floated the organization called Samajik Samrasata Manch (Social Assimilation Platform) to attract different sections of dalits for the purpose of developing 'Hindu' unity. Here we again observe two separate strategies, one for Dalits and the other for Adivasis. In both, the common factor is that their material problems are not addressed and an assertive cultural identity is brought to the fore. Amongst dalits the new middle class aspired for higher status within the Hindu social fold. Sanskritization process made them to ape for the imitating the upper caste, to ignore and forget the material plight of their deprived brethren. The deprived one's amongst them got swept in the cultural whirlpool of Swadhyay, Asaram Bapus, Swaminarayan type sects and Pandurang Shashtris who proliferated all over, duly supported by the section of affluent middle class. They did bring the traditional Brahminical values in modern garb, laced in sugary syrup of soothing discourses. These outfits have spread the idea of Hindutva and the pride in being Hindu, based on Hindutva ideology, cutting across different communities.

It is in this context that the anti-Christian missionary campaign was brought in. The argument that all those living in this country are Hindus was taken to the practical logic. The one's converting to 'other', 'foreign' religions were supposed to be doing so under the allurement of the money or other favors. Hinduism was projected as superior to other faiths as it neither does, nor believes in conversions. Here two birds are killed in one stone. Hinduism, i.e. Brahmanism, cannot undertake conversions in the real sense, as it is an exclusive club. The lower castes do like to convert to escape the social injustice imposed by the upper caste, practicing Brahminical ideology. The argument is cleverly twisted and the 'elite exclusivism' is presented as the virtue. So all those who convert are supposed to have succumbed to the guile or intimidation of the 'foreign religion' so they need to be 'reconverted back' to Hinduism by newly developed rituals after intimidating them. Also they have to be taught to throw away their old gods and taught the virtues of Ram, Gita and Acharyas. And in this direction the Christian missionaries need to be taught a lesson, few Bibles to be burnt, Nuns and Fathers beaten up etc. Gujarat-Orissa has seen all this more than the other places of India where the Religious fascism of RSS-combine is stalking the streets.

The RSS-combine has also used different social facilities like night schools and youth camps to subsume the Dalit identity into a Pan Hindu identity. Many a Dalits have started subordinating their caste identity and claiming them to be Hindus. The core philosophy around which RSS formed dalit organizations operate is that the caste struggle is not desirable and what we need is caste-harmony, Samajik Samrasata (Social Assimilation). This has trapped many a middle sections of dalits who have derived benefits of the reservation and other social avenues. These organizations floated by RSS have given a broad Hindu identity to the section of Dalits, who have accepted it as an avenue for upward mobility. The plethora of these organizations apart from organizing Hinduized versions of popular festivals also arrange the programs of inter-dining (Ram Khichadi) to make their social presence felt amongst the Dalit sections of society. The tendency to blindly worship Phule and Ambedkar has been taken full advantage of by Brahminizing them. RSS has no problems in worshipping these major contributors to Dalit movement so far as their teachings are kept under wraps.

The anti minority violence does create a social and political atmosphere of terror, due to which human rights and social movements get intimidated. The attacks in Adivasi areas and forays of RSS in Adivasi areas intensified from mid eighties when it was realized that by directly attacking Adivasis, the way they were attacked in 1980 and 1986 in Gujarat through caste violence, will be counterproductive at electoral level. The strategy evolved was to 'use' them as foot soldiers against Muslim minorities. At the same time electoral arithmetic brought to their attention this substantial chunk of population of Adivasis trying to come up through modern education and thereby disturbing the status quo, prevalent in the far off villages. It's due to this, that the Christian missionaries were perceived as a big threat to the project of Hindu Nation. Through the network of schools spread in the far off areas these Missionaries, whatever be their own motives, were instrumental in getting a section of Adivasis empowered and in the process the upper caste affluent base of Sangh was getting jittery.

The posting of RSS volunteers into the forest work was very systematic. Apart from attacking the Christian missionaries as foreigners the *Ghar vapasi* was brought in at a big scale in all the Adivasi areas scattered from Gujarat to MP to Orissa. Around this time many a swamis; descended in these areas, Lakkhanand in Phulbani area (who was killed presumably by Maoists recently), Aseemanand in Dangs (who is absconding due to his links with Malegaon blasts), and Aasaram (in whose ashrams children have been dying due to mysterious reasons) disciples in Jhabau and many other such efforts were unleashed. In Adivasi areas they resorted to threatening, you are Hindus, Hindu rituals are like this and so these have to part of your life. Dilip Singh Judeo type workers had been doing Ghar Vapasi, converting Adiviasis to Hinduism by newly devised baptizing techniques.

At the same time Hanuman has been popularized as the God in these areas and lately Shabri, the destitute women who had the privilege of offering wild berries to Lord Ram is being projected as the Goddess of Adivasis. The cultural symbolism cannot be missed in the selection of these deities. Hanuman was the unquestioning devotee of Lord Ram, with muscular power as the main virtue. He is capable of flying while carrying a huge mountain. But all the same he is carrying the mountain because he cannot identify the herb needed for treatment of

Laxman, Lord's younger brother. This is what is the signal to Adivasis, unquestioning loyalty to Lord Ram, no need to have education. So what are the Christian missionaries doing here? Why should they be trying to educate you? They are foreigners. So Pastor Stains is picked up for the treatment which they want to mete out to the white robed priests and nuns.

Shabri, the embodiment of poverty is being glorified on purpose. Your great ancestress had the privilege to offer wild berries to the Lord. She is your role model, poor, powerless and with blind reverence and devotion for the upper caste. The recently held festival in Subir, Dangs district of Gujarat, celebrated Shabri and lakhs of Advasis were brought from neighboring Adivasi areas for the festival. The local people were scared that Sangh's festival may create the trouble and they may try to forcibly do the conversions to Hinduism. It was declared that Christians and Muslim are foreigners and are a threat to Hindu religion. This Kumbh is meant to 'protect' the Hindus from the foreigners. In the beginning it was announced that conversions are the aim of Kumbh and than silence was kept on this point once various groups questioned their motives.

To conclude communalism aims, operates at various levels vis a vis caste. Firstly it wants to oppose the process of caste and gender transformation, so it presents the goal of Hindu Rashtra, which is opposed to equality. Most of the landmark years of communal politics have been in response to the rise of dalits, beginning of education, beginning of their social movements. These dalit assertions and progresses were answered by formation of Hindu Mahasabha and RSS respectively. They aimed to throttle dalits' rise around 1980s, by intensifying the rise of religiosity and anti dalit violence. Secondly through clever social engineering, attempts are being made to co-opt dalits and Adivasis. And these sections are again being used to commit violence against Muslims and Christians.

24

Commmunalism and Anti Christian Violence

I

Introduction

Orissa has witnessed unprecedented violence against the tiny Christian minority. On August 23, 2008, Swami Laxmananand along with his four followers was killed, probably by a group of Maoists. Immediately, anti-Christian violence began on big scale The way it began it seemed as if preparations for it were well afoot. It was systematic and widespread. It sounded as if preparation was already there, just the pretext was being waited for. So far many innocent Christians have been killed, wounded and rendered homeless apart from many Churches having been torched.

Christians are a tiny minority in India. Contrary to the perception that British brought Christianity to India, it is one of the oldest religions of India. Its spread has been slow. Not much was heard against this minority till the decade of 1990s, when suddenly it started being asserted that Christian missionaries are converting. Anti Christian violence has been occurring more in the interior remote places and is accompanied by another phenomenon, that of Ghar Vapasi (return home), which is the conversions of Adivasis into the Hindu fold.

It is from 1996, that this phenomenon has captured the attention of all of us. Suddenly, as if from nowhere has descended the 'threat of conversion to Christianity' by force or fraud. Simultaneously, attacks on priests and nuns have increased in distant interior places. It has been a peculiar phenomenon that while these attacks in remote places were being undertaken, the Christian institutions in cities – schools, colleges and hospitals – did not face such threats. The selective targeting of Christian missionaries in distant places was a matter of serious attention, concern and introspection. As the 'social common sense' started accepting, 'yes, they are converting', 'they have been converting', a sort of silent approval did accompany these attacks on the missionaries. One was used to hearing about attacks on Muslim minorities so far. How come a new minority is the 'source of trouble' now and hence, 'being taught a lesson'? How has this come to the forefront of social thought at broader level? The discerning observer did notice that it was the year when the BJP government for the first time came to power at the Centre, that the trend began more in BJP or BJP-allies ruled states and also in states like Orissa where the roots of RSS run very deep.

It did begin with isolated incidents like the attack on the Catholic Health Centre of India near Latur (1996), burning of Bibles and attacks on the Christian congregations. But most shocking was the burning alive of pastor Graham Steward Stains (1998, January) along with his two sons, Philip and Timothy, aged 9 and 7 years, who were sleeping in a jeep after a village festival. Gradually the pattern of these attacks started emerging.

In the remote places where Vanvasi Kalyan Ashrams (Society for Welfare of Forest Dwellers), an outfit of RSS, have been active and doing the propaganda work along with starting of Ekal schools and have been Hinduising Adivasis, the incidents were more pronounced and intense. The intimidating atmosphere went on to a serious degree and the gullible elements under the barrage of propaganda started calling in for stoppage of conversion activities. The then Prime Minister, Atal Bihari Vajpayee, a RSS trained swayamsevak (Volunteer) of the country went on to demand a debate on the conversions.

The violence against Christian missionaries has by now become a matter of routine. Unlike the anti Muslim pogrom it has been scattered, in space and time. Barring few dastardly acts like Pastor Stains' burning, Rani Maria's being hacked to death and beheading of another priest, the incidents were medium in intensity and did not take the shape of carnage or pogrom against the community till the recent one in Orissa (December 2007 and August 2008). The occurrence of these incidents was mostly in places that are far flung in Adivasi areas, with rampant poverty and illiteracy. The apathy in highlighting these core issues by a section of media was appalling. At the same time, by word of mouth the propaganda began that Christians were blowing up some minor incidents.

The attacks and finding of issues continue and it is clear that the message has spread that Christian missionaries working in remote places are soft targets and one can get away without much reprisals. Also the anti-Christian mobilization of Adivasi youth through cultural manipulation was the groundwork on which the anti-Christian violence could sustain. In the atmosphere created by the activities of RSS progeny, local communal groups have felt emboldened to pick up any small issue and to make a violent incident out of it. It's frightening effect on the victims is tremendous. It also begins to polarise the local communities into Christian and non-Christian camps amongst whom the seeds of tension are sown.

While primarily the violence has taken place in remote areas, very few incidents have come to light, which have occurred in cities. In one of the notable incidents, the Principal of a Christian school was intimidated by the Municipal corporator belonging to a communal party. The Shiv Sena leader of the area approached with a list of children who must be given admission in the school, irrespective of the admission criteria of the school.

The role of state agencies has been no different in these incidents. In most cases, the administration has looked the other way when communal goons were on the rampage. The administration most often provided enough leeway for them to wreck havoc, indulge in intimidation, violence and to get away with that. The adivasi areas, which were so far peaceful, started witnessing communal tensions. It also shows the map of spread of Vanvasi Kalyan Ashrams and Vishwa Hindu Parishads in an indirect way.

II

Hinduva and Anti Christian Violence

RSS had been floating different organisations for different sections of society; Vanvasi Kalyan Ashram to Hinduise Adivasi was founded in 1952 and the Vishwa Hindu Parishad founded in 1964 was to play an important role in the anti Christian tirade in times to come. Bajrang Dal which directly supported violence against Christians was founded by RSS in 1984. After the intimidation and browbeating of Muslim minorities, especially after the post Babri demolition Mumbai riots, they stepped up their social dominance and needed another community to target their trishuls for further expansion of their social and electoral base, and that was done by the bogey of forced conversions and accompanying anti Christian violence, which started coming to the fore from 1996 onwards. The targeting of minorities has played an important role in polarising the communities, in consolidation of the majoritiarian politics in various ways.

The beginning of anti Christian violence was slow and sporadic. With Bharatiya Janata Party (BJP) coming to occupy the seat of power intermittently at the Centre, the emboldening of RSS progeny was very visible. Each and every pretext was converted into an occasion for anti Christian propaganda and violence. The list of these incidents is long, and of course incomplete.[1] The initial and detailed reports of these started appearing in Communalism Combat, a magazine devoted to the issue of communalism in all its facets. Though the Human rights groups felt uncomfortable about these episodes, each and every episode could not be made an issue of national campaign or investigation.

The burning of Pastor Stains, in that sense was a turning point for Human rights groups, who so far were trying to grapple and respond to the anti Muslim violence. With this many concerned groups took up the investigations of the violence against Christians in the right earnest. As such, the first major investigation had to be undertaken by the BJP led NDA Government itself, in the aftermath of Stains murder. Initially, as a fire fighting measure, the functionaries of the government tried to give a clean chit to the Sangh Parivar. After the murder, the then home minister Lal Krishna Advani, stated that he knows Bajrang Dal very well and this act could not have been done by that organisation. To put a veil on the episode, the three cabinet ministers, George Fernandes, Murli Manohar Joshi and Navin Patnaik rushed to the site and proclaimed that the murder of Pastor is an international conspiracy to destabilise the BJP Government. This way they tried to bypass the real issue, i.e. involvement of Dara Singh, an activist of Bajrang Dal.

III

Inquiry Committee Reports

Wadhwa Commission[2] gave the report, which despite Justice Wadhwa's own leanings, did conclude that Pastor Staines was not involved in the work of conversions and neither did the population of Christians increase in the area where the Pastor was working. The report however, glossed over the association of Dara Singh with Bajrang Dal despite overwhelming evidence for that. Dara Singh had been a very active Dal member who had mobilised the Adivasi youth on the argument that their religion is under threat due to the activities of the Pastor. In the same region, Sheikh Rahman was also murdered on the accusation of cow slaughter.

Human Rights activists and groups were left with the task of opposing the communal killings, campaigning against the false allegations raised by the criminals during such incidents, to also bring out the truth behind the same and to make it known to as many people as possible. Most of the reports that came up in this period give an indication of the speed with which the anti-minorities trend spread like wild fire all around.[3]

The series of horrendous events that took place in Orissa woke up the Human Rights groups to the damage being inflicted by RSS progeny to the democratic fabric of this country. Many serious groups took up the investigation to different areas of the nation, the focus being Gujarat, where the Hindutva onslaught has been on its worst, hitting both the minorities simultaneously and declaring village after village of Gujarat as part of the Hindu Rashtra. The report of Nishant group was amongst the initial ones to bring to the fore these violations of human rights against minorities in a systematic way. It highlighted the nature of propaganda indulged in by VHP and company and the nature of atrocities committed by them. It did observe that some land disputes were converted to communal issues to have an upper hand in grabbing the property.

Inter-religious marriages, though few and far between were used as another pretext to the grist of the VHP hatred mill. Many incidents of communal violence against Muslims have been used by the traders to wipe away the competition. This report does point a finger to that and one recalls the settling of trade rivalries as a major aspect of Gujarat pogrom, which went on in a big way for the economic boycott of Muslims. It is no surprise that the petty traders are one of the major block supporting the RSS, VHP and Vanvasi Kalyan Ashram, in particular. Events like burning of Bibles, economic plunder of Adivasis etc. have come to light. The dangerous slogan, 'If one cow is butchered two Muslims will be done to death' floated in different parts of the country with intimidating aura.

Around this time a spate of events started occurring and Hindutva elements scattered far and wide started looking for a pretext to intimidate the Christian missionaries and Christians either during their prayer meetings or pilgrimages etc. The point to comprehend was that due to the rule of BJP led NDA, the RSS swayamsevaks (volunteers) started becoming more assertive and the message went around in a subtle manner that 'our' government will ensure that the culprits will 'get away', law will be made to sleep over these incidents. This fact was in conjunction with the communalisation of social common sense, which now added on the Christians too as a dangerous minority, out to convert this Hindu Rashtra into a Christian majority state. It is during this time that one heard from the then top functionary of BJP, a serious ideologue of RSS, Mr. Govindacharya that Christian missionaries have committed to convert over 1000 million people by the 2000 birth anniversary of Jesus Christ. Nothing could have been more ridiculous to believe. In a country of 1030 million where there are just about 2.3 crore Christians, to imagine that 970 odd millions will be added to the flock in a period of just two years was the stuff from some joke book for morons.

In Pali Naigaon, Maharashtra (1998) the Holi (festival of colours) revellers attacked the Christian pilgrims and the police further intimidated them to run off without booking their complaint. The local integrated customs, which are not monolithic and uniform prevail at different places and people have adopted the religious traditions according to local culture and ethos, on their own, even without being conscious of the same. It was observed that fasting for days in the area is usual but with the changing political environs, the things are changing and the incidents like this have polarised the communities in the worst possible way.[4]

The incidents that took place in Mumbai in a series of violence against Christian run schools are the real eye opener about the contrast in the pattern of violence in cities and villages. While in villages the idea is to make the missionaries run away and abandon their work of teaching etc., in cities they are harassed on opposite grounds. In various schools in Mumbai, the Shiv Sena corporators and other such leaders first intimidated and latter did what they are best at, the breaking of furniture, etc. The Principals of the schools were pressurised to admit children with political patronage in those schools[5]. In one of the small town mission schools, one RSS supporter, whose son was studying in the school, told the father Principal that they are doing a good job in running such schools, but why should they go and teach those 'animals', meaning advasis, in the interior part of the villages. The report makes such aspect of the Christian missions and education fairly clear.

'Then they came...,' the report of All India Federation of Organization for Democratic Rights[6] investigates the incidents from most of the states and also elaborates the demographic and other aspects of the problem. The report also highlights the RSS plan to oppose the Christian work in Adivasi areas, to start EKAL Vidyalayas and to force the re-conversion, Ghar Vapasi, (back to home, as such it means conversion to Hinduism) in different areas of their activities. The report takes these as starting points to come to the conclusions that these attacks are part of the political agenda of RSS politics which aims to consolidate its own base in the Adivasi area.

Dangs has been another area where all aspects of Hindutva offensive could be seen, the sinister propaganda, the attacks on Chapels and prayer meetings is brought out well in the report, Communal Carnage in Dangs by Peaceful Society, Goa[7]. This report is focused on Dangs and brings out the meticulous details of the issues as to how the local Christian community had to face the flak and how the administration made the matters worse by colluding with the rioters and also by giving permissions for rallies which turned violent.

When these incidents were happening all around, in a place called Ulhas Nagar, near Mumbai, the local unit of VHP and affiliates tried to create the fear of conversions. Investigations, by EKTA Inquiry Team, 1999,[8] showed that one case of inter-caste marriage was blown out of proportion, which started the hysterical reaction against the Christians. A section of local media bought the Hindutva version and contributed in aggravating the problem.

In the outskirts of Nasik, another city near Mumbai, one Christian prayer meeting was attacked on the ground that it is a ploy to convert people. Here also, investigation, Citizens Inquiry Report, Mumbai, 2000,[9] proved that there was just one family staying in Abhona where the attack took place. The BJP top leadership of the state tried to make a big issue out of that.

Dangs has been a subject matter for investigation by different Human rights groups due to the intensity of the problem there. It is here again that Mr. Vajpayee came visiting and gave the call for a 'National debate' on conversions. The National Alliance of Women's Organisations' report[10] takes many more issues for investigation and points out the planned nature of attacks, on rise in Christian population in the area, forcible re-conversion to Hinduism and the deep nexus between RSS and Hindu Jagran Manch (HJM). The report goes to the extent of calling for a ban on HJM, which have been the major violator of law and intimidator of minorities.

The rape and murder of one minor girl in Jhabua, by a boy residing in the nearby area gave a pretext to the local rabid elements to launch the anti- Christian tirade in the area. Since then Jhabua has been in the news and one has been hearing of the conversions there. The area lies in the vicinity of Gujarat where intense anti-Christian violence was witnessed. As a fall out of that, many Christians decided to shift to Madhya Pradesh, which at that time had Congress Government, resulting in the rise of local Christian population. This fact was twisted to show that conversions were going on and needed to be curbed. The report on Jhabua[11] brings out the complex dynamics of the local Christian population. The activities of the Church are fairly old, and the Church run school in nearby Meghnagar is very popular. Conforming to other areas, one can see here also that it is an area of rampant poverty, where the Adivasis are able to make both ends meet with great difficulty.

Rajendra Sail's report [12] on the Chattisgarh conversion took all the pain to put forward the demographic facts to counter the myths surrounding conversions. He had a tough job on hand the myths surrounding conversions. He had a tough job on hand as Chattisgarh came into being recently; earlier it was part of Madhya Pradesh. With deft logic and advocacy of correctness he demonstrates the false nature of the allegations of conversions.

IV

Orissa: The Boiling Cauldron

Gladys Stains is a name etched in our memory for wrong reasons. Her husband and two sons were torched to death around a decade ago in Keonjhar Manoharpur Orissa. Recently she wrote to Prime Minister Man Mohan Singh, to ensure that communal peace is restored in Orissa. This she did in the backdrop of the scattered attacks on Christians, over 40 churches torched in Orissa (24 Dec. 2007). In the violence which broke out, many of the people have been severely injured. Some of the priest and laity have run for shelter, leaving their homes and hiding in the forests in the biting cold. All this has happened in the Adivasi area in and around Phulbani and Kandhamal. The timing was around the Christmas celebrations, 2007.

It is no coincident that the BJP is part of the ruling coalition in Orissa, and those involved in the vandalism are part of some or the other organization directly affiliated with the RSS. The major such are Vanvasi Kalyan Ashram, Bajrang dal and their local variants. While the media reports are sketchy, the Citizens Inquiry team, which was to visit the area has been denied permission to visit the districts and was escorted out of the area.

The attacks on minorities and weaker sections is launched for short term or long term political goals, but the care is taken that a pretext is manufactured and then the attacks are unleashed. In this case it has been said that Swami

One is supposed to believe that a Swami from the majority community, with sizeable following, will be attacked by the section of miniscule minority!

The Christmas season is the chosen time for anti Christian attacks. Earlier also such occasions have been chosen for beating and attacking the Christian community, notably in Dangs in 1998. This time in Phulbani and Kandhamal area the declarations being made by the Swami and associates is that the presence of Christians will not be tolerated in the Adivasi areas.

The case of Orissa was specifically investigated by India Peoples Tribunal[13], led by Justice K.K.Usha (retired) of Kerala High court in 2006. This tribunal forewarns about the shape of things to come. "The tribunal assessed the spread of communal organizations in Orissa, which has been accompanied by a series of small and large events and some riots...such violations are utilized to generate the threat and reality of greater violence, and build and infrastructure of fear and intimidation." It further notes that minorities are being grossly ill treated; there is gross inaction of the state Govt to take action. Outlining the mechanism of the communalization, it points out, "The report also describes in considerable detail how the cadre of majoritarian communal organizations are indoctrinated in hatred and violence against other communities it holds to be inherently inferior. If such communalization is undertaken in Orissa, it is indicative of the future of the nation... the signs are truly ominous for India's democratic future." (p 70)

The after-effects of the anti Christian violence (2007) in Kandhamal district of Orissa are not over, so to say. Recently the Archbishop Cheenath of the state said that the elections in the Kandhmamal district should be postponed as the refugees living in the camps are not able to return. The reason is that living in the camps are not able to return. The reason is that many of them who returned were threatened by the local Bajrang Dal workers and associates. They were told to renounce Christianity, convert to Hinduism pay the fine, withdraw the cases and vote for the candidate who they will be told to, obviously BJP candidate. Many of those who tried to return with such hostile conditions awaiting them if they return, came back, some to the camps others to unknown destinations.

Meanwhile BJP candidate of the area, Ashok Sahu, when he came to know about his likely arrest for 'Hate speech' first absconded for few days and then was arrested just three hours before the campaign was to be over (14th April 2009). He told his followers to keep calm; else the elections will be postponed, as being demanded by the Archbishop.

One also recalls a similar situation in the post Gujarat violence. There, while state Government claimed that normalcy has returned, the Chief election commissioner James Michael Lyngdoh was visibly upset when he saw the condition of the Muslims living in the camps and their inability to be able to be part of the electoral process.

In Orissa the violence has taken a heavy toll of the amity of the region. The violence which began August 2007 continued till December. It resulted in death of close to 6-7 hundred Panos (Christians) and 90 Churches, 100 other Christian institutions were destroyed. The pretext was that Swami Laxamananand, the VHP swami working in the area has been murdered by Christians. At the same time the Maoist group claimed that they own the responsibility for the act. Since some pretext was needed to launch the attacks, the claim of Maoists was not considered and the VHP, BJP and company kept harping that it is the Christians who have committed the crime. As such the matter is tragic but simple. Who so ever has committed the crime should be punished. Why the whole Christian community has to be targeted and attacked for the act of some group or an individual.

Since at that time BJP was part of the ruling coalition it had its way. The death procession of swami was taken through a long circuitous route. The idea was to communalize the atmosphere in maximum area. This again is quite akin to Gujarat. After the Godhra train tragedy the dead bodies were taken in a procession to Ahmedabad, with VHP, BJP workers shouting provocative slogans. The whole hell was encouraged-permitted to be unleashed. Here also a long route was deliberately taken and police and other state authorities acted as the bystanders when the mayhem broke out. Surprisingly the VHP's Praveen Togadia was permitted to go to the area while the Central Minister of State for Home affairs was not permitted to visit the area.

The violence in Kandhmal is a case of how communal forces can divide and come to dominate, become strong through orchestrated violence. The Kandhs, (Adivasis) are close to 50% of population, and dalits, most of them Panos are 16.9%. Kandhs and Panos are the two major communities in the area. The remaining 30% are called Oriyas, since they don't speak the languages of these two major groups, the local Kui language. These are from various urban regions, traders being a big chunk of them.

The Kandhs, Adivasis were mainly food gatherers. Panos were landless outcastes who came to hills in search of livelihood, close to two centuries ago; Kandhs put their land at the disposal of Panos, since Kandhs themselves were not into agriculture. Panos came as servile labor. The communalists have propagated that Panos are grabbing the land of Kandhs. Kandhs come under the schedule Tribe category while Panos are dalits.

Today Kandhs own close to 9% of land, while the traders, Oriyas, control much more of Adivasi land. The major land grab from Adivasis has been by traders, but no agitation has ever been done against that by the RSS affiliates.

Many of these dalits took to Christianity and many of them benefited due to education, and the consequent jobs. As noted they also came to posses some land over a period of time, still their land holding is much lesser than that of Non local Oriyas. A massive propaganda has been going on in the area that Panos have grabbed the Adivasi land that they are trying to manipulate caste certificates to take advantage of status of ST's. As a matter of fact both the Kandhs and Panos speak Kui. State has declared ST category for Kui's, due to which some Panos also got some ST concession, it has not been a deliberate act.

These two issues were exploited by the VHP, Bajrang dal people who have been spreading the Hate against Christians in the area. It is important to note that Christian missionaries have been working in the area from over two centuries. Missionaries never used violence for conversion, while the RSS affiliates have resorted to all sorts of intimidation to convert them to Hinduism through newly invented conversion rituals. And asserting their political definition of Hinduism, they say that Adivasis are Hindus, who have drifted away due to allurement, so Adivasis coming to Hinduism is not conversion but a Ghar Vapasi, 'return home' for these misguided ones'.

Swami Laxmananand came here from last few decades and began his campaign of Hate against minorities. The result is there for all to see. The report on Kandhamal violence has recently (March 2009) been published by various human rights organization, "From Kandhmal to Karavali: The Ugly Face of Sangh Parivar". It points out "that the violence was committed by Sangh Parivar organizations, mainly Bajrang Dal...police watched benignly as the arson took place in public. The ideology and organization of their mentor RSS pervades in the media...the press has reported the violence in the manner that put the onus on victim, they were at fault and had it coming" (page 3) what is spread to create hate is the distorted version of country's history and the falsehood about our society.

Today we are witness to the process where by people like Asok Sahu have not only spread their political tentacles through "Hate Other" ideology, but also that they are violating the laws of the land for their political benefit. Tragically the distorted version of History has been one of the main weapons of the social common sense, which forms the base of communal violence. One hopes that in due course society and all those concerned with preservation of plural values not only look at the immediate causes of Hate other ideology, but also the deeper propaganda against the minorities widely prevalent through various organizations practicing politics.

V

Conversions:

Conversions have been in news for the last few years or so. The general points being raised are that there are a lot of conversions due to inducement and allurement by the Christian priests, that these conversions are contrary to the spirit of the constitution and that these forcible acts of the missionaries are the reason behind the conflicts between the converted and their old communities. Though there is a freedom to profess and practice one's religion, the conversions show disrespect and intolerance for other's religions.

Most of the assumptions in this argument are based on premises, which have nothing to do with the reality. First, let us note that the bogey of conversions has begun all of a sudden from 1996. The very suddenness and countrywide spread of the phenomena definitely needs to be given a careful thought, more so after the realization that there is no particular increase in Christian population as reflected in the census data and the data from Justice Wadhwa Commission of inquiry. As per this, we note that the All India Christian population in 1971-2.6%, in 1981-2.44% and in 1991 2.32%. This shows a marginal decline in the all India population of Christians. It is remarkable that a tirade against conversions can be raised when there is an actual decline in the population of Christians. Secondly, in Manoharpur in Keonjhar district, where Pastor Stains was doing his work amongst the lepers, where he was burnt along with his two minor sons on the charge that he was indulging in conversions, Justice Wadhwa report gives an interesting statistics- there is a rise of Hindu population by 2.52%, and that of Christian population by .008% between the years 1991 to 1998. These figures totally demolish the foundation of the argument that massive forced conversions are on.

The second point to be noted is that the conversions are projected to be a purely passive process in which the poor Adivasis are converted by inducement and allurement. This again is a point which gives the image that those converted are mere passive beings bereft of intelligence just because they are poor and so susceptible to the 'anti-National' activities of the missionaries. A slight peep into the history of conversions in India will make the matters clear for us; whether the conversions are an active or a passive process. If we recall, a while ago the major justification for anti-Muslim tirade was that Muslim Kings converted the Hindus by the sword, and this was the major component of the propaganda, which formed the base of the anti Muslim sentiments in the 'social common sense'.

Conversions have been used by communal forces under different guises. Hindu communal forces take the cake in this matter. As such Hinduism is based on caste system and

Brahminism has been the dominant factor. It is not a prophetic religion, and thereby spreading it is not the norm of the religion. Earlier Brahmin groups, being the elite, insisted more on 'exclusion' of others rather than on proselytisation. Other 'Indian' religions that were prophetic (Jainism, Budhhism and Sikhism) did believe in propagating and that's how Budhhism in particular spread far and wide, to other countries. Hindu and Muslim political forces in the early part of 20th century did undertake conversion (shuddhi,-tanzim and tabligh). The shuddhi was more to attract those lower castes who had adopted Islam or Sikhism as their religion. The current Ghar Vapasi campaign of VHP draws its legitimacy from the assertion that Adivasis are Hindus. Religion is determined by one's beliefs, deities, holy books, communitarian celebrations and rituals. Most of the Adivasis have been beef eating, are unaware of Ram and other Hindu deities of Hindu religion, do not celebrate Diwali and other Hindu festivals, are oblivious to the wisdom from Gita, Ramayana, Mahabharata and Vedas, have been practicing the animism in their own way. How can they be called Hindus except as an outcome of political machinations and the necessities of Hindutva onslaught that is trying to match Islamic fundamentalism in its pernicious methods?

What is remarkable is not that conversions as a marginal phenomenon have been part of the Indian reality from ages, but the fact that a political wonder called Sangh Parivar can make it an issue for consolidating its base (earlier Islam with Sword, and now the Christian priest with a blanket and a tablet of aspirin). What is remarkable is that this political multithreaded hydra can make the forced conversions an issue to build its political base even at a time when the actual percentage of those being targeted is on the decline.

The current anti Christian tirade has been preceded and accompanied by an aggressive anti-Christian propaganda against

Christians and against conversions. Conversion is violence, it is illegal, Christian population is rising in proportion, it is done by forcible means, converts are seduced by money, the converts are traitors and a whole new gamut of propaganda is dished out on regular basis. All these are absolutely false and carefully manufactured to achieve the goal of spreading hatred.

It is true that during British rule Christianity was looked up with respect, but it was not a state religion. It was not promoted by British rulers per se, though a missionary here or a missionary there might have got some benefits to start his work. In many pamphlets and publications, Gandhi has been quoted in a very effective manner to convey something that was contrary to his beliefs. Gandhi is quoted extensively by Hindutva forces to oppose conversions. The quote, which is a fragment of the whole, is from Gandhi's collected works, Volume XLVI p. 27-28[14]. In an interview dated 22nd March 1931, given to The Hindu, Gandhi apparently stated that if in self governing India, missionaries kept 'proselytising by means of medical aid, education etc., I would certainly ask them to withdraw. Every nation's religion is as good as any other. Certainly India's religions are adequate for her people. We need no converting spirituality." This is the first part of the quote and the lines that follow give the totally opposite idea, the ideas, which Gandhi held. Gandhi goes on to write, "This is what the reporter has put in my mouth... All that I can say is that it is a travesty of what I have always said and held." He goes on to explain, "I am, then, not against conversion. But I am against the modern methods of it. Conversions nowadays have become a matter of business, like any other... Every nation considers its own faith to be as good as that of any other. Certainly the great faiths held by the people of India are adequate for her people. India stands in no need of conversions from one faith to another." And then he goes on to list the faiths of India, "Apart from Christianity and Judaism, Hinduism and its offshoots, Islam and Zoroastrianism are living faiths."

The Hindutva onslaught spreads the canard of conversions as an excuse for the attacks and intimidation of the Christian minorities. Many a time, the arguments are so twisted as to blame Christians themselves for the atrocities committed against them. In response to the rape of nuns in Jhabua, B.L.Sharma 'Prem' of VHP said that it is an act of patriotism against those anti national forces. Again VHP's Giriraj Kishore gave a call that foreign missionaries should be removed from the country. It is also pointed out that Missionaries denigrate Hindu religion and do not believe in equality of religions. So they indulge in conversions as they regard their religion as the superior one. These outbursts of Hindutva forces are in dire contrast to the pain and anguish of the then President of India, Dr. K.R. Narayanan, who expressed his sorrow in the aftermath of Pastor Stains murder by stating that, "this act belongs to 'World's inventory of black deeds'."

VI

Reconversions: Ghar Vapasi

Arguments have been put forward to convert the Adivasis to Hindu fold. These arguments are not unlike the one designed in the peak phase of communal politics in which the conversion to Hinduism was brought in the name of Shuddhi. The clever point here is that the basic presumption that all are Hindus and then they are 'taught' Hindu rituals etc. Actually the big conversion going on today is Ghar Vapasi, where the presumption is that Adivasis are Hindus who have either forgotten the Hindu norms because of staying in forests or that they have been misled by Christians. To bring them back under Hindu fold is accomplished by the newly designed re-conversion techniques. This is what is going on at massive scale by the likes of Dilip Singh Judeo or Swami Aseemanand. Aseemanand gives the deeksha (initiation) after they are given holy bath in the garamkunds (hot springs), where the activists of VKA take them in jeeps. The point to be noted here is that while Adivasis are basically animists, when they are initiated into Hinduism through Ghar Vapasi they return as followers of Ram or Hanuman.

The theoretical conversions were done through the census. Adivasis were earlier mentioned as Animists. From 1951 census, they started being grouped as Hindus. The process of Ghar Vapasi is the culmination of various components. At one level it is a mere political imposition; at the same time VKA and other organisations have initiated the process of Sanskritisation, the cultural manipulation of Adivasis into the fold of Hindutva. The main attraction for Adivasis towards Christianity has been the availability of educational and health care facilities offered through their schools, hospitals and health centres. One Sarna dharma is also being promoted as a counter to Christianity. The influence of Hinduism is substantial in this process. Similarly Bhagat movement earlier started by well meaning people was infiltrated by Hindutva elements to co-opt the Adivasis. Their places of culture have been converted to Hindu temples and a good deal of funds are being diverted to these places for building temples and celebrating Hindu festivals like Ganesh puja, Durga Puja, etc.

The Sanskritisation process is done through various mechanisms apart from the celebration of Hindu festivals and the promotion of the worship of Hindu Gods, like Ram and Hanuman. The educational network of Ekal Vidyalaya (single teacher school), Sarswati Shishu Mandir and Sarswati Vidyalayas has been very extensive. Similarly the influence of communalisation process prevalent in Gujarat is also visible. Apart from other ways, the followers of Asaram bapu have in particular made inroads to the Adivasis areas extensively. Similarly some of them go to Gujarat for employment and there they come in contact with the widely prevalent network of VKA (Vanvasi Kalyan Ashram) and VHP.

VII

Conversions: Cultural Cooption

Why the attacks on Christians at this point of time, is the core question. Why is Hindutva, which has spent most of its energies in attacking Muslims at various levels, targeting Christians now? It is clear that some ideological groundwork was done by earlier ideologues of Hindutva like Golwalkar. Its practical implementation began with the formation and activities of Vanvasi Kalyan Ashram, which wanted to counter the missionary work in the Adivasi areas. While Christian missionary work was more on the level of social service, VKA's focus was on indoctrination and cultural manipulation through different mechanisms. The need to target the Christian missionaries got concrete expression especially from 1996, the year BJP first came to power at the Centre. There are multiple reasons for this newfound attack. Its foundations were laid with the formation of VKA, only the outward manifestation is coming to the fore now and is polarising the communities along various lines in Tribal areas.

The forays of RSS in Adivasi areas intensified from mid eighties when it was realized that by directly attacking dalits, the way they were attacked in 1980 and 1986 in Gujarat through caste violence, will be counterproductive at electoral level. The strategy evolved was to 'use' them as foot soldiers against Muslim minorities. At the same time electoral arithmetic brought to their attention this substantial chunk of population of Adivasis trying to come up through modern education and thereby disturbing the status quo, prevalent in the far off villages. Its here that the Christian missionaries were perceived as a big threat to the project of RSS, which wants to maintain status quo vis a vis Adivasis dalits and women. Through the network of schools spread in the far off areas these Missionaries, whatever be their own motives, were instrumental in getting a section of

Adivasis empowered and in the process the upper caste affluent base of Sangh was getting jittery.

The posting of RSS volunteers into the forest work was very systematic. Apart from attacking the Christian missionaries as foreigners the Ghar vapasi was brought in at a big scale in all the Adiviasi areas scattered from Gujarat to MP to Orissa. Around this time many a swamis, descended in these areas, Lakkhanand in Phulbani area, Aseemanand in Dangs, Asaram disciples in Jhabau and many other such efforts were unleashed. In Adivasi areas they resorted to intimidation, you are Hindus, Hindu rituals are like this and so these have to part of your life. Dilip Singh Judeo, of VHP of Chattisgarhg, had the record number of Adiviasis converted in to Hinduism by newly devised baptizing techniques.

At the same time Hanuman was popularized as the God in this area and lately Shabri, the destitute women who had the privilege of offering wild berries to Lord Ram is being projected as the Goddess of Adivasis. The cultural symbolism cannot be missed in the selection of these deities. Hanuman was the unquestioning devotee of Lord Ram, with muscular power as the main virtue. He is capable of flying while carrying a huge mountain. But all the more he is carrying the mountain because he cannot identify the herb needed for treatment of Laxman, Lord's younger brother. This is what is the signal to Adivasis, unquestioning loyalty to Lord Ram, no need to have education. So what are the Christian missionaries doing here? Why should they be trying to educate you? They are foreigners. So Pastor Stains is picked up for the treatment which they want to mete out to the white robed priests and nuns.

Shabri, the embodiment of poverty is being glorified on purpose. Your great ancestress had the privilege to offer wild berries to the Lord. She is your role model, poor, powerless and with blind reverence and devotion for the upper caste. The recently held festival in Subir, Dangs district of Gujarat, celebrated Shabri and lakhs of Advasis were brought from neighboring Adivasi areas for the festival. The local people were scared that Sangh's festival may create the trouble and they may try to forcibly do the conversions to Hinduism. It was declared that Christians and Muslim are foreigners and are a threat to Hindu religion. This Kumbh is meant to protect the Hindus from the foreigners. In the beginning it was announced that conversions are the aim of Kumbh and than silence was kept on this point once various groups questioned their motives. This was boldly stated in the CD produced by Shabri Kumbh organizers. By the time the court ruling came to ban this CD was given, lakhs of its copies were already circulated and had the desired effect of threatening the Christianity community.

The Shabri samiti distributed saffron flags to the villagers and spread the word that those who do not put the flag will be regarded as anti Hindu, those who do not visit the Kumbh will also be regarded as anti Hindu. In this intimidating atmosphere the intervention of Human rights groups resulted in the Central government sending its observers. Also the Adivasi leaders realized the game being played by Sangh and mercifully a large section of native adivasis kept away from the festival. But Sangh has succeeded in spreading the seeds of hate and intimidation far and wide.

During Kumbh the inflammatory speeches were delivered by different leaders of Sangh. It remains to be seen as to what will be the long term impact of this festival. One thing is sure that the whole Adivasi area at some level has been shaken by this festival in which the major organizers were the city based traders, contractors and other supporters of Sangh. The native Adivasi festivals and gods are being undermined in various ways.

Adivasis never used to have the temple or place of prayer within the four walls, most of their Gods were in the open. The festivals, dancing and feasting also were held in the open. With the new influence things are changing. The rift between the 'Hindu' and 'Christian' Adivasis is widening which surely will have adverse impact on the life in the area. In pursuance of the same tactics, now summer festival and Anjani mahotsav (festival) are being planned. Anjani, mother of Hanuman was never the object of veneration. Now she will be occupying a place amongst the deities.

During the festival of Shabri (Feb 11-13, 2005) in Ghubadiya, a place near Subir, the graveyard was dug up, the crosses on the graves were burnt. Not much notice of this has been taken in the local media and administrative circles. The increasing influence of Sangh and the religiosity is taking deeper turns. One understands that from the villages young girls in the age groups of 14-15 are being picked up to be trained as Sadhvis who can give recitation of Ramayana and other Hindu scriptures. The whole emphasis is on the cultural manipulation and the basic issues of Adivasis like land, education and health are being cleverly sidetracked through this culturo-religious manipulation.

VIII

Conclusion

India is faced with a peculiar situation today. The identity politics, which should be declining in democracy, is coming to the fore in a strong assertive way. The anti Christian violence has been having serious sociological repercussions in small towns and villages, especially the places where Adivasis are large in number. Anti Christian violence is in the continuation of RSS agenda of Hindu Rasthra, Pehle kasai Phir Isai (First the Muslims then Christians). There is an additional factor in the anti Christian violence. One concedes that there may be many a Christian groups who might be focusing on the conversion work, within the bounds of Indian constitution, of course. The major problem is that the effort of missionaries to reach education to the adivasi areas. Educated Adivasi, empowered Adivasi will be more aware of her rights and that's precisely what RSS combine cannot stand.

Total processes unleashed in these areas comprise of Ekal Schools, sanskritisation, and political intimidation. It is remarkable that many Christian missionaries have withstood the pressure in their stride. Immediately in the aftermath of Pastor Stain's murder, Gladys Stains, his wife, not only forgave the culprits and continued to work for the Leprosy patients without a break for good many years. It is another matter that law has to take its course and Dara Singh, despite the patronage from Hindu rightwing political forces was indicted and is facing life imprisonment. He has been deified, 'Hindu Dharma Rakshak'; (Protector of Hindu Faith) and made a hero which shows how the VHP, VKA and associates operate.

The issue is not just the protection of people doing charity work in remote areas, but also to have a deeper look at the social processes under way, in these areas. Needless to say these are precisely the areas where poverty, hunger, disease and misery abound, where the land issue of Adivasis needs to be urgently redressed. The awakening of a section of adivasis to their rights, the rise of Hindu right wing in these areas and the consequent sidetracking of the social, economic issues, sum up the whole story about the agenda of those behind the attacks!

References

1. Praveen Swami, A catalogue of Crimes, Frontline, Feb 12, 1999, AIFOFDR, Then they Came for Christians, Mumbai,1999.

2. Wadhwa Commission Report, in MP Raju. Media House Delhi, 1999.
3. Puniyani, Ram The politics behind anti Christian Violence, Media House, Delhi 2006.
4. Indian People's Tribunal, "Report of the Fact Finding committee into the attack on Pilgrims to Pali Naingaon, Maharashtra, 1998, Mumbai.
5. EKTA, VOTE and CDRA, Attacks on Schools run by Christian Missionaries, 1999.
6. AIFOFDR, Then they Came for Christians,, Mumbai ,1999.
7. Peaceful Society, Goa, Communal carnage in Dangs, 1999.
8. EKTA, Inquiry into Ulhasnagar violence, 1999.
9. Citizens Inquiry Report, into Attack on Girls School in Nasik 2000.
10. National Allaince of Women's Organisations, 1999, "Violence in Gujarat: the case for larger Fundamentalist Agenda.
11. People's research Society, Bhopal, "On Jhabua incident", 2004.
12. Rajendra Sail, "On the Conversions in Chhattisgarh-At the root of Controversy.
13. Usha K.K., Chatterjee A. and Desai Mihir, Communalism in Orissa, IPT Mumbai 2006.
14. Gandhi, Mahtma, Gandhi's collected works, Volume XLVI p. 27-28.
15. Citizens Inquiry Committee, "The Untold Story of Hindukaran", Anhad, Delhi 2005.

25

Communal Ideology and Violence Against Women

In many a third world countries in the name of religion, communal politics is having a field day. One of the major components of communal politics is the perpetuation of patriarchal values. By patriarchal norms we mean a value system in which men have control over the lives of women. With secularisation process, which began the world over from 18th Century onwards, a ground has been laid whereby the patriarchy can be questioned and challenged. In many a third world countries reaction to secularisation process (which stands for the values of Liberty, Equality and Fraternity) has occurred in the form of rise of communal and fundamentalist movements. These movements, which initially found their support base amongst the declining Feudal elements of society, are lately being spearheaded by the affluent middle classes and the section of society which thrives on the percolation of retrograde norms, in the name of religion. The Fundamentalist ideologies are based on the norms selectively culled from religious practices, norms that can sustain the domination of the elite males of the society in the name of religion. Communal politics has a large overlap with this fundamentalism; it is based on the hatred of 'others' religion' and is inherently oppressive to the weaker sections of society, including the women. This ideology is upholder of patriarchal norms and thereby is oppressive to the women in a subtle manner.

This ideology inflicts both covert and overt violence against the women. Patriarchy as such builds the identity of community through the bodied of women and through that route the hatred of those belonging to others' religions gets compounded by the idea that women are the property of men. It is this which makes women's life a living hell in the highly communalised atmosphere. The worst of this violence is seen in the manifest form in the communal riots, where women are the victims in the multiple ways. Violence against women of 'other community' in these cataclysms becomes a part of the pogroms against the minorities. There are ghastly stories at the time of partition where women from both sides of the divide were subjected to humiliation of the worst kind and on the top of it, many of them were subjected to being tattooed on different parts of there bodies as an act of 'achievement' and some of the culprits even went on to tattoo their names on the hands of victims. It must be recalled here that in the rehabilitation process, the women who were left behind in both the countries were not easily accepted by their relatives on the grounds that by now they must have become 'impure' in the hands of the 'enemies'.

It is interesting that many a communal violence have been sparked off by spreading the rumors that women of 'our' community' have been 'defiled' by the men of 'other' community. The recent rumors (! truth) about the rape of Muslim women in Surat riots, in the aftermath of Babri demolition were a big eye opener as to what this communal ideology can do to pervert the minds of those indulging in these barbarian crimes. As such communal ideology justifies these acts on the weird ground that these are the best preventive measures to protect 'our' women. One of the ideologoues of communal ideology while commenting on Shivajis's noble act of 'letting go' the daughter-in-law of Nawab of Bassien went on to opine as follows (from Dhananjay Keer "Veer Savarkar", Popular Prakshan,1966, p. 539) "...had expressed his opinion that the liberal policy adopted by Shivaji in case of Muslim women was wrong as this cultured and human treatment could not evoke in those fanatics the same feelings about Hindu women. They should have been given tit for tat, he observed frankly, so they might have realised the horrors of brutality." This spine chilling prescription of dealing with "others' women" can come only from the ideology of hate which generalises the communities, projects a uniform enemy image of them and then also goes on to underline that women are essentilly a property of men, so protecting one's property and defiling 'others' propery are two sides of the same coin.

The attitude of communal ideology vis a vis the women becomes painfully obvious by different incidents which we will like to narrate in brief. Recently the 'Self Respect' killings are in news from the media. In areas of Pakistan those women who face Talaq and their husbands abandon by their husbands have been killed or being encouraged to commit suicides, by fundamentalist sections of society on the plea that it is better to die with respect rather then live the life after being divorced. Similarly we can also remember, few years ago Roopnwar was burnt on the funeral pyre of her husband. This came under intense criticism from the progressive sections of society. Surprisingly one top functionary of a Communal party not only defended the act but she also went on to arrange a demonstration in front of parliament, the slogan of the demonstration was 'It is not only the honor but also the right of Indian women to commit Sati (Being burnt on the funeral pyre of husband). Lately in the intense anti-Christian atmosphere few nuns were raped in Jhabua in M.P. As condemnations poured in, similarly in came the appreciation from one MP of a communal party. He went on to call this rape as an act of Patriotism!

Coming to the communal holocausts which our society has been witnessing; it has been an elementary observation that women of minority community are victims of 'double' attack. On one hand the violence coming from Majority community shatters their bodies and souls and leaves many of them without the breadwinner in the family. On the other the communal elements of their own community later blame them for not sticking to the religious tenets (as interpreted by these elements) because of which these acts are taking place. Also these incidents give them more ground to restrict their lives further for the fear of the majority community. Also as communal ideology is founded on the selectively picked up precepts and practices which give more power to the men, this ideology justifies the 'low intensity covert violence' against the women. There are leaders of so called Women's movement affiliated to communal politics who justify wife beating, dowry etc. (Mridula Sinha: Telegraph Interview;1993) She went on to say that domestic violence is meant to bring the women on the proper track for the smooth running of the family, she also conceded having given dowry for her daughter and having received the same for her son's marriage!

As the primary relationship in this ideology is that of 'ownership' of the women, the inter-religious marriages are seen through the angle of 'loss' of 'our' property (woman), i.e. the appropriation of 'our women' by the 'others'. It this mindset which resulted in the terrorization of some Muslims in Gujarat villages where few adivasi girls got married to some Muslim boys, and the punishment of this crime was meted out to the villagers belonging to the minority community. The starting point of communal ideology is the subordinate position of women, and having accepted that the women's wings of these organisations operate within the defined limits of the male organisations, which prescribe the overall framework in which these organisations have to operate. This politics claims to be respectful to the women but this 'respect' is proffered only when the women live within the prescribed limits imposed on them. And this is the ground on which both covert and overt violence is unleashed against the women of their 'own' community and women of "enemy's" community.

It is puzzling as to how many a women can be 'taken in' by communal ideologies despite the fact that these ideologies are against their interests. Here one has to appreciate that communal politics operates in the name of religion. As Ayesha Imam (Making the links-Anti Racism and Feminism; Paper presented at CRIAW-Toronto-1991), "....Religious beliefs are not simply imposed but generated and developed in the process of appropriation and reconstruction of social and personal experience........Fundamentalist groups can provide security in having a total way of life set out, giving a focus for identity and relief or empowerment therein as a welcome value placed on much of women's unrecognised labour in the domestic realm."

While most of the religion's can also be interpreted in a way where the status of women and men is on par (Shramanic traditions from Hindu religion and the basic tenets of Islam as interpreted by many liberal Islamic scholars) the practices which go on in the name of religion are highly discriminatory against the women. These are worst compounded in multi-religious societies where in the prevalent political situation and power play, elite of the society resort to communal politics and use (!misuse) the name of religion to perpetuate their hold on the social affairs and in the resulting inter-community clashes the violence which takes place against women is the most ghastly and condemnable.

26

Communal Mind Set and Place of Women

Shri Ram Sene Beats up Girls in a Pub

Hitler, the epitome of sectarian politics had set many a norms, practices, which underlined his agenda of Fascism. He targeted the 'outsiders' (Jews, Communists) and suppressed the 'insiders' (workers, women). While what is most visible of his crimes is the genocide of Jews, what was also very damaging was that he suppressed the rights of women and workers. About women he famously went on to pontificate that German women, love to be mothers and that their sphere of activity should be around Kitchen, Church and Children.

Another sectarian outfit, the Taliban after capturing power banned the women from public sphere, asking them to be in the confines of home; else severe punishment will be waiting for them. The fundamentalist groups like Dukhtarane Millat in Kashmir went on to throw acid on the face of the girls refusing to accept the Burqua. Controlling the lives, dress of women, to relegate them to subordinate position, is the common agenda of fundamentalist, fascist politics, irrespective of their religion or race. Apart from other things this politics overall imposes the patriarchal norms in most aggressive way.

Nothing could have brought to our notice these facts more than the act of Shri Ram Sene, in Mangalore, when they beat up girls in a pub in Mangalore (25th Jan 09). Their argument, as articulated by their Chief, Pramod Mutalik is that this is against our Hindu culture. Since the time the BJP government has come to power, these groups have got a message that they can get away with their criminal activities due to the patronage of their ideological-political mentors. Earlier these groups have vandalized churches. Now, while the hooligans attacked and took liberties with the girls, their chief, Mutalik, was arrested initially on some other charges not for this crime by his outfit, Shri Ram Sene. It's only later that due to the pressure from media and the pressure of social opinion that he was also charged for this attack on girls. Not all the sainiks were arrested and even those who were arrested from amongst them many were released on bail, such was the attitude of the BJP government.

The trajectory of the 'career of Mutalik also shows the deeper connections of RSS and others. He is a RSS trained swaymasevak, who later joined Bajrang Dal, and then Shiv Sena before floating this Shri Ram Sene.

BJP, and RSS spokesmen criticized the action of the hooligans taking the law into their hands, but at the same time upheld the 'cause' of protection of Indian culture, women should behave accordingly. They also justified Mutalik's ideology. RSS-BJP distanced themselves organizationally from the Shri Ram Sene. Same Mutalik who has been the aspirant of BJP ticket, might now become persona non grata for RSS-BJP, irrespective of the fact that he is a RSS trained swayam sevak. RSS operates for its goal of Hindu nation through a clever mechanism. It trains volunteers into the ideology of 'Hate Other', for creation of Hindu nation, and then these volunteers in turn go and set up different organizations to fulfill the goal of RSS.

The advantage in this technique is that if some progeny of RSS does a thing which is against law, against which public opinion is strong, they will quietly disown the person. Beginning with Nathuram Godse, the killer of Mahatma Gandhi, this has been the method. Even Dara Singh of Bajrang Dal was disowned by RSS-BJP combine once he did the ghastly crime of burning Pastor Graham Stains. It is a 'brilliant' and shrewd strategy. One of their warriors, Babu Bajrangi, who played a major role in Gujarat carnage, has been very active in attacking the couples in Gujarat. This mechanism, where by RSS trains them to impose the elements of Hindu nation by playing different roles, helps it spreading the tentacles of its sectarian politics without facing the consequences of the criminal acts.

As such the ideological clones of RSS have been vandalizing and attacking cultural activities, gazal programs, painting exhibitions and film shows on regular basis. Girls, women have also been facing the brunt of this offensive. There have been the attacks on couples involved in inter-caste, inter-religious marriages. They have been creating ruckus on Valentine day, and against girls wearing jeans. It is not that the RSS affiliates have been very active in violence against Muslims and Christians, alone. Having intimidated those communities severely, now atrocity against women may become the central focus of their activities. The aim of, such crimes is to browbeat them into receding from social space. Now this may be the major agenda of RSS-combine. What role this intimidation of girls plays? It is clear that with such attacks, the girls will feel intimidated to freely move out; their parents will put more restrictions on them curtailing their freedom.

All this is being done in the name of Hindu traditions. These self appointed custodians of Hindu culture neither know Hinduism, nor do they have any idea of Hindu traditions. They are projecting their political agenda of Fundamentalism, the agenda of subjugation of women through these actions. One letter writer has pointedly asked do these attackers identify the practices of female infanticide, wife beating, and bride burning as practiced by many Hindus as the culture of Hinduism. Is it due to this that they have never taken up campaigns against these ills of Hindu society? Is it because of this, that we never here the protest against these evils from these self proclaimed custodians of Hindu culture.

The agenda of 'politics in the name of Religion', aims to suppress the rights of women. Vijaya Raje Schindia, the BJP Vice President had upheld Sati, Mridula Sinha of BJP Mahila Morcha had upheld wife beating, dowry, and advised women not to work outside unless it is a must. The RSS subordinate organization for women is Rashtra Sevika Samiti, where the word Swyam (self) is missing in contrast to the male organization, Rashtriya Swayam Sevak Sangh. The clear indication of Patriarchal values which the Hindu Right wing uphold. Those concerned with women's welfare need to stand against the evil practices of dowry, bride burning, and female infanticide, while these attacks aim to abolish women's freedom, whatever little they have managed to get through their struggles. These attacks are meant to curb their right to choose their way of life and to impose controls of all sorts over them.

The institution of religion stood for subordinate position for women. Fundamentalism, coming from any religion has the similar social-political agenda. The nitty gritties of disowning apart, the superficial differences of Mutalik and BJP apart, they are guided by same ideology of Hindutva. No wonder the same Mutalik had links with the Malegaon blast accused Lt Col.

Prasad Purohit, who holds Mutalik in high esteem. Unfortunately as the present matters stand the matter may create some furor in the country, which will die down over a period of time as BJP govt. will ensure that their foot soldiers, storm troopers of its ideology get away without any serious punishments. After all they are ideological brother; they are children of single father, the RSS, the ideological parent of Hindu Rashtra.

27

Shivaji's Statue in Arabian Sea

Maharashtra Government has taken a decision sometime back that it will erect the statue of Shivaji, in the Arabian Sea, a la Statue of Liberty. Shivaji is the greatest icon from Maharashtra medieval times. This statue is estimated to cost around 300 crores as per present projections. This decision of the Maharashtra Government was hardly debated. Even those who feel that there is a bigger need for funds for other development issues, kept quite as by now Shivaji has become a matter of big identity politics in Maharashtra. Every party with Maharashtrian identity swears by him. While one is generous in criticizing the statue raising spree by Mayawati, statues of dalit icons and of her own self, about Shivji there is hardly a ripple of protest, whether the debate about public money of such a big magnitude to be spent on the statue has remained on the margins.

What surfaced as the debate took the form of caste issue. There was a talk that Babasaheb Purandare, a Brahmin, who has written some popular material on Shivaji will be made as the Chairman of the committee. Maratha Mahasangh and Shiv Dharm officials, Purushottam Khedekar and others like Mete, had objected to a Brahmin heading the committee for a statue for Maratha warrior. They had also threatened to use violence in case their fatwa is not followed. Not to be left behind the other leader of another violent outfit, Raj Thackeray gave a counter threat, that Purandare must be retained on the committee.

It goes without saying that Khedekar, Mete and Raj Thackeray they all sail in the same boat of intolerant politics, which needs to be condemned. Also the caste angle of controversy should be opposed. Still one will say that Babasaheb Purandare should not be on the committee. The reasons for that lie not in the fact that Purandare is a Brahmin, but because Purandare's presentation of Shivaji is through and through communal. It picks up from the tradition of British Historiography. In Maharashtra itself there are as many Shivaji's as the number of political streams. Purandare's Shivaji, as manifested through his play Jaanta Raja (All knowing king) is primarily anti Muslim King. Shivaji is also presented as the great worshipper of Brahmins and cows. His total slant is that Shivaji wanted to build Hindu nation etc. which is not only far from truth but also a very divisive way of presented our past. As a matter of fact Shivaji is popular amongst people, not because he was anti Muslim or worshipper of Cows and Brahmins, but because he reduced the taxation on the poor peasants.

Shivaji adopted a humane policy in aspects of his administration, which did not base itself on the religion. In the recruitment of his soldiers and officers for his army and navy, religion was no criterion and more than one third of his army consisted of Muslims. The supreme command of his navy was with Siddi Sambal, and Muslim Siddis were in navy in large numbers. Interestingly his major battles were fought with the Rajput army lead by Mirza Raja Jaisingh on behalf of King

Aurangzeb. When he was detained at Agra forte, of the two men on whom he relied for his eventual escape one was a Muslim called Madari Mehtar. His confidential secretary was Maulana Haider Ali and the chief of his cannon division was Ibrahim Gardi.

His respect for other religions was very clear and he respected the holy seers like 'Hazarat Baba Yaqut bahut Thorwale', whom he gave the life pension and also Father Ambrose, whose church was under attack in Gujarat. At his capital Raigad he erected a special mosque for Muslim devotees in front of his palace in the same way that he built the Jagadishwar temple for his own daily worship.

During his military campaigns Shivaji had issued strict instructions to his men and officers that Muslim women and children should not be subjected to maltreatment. Mosques and Dargah's were given due protection. He also ordered that whenever a copy of Koran came into the hands of his men, they should show it proper respect and hand it over to Muslim. The story of his bowing to the daughter-in-law of Bassein's Nawab is well known to all. When she was brought as a part of the loot and offered to her he respectfully begged her pardon and asked his soldiers to reach her back from the place from where she was forcibly brought in. Sardesai in his book New History of Marathas writes "One thing is quiet clear that in defending the Hindu religion, Shivaji was in no way actuated by any hatred towards Muslims as a sect or towards their religion. All this goes on to show the values of communal harmony which Shivaji pursued, and that his primary goal was to establish his own kingdom with maximum possible area. To project him as anti-Muslim and anti-Islam is travesty of truth.

Today rank casteist forces are also in the bandwagon to 'use' Shivaji' issues for their political goals. The Human rights activist Teesta Setalvad had prepared a hand book of History for the school teachers some time back. In this she pointed out that since Shivaji was a Shudra, the Brahmins refused to coronate him, so a Brahmin had to be brought from Kashi, who did the coronation ritual, but that too with the toe of his left foot. The local Shiv Sena went on to oppose this handbook on the ground that the writer is calling him a Sudra. It is true that he was a Sudra and this incident is true. Similarly Bhandarkar Institute was attacked by the same people, Khedekar and company, on the pretext that this institute had helped James Lane write a book on Shivaji. It is well known that this book mentioned a rumor about the real parentage of the King.

One hopes the Government thinks of using the public money in a better way than raising statues. The money for the statue should be raised from people by the committee. The public money should not be spent on this.

28

Communalism in India: International Dimensions

The World has witnessed two major occupations after invasions and one attack on a country during last 15 years. First Iraq was attacked on the pretext that it has occupied Kuwait; thousands died and millions worth of property was decimated. Later on the excuse of catching hold of Osama bin Laden Afghanistan was attacked, bin Laden escaping successfully, while over sixty thousand people perished. Despite the report of UN inspectors that Iraq does not have the Weapons of Mass Destruction (WMD), biological weapons etc. Iraq was attacked and occupied by US and its ally armies.

At the same time the phenomenon of Al Qaeda has reared its head in a menacing way. Attack on World Trade Center, the attack on London tube stations and the aborted attack in Australia are few amongst the examples of the same. This is running parallel to the notion that Islam is a violent religion, Muslims are terrorists and also that Islamic civilization is the retrograde backward one which is the threat to the World.

Samuel Huntington in his book Clash of Civilization puts forward the thesis that the current phase of World politics is the phase of backward Islamic civilization attacking the advanced Western civilization. It is the phase in which different Islamic terrorist groups have come in different parts of the World. India is also one of the places where terrorism emerged from Kashmir and has been supplemented by the one in response to the communal carnages here and three.

This clash of Civilization thesis came into being after the demise of USSR, after the Socialist block collapsed. This post 80s phase has been marked by various phenomenons. The first major is the globalization, the economy assuming more global form with the domination of US in most areas of economy. The public sectors which had come up for installing the industrialization, as the Industrial bourgeoisie was too weak to undertake this task, started being looked down and also the bureaucratic tangles led many of these into economic losses and consequent policy of the Governments to close them down. It was accompanied by the decline in the social welfare schemes. The second painfully visible part of the global scene was decline in the moral and political power of United Nations. U.S. flaunted the authority of UN and went on to undertake its aggression bypassing the UN. The third one was the increasing stranglehold of U.S. and its allies on the oil fields of Middle East. US oil corporations have been given the oil wells on the platter after US aggressions in one after the other country. Now one can perceive that U.S. is planning to attack Iran and Syria for their violation of nuclear policies. The decision maker about these countries' policies is again the US, giving itself legitimacy through its brute force.

It is claimed that US is doing this to install democracy in these countries. The claim is that it is the mission of United States to spread freedom and democracy all over the World. In the countries which it has invaded the earlier dictatorial regimes have been crushed for the sake of democracy implanted there courtesy the U.S. army. The motives of U.S. are presented to be to confront the despots and to promote the democracy. In turn by now it has also been popularized that Islamic terrorism is *the* threat to the World.

As a small aside, India has also witnessed the similar phenomenon. Here the Right wing politics has asserted itself, the communal violence has gone up, and at places the hurt and humiliated Muslim youth have resorted to the insane path of terrorism. The response to Kashmir problem has added on to the prevalent notions of Islam being the religion of terror. The global and local phenomenon have started looking similar. Islam and Muslims seem to be common culprits. And that's where Samuel Huntington gets legitimacy as the philosopher, ideologue of present times.

What is the truth? Colonial powers that were out to plunder and exploit the World, used the language of civilizing mission in the East, the White man's burden to civilize the barbarians of the colonies. With the independence of the colonies the Nationalism came to the fore in these regions, the language of this was Left oriented. Many a places this was inspired by the revolutions of Russia and China. Vietnam came as one more inspiring example of the same. Current global politics is stalking in the language of religion all over. The economic and political interests have been given the veneer of religion. The identity politics has come to the fore with undermining of the real issues of the poor and oppressed sections of society. The culture and social values are in a reverse gear due to the present political agenda of the dominant countries of the World and dominant sections within the country.

The real reasons for US polices lie in its lust for oil. The clash is not between the civilizations, it is between the economic and political interests of different layers of society and different countries. The reasons for terrorism have to be looked in the underlying social deprivation, the conscious training of outfits like Al Qaeda by CIA to oppose the USSR occupation of Afghanistan. In countries like India it is the politics in the name of religion which is dominating the scene and it is that which hides the political agenda of opposition to the social transformation for caste and gender equality. Huntington at global level and Religious right wing and national level converge on this point of projecting Islam as the enemy of civilization, it is the defense for their own political agenda.

Clash of Civilizations:

The politics after the decade of 1980s has seen the gradual intensification of the US interference in the Middle East. The overt action was the attack on Iraq 1991 and subsequent imposition of sanctions which crushed the Iraqi society. This was to be followed few years later to attack Afghanistan, on the pretext of catching Osama Bin Laden. Incidentally in this invasion over 60000 Afghan civilians, children, women, old people and others were killed, while the 'real target' of invasion, Osama continued to live in the pink of his health. Then came the massive operation involving over two lakh, American forces to 'liberate' the people of Iraq from the atrocities of Saddam Hussain.

During this period the 'terrorist' acts, which were labeled as Islamic terrorism came up, Al Qaeda, Lashkar-e- Tayyaba, Hamas were seen launching most virulent actions. It was propagated that Islam is the root of violence, Muslims are aggressive and the acts of terror are due to Islam and Muslims. It is this backdrop that American ideologue Samuel Huntington, while commenting on contemporary politics stated, "The twenty First Century is at least beginning as the century of culture, with differences, interactions and conflicts among cultures taking center stage. This has become manifest, among other ways, in the extent to which scholars, politicians, economic development officials, soldiers, and strategists are all turning to culture as the central factor in explaining human...behavior (Huntington, 1999) and further, "The rivalry of super powers is being supplanted by the clash of civilizations."

It was again for first time that the global political interests were being presented as the clash of civilization. Earlier human society has seen the clash between kingdoms in the garb of Crusade, Jihad or Dharmudh, the aggression of imperial powers in colonizing the large chunk of globe in the language of, Civilizing mission in the East and the preservation of Imperialist interests in the garb of defense of freedom. This essay examines the intent behind the Huntington's theorization.

World Scenario-Contemporary Times

Political perception got a turn on the terrible Tuesday (September 11, 2001) on which nearly three thousand innocent lives were lost due to the terrorist attack on World Trade Center. In retaliation, America launched a war on Afghanistan, 'Operation Infinite Justice', a war on terrorism, which was supposed to catch Osama bin-Laden, who is accused of masterminding this despicable crime against humanity. It is another matter that America is not showing the evidence of this to the World community.

Last two decades have been very turbulent phase in the History of the World. On one hand we have seen most of Socialist economies collapsing, we have also witnessed the rise of religious fascism or Fundamentalism, also known as Religion based Nationalism, and at yet another level the phenomenon of globalization has been causing havoc on the lives of poor, eliminating the large workforce from the field of employment. Is there a deeper linkage between these phenomena or their taking place in the same span of time is a mere coincidence? It is probably necessary to begin with understanding the Industrial revolutions to place the things in their proper perspective.

Terrorism and War

On global scenario terrorism has been on the rise. Starting from the formation of Israel and displacement of the Palestinians, the terrorism at global level has been on the rise and assuming more dangerous forms continuously. It is not easy to define the term Terrorism though it has been used most often. The state machineries have generally been using the term terrorist acts and in the process avoiding defining the term terrorism. What does it mean exactly? Terrorism can be defined as, violence or threat of violent act by an individual or a state against the non-combatants, in pursuit of their political goal. In the purview of this fall many an acts by state or rather different states have been the major perpetrators of terrorism in one form or the other. It is true that last few years we have seen more terrorist acts coming from those owing allegiance to Islam. And in subtle and overt form it is being said that it is Islam which gives rise to terrorism.

Terrorism and Religion

How is Islam related to terror, or for that matter how is any religion related to the cult of violence? Were the crusades undertaken by Christian Kings to promote Christianity? Did Muslim Kings undertaken Jihad to promote Islam? Were the *Dharmayudhs* by Hindu kings undertaken to promote Hindu religion? By no stretch of imagination any war related violence could be attributed to these religions. It is the Kings whose basic goal was to expand their Kingdoms, who undertook these wars and misused the names of their religions to get more people involved in the same. Timothy Mc Viehg, Oklahoma bomber was not serving Christianity, neither Dhanu was serving Hinduism when she acted as a live bomb killing Rajiv Gandhi and innocents around him, nor was Bhindranwale serving Sikhism when he promoted the cult of violence which led to murder of Indira Gandhi and then the butchery of thousands of Sikhs, nor was Osama bin-Laden serving Islam when he thanked Allah in the wake of the WTC tragedy, nor are the Kashmiri militants serving Islam when they maim and kill innocent Hindus and Muslims in the Valley of Kashmir. Terrorism is the product of social and National discontent, discontent, which flows though the barrel of the gun or explodes with the bomb of terrorist when the democratic channels are not available for its expression for the victims of Injustice. People belonging practically to all the religions under the sun have resorted to terror in the name of their religions. It is not that only one religion has the distinction for this misuse.

In Indian context the terrorism of Khalistanis could be contained when the dealing with the militants could be combined with winning over the hearts and minds of people and by making available the effective democratic options to the people at large. The present terrorism by the self proclaimed Jihadis is definitely a slightly different ball game. The role of Pakistan in this is very discernible. But here our myopic vision stops and fails to see the imperialist designs in promoting the terrorism and routing this through the conduit of Pakistan. We are unable to see the deeper imperialist goals of control over oil resources, which has nurtured Talibans. Right since the formation of Israel and its being backed by US the signals were around of its designs in the Middle East and then in the sub-continent. Israel went into violate all the UN resolutions, attack Arab world repeatedly, to capture the Palestinian lands and to cause the loss of home and hearth of close to a million Palestinians. In due course U.S. started tightening its grip on the resources of the region. US has crushed the democratic aspirations of the countries in the oil rich region to promote its interests, those of controlling and appropriating the oil wealth.

'Peace as War'

In the wake of the attack on the World Trade Center (WTC), U.S. immediately decided to attack Afghanistan. U.S. projected that this terrorism is a big threat to the world 'Peace' so to preserve the peace in the world it has decided to launch the aggression. Those killed in this war were mainly the bruised and battered people of Afghanistan. The major world powers came to the support of the US aggression. Interestingly the World body, United Nations was not approached, neither was the World shown the evidence of involvement of Osama Bin-Laden. Afghan regime did offer to hand over Osama bin-Laden to a neutral country if the evidence implicating him in this attack was shown to them. U.S. refused that and ignoring the peace calls from Fidel Castro, Dalai Lama and Pope John Paul, launched the attack. In the attack nearly sixty thousand Afghan people died and the new Govt. has been put together. This new regime is a puppet of U.S. The 'dreaded' terrorist, bin Laden, has so far not been caught!

Has this act of U.S. been to control the terrorism? Why does terrorism come up in the first place? What have been the real intentions of U.S. in this war? We need to go through a bit of the history to find answers to some of these questions. U.S. has taken advantage of the popular anger against the WTC attack to fulfill one of its core agenda of controlling the oil resources of the world. We will see that the attack by U.S. has been deliberately projected as the clash of civilizations. There is a deep linkage between the imperialist designs of yesteryears which colonized the world for plundering the raw materials of the colonies and the present US move which aims to control the world oil wealth.

'White Man's Burden'

While these countries, mainly of Europe, were industrializing, they also set out to colonize rest of the World.

World became divided into spheres of influence of different powers. In colonies some social transformation began along with the industrialization, which the colonial masters had to initiate to fulfill their agenda of plunder in the colonies. But here the process was much more complex and painful. The colonial masters were not interested in the transformation of social relations towards those of equality. They had alliance, generally with the feudal elements of the colonies. They did bring in some cosmetic reforms in the social practices but the basic structure was left untouched. Colonies were used by the masters to plunder the raw materials and also as a market for the products of their industries. To ensure their rule and goals, the processes that had to be brought in also gave rise to the 'modern' classes, mainly workers and industrialists. But the secularization process remained weak and unfinished one. The introduction of needs of the colonial empires in the colonies was done under the ideological banner of 'White Man's Burden' (to civilize the backward countries) and the real plunder and exploitation of markets was the processes hidden behind the curtain of ideas created by media and other mechanisms which supported the formation of Social common sense.

'Socialist Economies'

In many a countries, especially Russia, China, Cuba and Vietnam, socialism came as the Nationalizing force, as the force which took the responsibilities of Industrialization and transformation of social relations towards the one's of equality. The economies in these were not controlled by market, but by the state. This control was no match to the flexibility and guile of the 'market economies' of the 'free world'. It should be noted here that though the few countries could achieve Independence from the direct political grip of the colonial masters, the economic domination of the Imperialists continued in direct and subtle forms.

Control for markets led to the two major World wars and America emerged as the major power at the end of Second World War. Towards the end of the war it dropped atom bombs on Hiroshima, Nagasaki to assert its hegemony over the World. At the end of Second World War the other major change in the political geography was creation of Israel from the land of Palestine and Partition of India to create Pakistan. Both these states were the blue-eyed boys of the Imperial powers, and played to their tunes, acting as custodians of Imperialist interests in the area. Even Soviet Russia, the leader of Socialist block supported the formation of Israel. In the ensuing battle between the Imperialism and Socialism the 'cold war' saw the world going ding dong, from one pole to the other but no major overt war took place. America's emergence as the leader of 'Free' World also saw its actions which though were laced in the language, 'to protect Freedom' from the 'Totalitarianism of Socialism', time and again tried to crush the Nationalism and social transformation towards the values of Modernity. No Nation could live its travails in an isolated way. Imperialism on one hand and Socialism on the other did hegemonise most of the weaker states in an unambiguous way.

'Defending Freedom and Democracy'

During this phase, with the emergence of US as the major player of free market, many emerging Nationalisms were suppressed by it. Since some National movements were taking support of Socialist ideology, the collective National bureaucracy undertook the task of implementation of Industrialization and social transformation of social relations. These nations were slipping away from the control of the colonial powers. The case of Vietnam and Chile best exemplify this. In Vietnam, US launched a war to crush the National movement under the flagship of 'defending freedom' and to save the world from the demon of 'totalitarian socialism'. This 'defense of freedom' came by trying to crush the Viet Cong led by Ho Chi Minh who was ushering the Vietnamese Nationalism in the name of Socialism. Uncle Ho finally made Uncle Sam bite the dust despite the limited resources. A decade later the 'Freedom' was 'defended' again in Chile by overthrowing the democratically elected Salvador Allende. The real aim being to perpetuate its control over the copper mines needed for US communications industry.

The economic compulsions have generally been blinding the World powers and they have been trying to live the adage that all is fair in war and love (for profits). The socialist economies suffered two major handicaps. One, they came in, in Nation states, which had been ruthlessly exploited by the 'defenders of freedom' during the phase of colonialism and second, that the regulating mechanism of market was absent from these countries. It is here that these countries started lagging behind the 'Free World', which by now had strong markets and stronger economies. With collapse of Socialist economies, more due to inner dynamics, the cold war came to an end.

Meanwhile the during Cold war some semblance of bipolar world did make it possible for the emerging Nations to breathe free and even to create the third pole of Non-Aligned movement. UN, despite its limitations could also play some role more rather than just providing the first aid to the victims of the wars around the world. It did show potential to become a World democratic Govt., but of course it has been too much riddled with the non-democratic structures like Security council, it does not have the proper representation based on the population of the countries and does not have distribution of proportionate power as per the population of the nation states.

Oil 'Hunger'

During cold war period also 'Free World' ('FW') has 'defended' democracy in various 'imaginative' ways. Apart from preventing the democratic Govt. coming into being wherever possible, it proactively overthrew the regimes with democratic potentials. In 1953 a CIA coup replaced the democratic Govt. of Mohd. Mossadegh in Iran and the rule of Pehlvi dynasty was installed. The former was considering nationalizing the oil industry. And that would have spelt doom and caused 'oil deprivation' to the US. The Shah who took over, courtesy the CIA, Westernized the society in a superficial way, while the deeper problems of society remained and America kept dominating the state. The protest, which built up, for the lack of democratic channels, got manifested through the religious clergy; the only available institution in such a society and Ayatollah Khomeini established a Fundamentalist regime, which now is gradually opening up. During this period itself this leader of free world cultivated oil Sheikhs in the Gulf region, the Sheikhs for whom even the D of democracy is the equivalent of a devil, but that does not matter so far as 'these suppressers of Democracy' are sitting in the lap of Uncle Sam. For FW, Freedom is safe with the despots, Sheikhs and dictators of every hue. In a way for FW democracy has been too precious to be had by the other countries, especially the one's rich in natural resources

In this march to economic hegemony Oil has played an important place in the policies of the World. None other than US and its cohorts know the importance of controlling the oil resources better. One of the reasons for the earlier colonial powers making the journey to the places far and wide to colonies the World was to control the resources of the World. Now, this came in the form of controlling Sheikhdoms or installing regimes, necessarily retrograde in social and political outlook, at the cost of relatively more progressive regimes. It more or less became a thumb rule for big Bully, the champion of Free World. And here the instances abound. Incidentally since these countries, around the oil triangle happen to be predominantly

Muslim, and so new theories and mechanisms had to be manufactured. Already at the end of Second World War Israel had been created at the cost of Palestine. Later one witnessed the promoting of Fundamentalist regimes by the World Imperialist forces. Meanwhile in 1991, Kuwait, acting as a minion of US was draining oil from the wells shared with Iraq. Saddam Hussain, unable to tolerate this, captured this small state and declared it as the 23rd state of Iraq. To give 'justice' to the Sheikh of Kuwait US launched an aggression on Iraq in which nearly two Lakh people died and five lakh children suffered due to the after effects, sanctions etc. 'Justice' was done and freedom of Sheikh of Kuwait (to gift its oil to US) was restored.

The story of Afghanistan, currently facing the death from the bombing is very peculiar. In 1978 People's Democratic Party came to power and went in for democratic reforms on secular lines. Following year, this Govt. was overthrown by conservative elements. Soviet Russia sent its army to bring back the rule, which could go in for social reforms. America decided to promote the most fundamentalist sections of rebels; Osama included, and helped them through and through to overthrow the Russian army. And that brought in the rule of Taliban, which was nurtured by US through the conduit of Pakistan. Meanwhile US did practically everything to violate the unwritten and written rules of the International behavior. Be it the checkmating of Nasser in Egypt, opposing Nationalist upsurges in Algeria, Syria and Lebanon down to bombing the pharma factory in Sudan.

The mighty have their-own logic. One thought with the decline of feudal empires the democratic constitutions will guide the nation states and a democratic UN would guide the international relations. But that does sound Utopia today.

Since the formation of Israel and later US role in most of the Islamic states, US policies started having their impact in the psyche of the section of Muslims. US identified closely with Israel's highhandedness in the Gulf region. It turned a blind eye to the atrocities of Israel and violation of the Human rights of Palestinians. Meanwhile with the collapse of Socialist States, Islam was given the status of 'enemy number one' by the propaganda machine of US. This was to explain the ill effects of it's own policies vis-à-vis Palestinians. The sum and substance of US policies in supporting the repressors of Muslims (Palestine), bombing the Pharma factory in Sudan, aggression on Iraq and supporting the Shah regime in Iran did lead to a sentiment amongst Muslims that US is standing to oppose and suppress their interests, world around. Even the Afghan adventure of US is more an exercise to control the oil resources from Uzbekistan. U.S. and its cohorts are the main backers of the Saudi Arabia, where the repressive governments. claims to rule according to Shariah. It has been responsible for supporting and financing a movement based on an ultra orthodox version of Islam, the Wahabi movement. Generally speaking the Islamic countries geographically distant from oil wells have been more successful in preserving and nurturing elements of democracy. Has it something to do with the fact that the prying (for oil) eyes of CIA do not relish the smell of development of democratic processes? At the same time US establishment can mouth the adages of defending the 'Free World' at the top of their voices, duly adored by their media, which in a way has specialized in 'Manufacturing consent' for the broad approval of U.S. policies which are a necessity to satiate the power and Oil hunger of Uncle Sam.

Fundamentalism in different countries

The coincidence of overlap in the time scale of Intensification of process of Globalization process and coming up of Fundamentalism is too obvious to be ignored. Shah, installed after the coup to thwart the proposed Nationalization of the oil industry was a 'good boy' for the West and more particularly for U.S. His selective modernization program created a deep chasm in the society, in which the elite benefited immensely and the poor got further marginalized. Inflation, intensification of poverty and unemployment led to massive social unrest. Due to the suppression of Democratic channels, the religious clergy remained the only established channel, which could be resorted to as a medium of protest. They gave a religious color to the movement, which overthrew The Shah regime and installed Khomeini to power. This was the major use of religion in the politics though under different circumstances. Selective use of *Shariah* is also made in many countries in Gulf region to suppress the Human rights of women and other subaltern sections of society. And these do against the democratic ethos.

In India again it was the decade of 80s when this phenomenon, fundamentalism, started growing in an overt way. Here the elite, upper caste, affluent middle classes feared the struggles of Dalits and women. The enemy was discovered in the hapless Muslim minority and the communalization of society on the ground of 'hate Muslim' started picking up, cúlminating in different Rath Yatras. Meanwhile to balance the power equations of the coalition Govt., Mandal commission was implemented. The upper caste/class consolidation, which was already building up took this as a big threat and rallied around Sangh parivar in a bigger way. This transformed the upper caste/ class psyche and the religion-based politics of Sangh parivar came to the center stage of the society. The demolition of Babri masjid gave the flesh and blood to this fundamentalist force, which duly occupied the seats of power at the center, unleashing an era of communalization of society and in due course manipulating the education and other cultural expressions of society to root the communalism at deeper level.

Globalization comes to Fore

The very system of Capitalism is a Global phenomenon. No economy can survive in isolation. Though the major rules are determined by those mightier economically and politically, there are some degrees of autonomies at local level. These autonomies are manifest more in the implementation of the policies rather than in the making of policies themselves. With collapse of socialist economies the phenomenon of globalization became more pronounced and its ill effects on workers and other weaker sections of society started becoming more apparent, despite the theories of apologists of Globalization, who welcomed it as heralding a more progressive Capital. The terms of trade are lopsided, going against the interests of the weaker Nations. During this period many an overlapping events happened the roots of which were already laid during the cold war and also a bit later. These apologists of Globalization totally ignored the political instance of the phenomenon of the World. For them, economy is the sole and only determinant of the World affairs. The role of political might of G7 and more so US in manipulating the economy in a way, which is unfavorable to the weaker Nations is crystal clear.

Huntington's Thesis

"It is my hypothesis that the fundamental source of conflict in this new World will not be primarily ideological or primarily economic. The great Divisions among humankind and the dominating source of conflict will be Cultural. Nation states will remain the most powerful actors in world Affairs, but the principal conflicts of global politics will occur between Nations and groups of different civilizations. The clash of civilizations will dominate global politics. The fault lines between civilizations will be the battle lines of the future." These gems are from Samuel Huntington the new ideologue of this era representing the age in the World when America's economic and political domination is close to complete. It is an era where America along with its minions is calling the shots. It is an era when the Non-Aligned movement of yesteryears has been well forgotten and the possibility of World Democratic order seems to be a

Utopia. The injustices done to large section of Muslims in the Gulf region and Africa have been showing its repercussions. The militant opposition of Palestinians initially got expressed in Yasser Arafat and other movements for the rights of Palestinians.

The other acts of commission by U.S. and other hegemonic powers have left a sense of injustice amongst a large section of Muslim masses. Also one is aware that the chances of International grievance settlement channels practically do not exist with UN being reduced to the desk in the state Dept. of the US and its Secretary General helplessly watching the might of imperialist powers attacking Iraq, and soliciting UN sanction for its terrorism. The same man watching from the sidelines, America's aggression on Afghanistan and the aggressor this time not even bothering to get it ratified by the World body, the facade, which it kept so far. And this person, was with Nobel for peace, for keeping quiet when the U.S. is on rampage in country after country. In this phase what is the way for the people of the World, which is feeling that injustice has been done it? How should they protest? Which doors they knock for grievance rectification?

This is aggressive terror aimed to dominate and control the World. This is the terrorism of the mighty out to enslave the weak. This state terrorism kills the innocent non-combatants, like the ones' in Hiroshima and Nagasaki, like the one's dying in the U.S. aggression on Iraq in 1991, like the one's dying in the streets of Baghdad currently. The other terrorism is of the one's who has been victims of the unjust policies of Nations and World, those whose ethnic aspirations have been suppressed, those who have been deprived of their home and hearth due to the greed of the World powers.

Today the ideological cover of 'defending Freedom in the World' is no more adequate for its interests in oil and other hegemonic goals. The resistance of the weak has to be dubbed in a more scathing manner to justify the Terror of the Mighty, and so the 'Clash of Civilizations' thesis. The ideology of the imperialism, in the times of Oil 'hunger', ideology of the hegemonic powers to crush the resistance in places where they want direct and indirect control over the resources of the World. So the 'backward Islamic civilization' is clashing with the Modern West, say the new ideologues of imperialists. Here in the clever maneuver, for those having oil wells, religious identity is imposed and those who aspire to satisfy their oil hunger by buying it for peanuts, the geographical category is used. Nothing new! The colonial Historians did the same trick here when they divided the History into Hindu, Muslim and British period. And then comes the next stage in which the followers of Mohammad are painted with the uniform brush. The Muslims today, a two billion strong, are reduced to a stereotype, clones of Osama bin-Laden or members of Taleban. The diversity recognition amongst the target group is dangerous for the oppressors. So even in India we see the Muslims being projected as a uniform community. It is easy for the dominant group to deal with the monolithic image of minority. More backward the projection of the image, the better it is. It helps in all the ways including during the times when violence and other suppressions have to be unleashed in pursuance with their politics.

So the Muslims in Iraq, Iran, Saudi, Indonesia, Bangladesh all become cast in a single mould. And now the next step becomes easy, since Muslims as a community can be projected to be opposed to Modernity. They are terrorists so there must be something in Islam, which promotes violence and terrorism. And so when the pogroms are unleashed against them in the form of communal violence or aggression is launched against innocent Iraqis or Afghans, consent gets easily manufactured for the devilish acts of the super powers. The political ratings of the one saying 'you are either on our side or on their' (terrorists) soar to maddening heights and those accepting social common sense clap with each missile hitting the home for the old or shelter for the people or the hospital. Some applaud the 'beauty ', the precision with which the missiles do their job; others rejoice that 'they' (the Muslims) deserve this lesson. So on overt level Uncle Sam retreats back after endorsing the 'clash of civilization' and to appear politically correct, the boss reverts to 'Infinite Justice' as the ideological cover for bombing the hospitals and children and the old people's homes.

White Man's burden thesis came up with the colonization, 'Defending freedom and democracy' came up while suppressing the rising Nationalisms and now the clash of civilization is being put forward when US is trying to control the taps of oil resources. There are many an Islamic counties in and around these resources, who had to be rubbed the wrong way, in order to maintain and extend the flow of oil towards fuel tanks of the powerful countries of the West. Keeping in mind this projection, which exploiters have generally kept for their own interests some ideological cover has to be maintained. If colonial masters are usurping the resources of colonies, it is White man's burden to civilize the people of the colonies, if Imperialism is crushing the Nationalist sentiments to be able to continue its hegemony on the World; it is fight for freedom of the World. Here both these have been used as a cover for the proactive deeds of Imperialism. Now the 'Clash' theory is there to explain the 'reaction to the injustices' done to the section of Arab world. One knows that most of the Muslim Nations are with the US in its efforts to control the Afghan territory through the new puppet, which will be pro-US. One also knows that the Muslim dominated countries like Indonesia, Malaysia and many significant one's are with the US for its 'sacrifices to save the freedom' in the World.

Summing Up and Future Perspective

The birds' eye view of the last few centuries can give us many an insights into the present morass in which we have landed up. The choices before us are very tricky. From a progressive angel one will like to see the condition of Human rights of all the people of the World improving. One longs to see a World community where the social relations of Liberty, Equality and Fraternity (community) are achieved at substantive level. One also longs for a society of abundance, the society bereft of hierarchies, a society where Equality and Freedom walk hand in hand.

The events of last few decades have thrown up very new phenomenon. In this ever-changing society new paradigms have to be grasped with new intellectual frameworks, which can cope up with the demands of the time. The World is witness to combined and uneven trajectory of development. It has seen the Industrialization process and the accompanying social relations halted in the tracks. Feudalism goes with the birth based hierarchy, Bourgeoisie Nationalism with formal Liberty Equality and Fraternity, which gives the ground for struggles, which can lead towards substantive Liberty, Equality and Fraternity. But as some Nations achieved these Industrial revolutions they did block the same in other countries, which were colonized. Some countries under the illusion of Socialist dream could sidetrack the rules of Market economy to bring in a collective bureaucracy and consequent industrialization and nationalism. Here the emphasis on social welfares prevailed but these states proved to be unviable in the global economy where 'Free Market' prevails. Last two decades saw the unique phenomenon of collapse of these economies, and rise of Middle sections of society in the garb of Traditionalism, under the flag of Religious Nationalism, basically to oppose the transitions towards equality, to suppress the process of change, to strengthen the status quo. In some other countries, especially the oil rich one's the Imperialism ensured the sustenance of pre-modern authoritarian regimes to fill the coffers of G7 countries. The simmering discontent, the blockade of democratic channels led to rebellions, which due to the lack of democratic channels are being expressed through the horrible 'Terrorism', which in a way is the concentrated expression of injustices perpetuated on large section of people. For a sane world the choice is not between War and Terrorism but the only goal can, the only alternative is Democratization, from the smallest area to the World level. It has to be the substantive Liberty Equality and Fraternity (community) through popular struggles for the Human rights of all the sections of society.

References

Ahmad, Aijaz: Iran Afghanistan-The imperialism of Our Time,Left Word, Delhi 2004.

Ali, Tariq:The Clash of Fundamentalisms, Rupa 2003 Delhi.

Amin Samir, US hegemony and the response to terror, Monthly Review, Nov. 2001.

Castro Fidel, Terrorism and the War Crisis, Monthly Review, Nov. 20001.

Chomsky Noam, Interview Monthly Review, Nov. 2001.

Durran Khalid, The Globalization of Terrorism, In Review, Fall 2000.

Engineer A.A., Islam And Modern Age, Vol. I, 1998, Mumbai.

Grare F., Manohar, New Delhi, 2001.

Huntington Samuel, The Clash of Civilization, Simon and Shuster, NY, 1996.

Huntington Samuel, Key Note Address, Colarado College's 125th Anniversary Symposium.

Koshi, Ninan: The War on Terror-Reordering the World, Left Word, Delhi 2003.

Lokshahi Hakka Sanghatana, The Assault on Afghanistan and the Real Intent behind it, Dec. 2001. Mumbai.

Lopez B. and Shahid M.Z., Combating Terrorism and Humanity, DRTC, Mubai Jan 2002.

Mamdani, Mahmood: Good Muslim Bad Muslim, Permanent Black Delhi 2005.

Zakaria Rafiq, Victims of Prejudice, Asian Age June 4th , 2001.

29

Dialogue for Peace in Action

Violence Threatening Social Peace and Need for Amity

Last two decades have seen a very negative trend World over. Immense violence has been unleashed, and that too in the name of religion. When two planes strike the World Trade Center and 3000 innocent persons die, Osama bin Laden expresses his joy and declares that what is going on is Jihad. In the name of Crusade, George Bush President of US launched an attack on Afghanistan. In this attack over 60000 innocent people get killed. In India, in 1992 December 6 the rampaging mob of 3 Lakh people led by Lal Krishna Advani, mobilized by RSS combine (RSS combine word stands for RSS and all those organizations which are driven by the political ideology in the name of Hindu religion, whose volunteers are trained by RSS for the goal of Hindu Nation). This demolition of Babri mosque has been regarded as the glory to Hindu religion by them. In Orissa (July, December 2007) a massive aggression is launched on the Christian community on the pretext of the murder of Swami Laxmananand. All through the name of religion is in the forefront of the violence.

Accompanying the violence a thesis "Clash of Civilizations", that the present era is the one where civilizations, religions are clashing is supposed to be describing the present phenomenon. This thesis propounded by Samuel Huntington, sees the current state of global affairs as one of conflict between civilizations, unmindful of the fact that civilizations don't clash it is barbarisms which clash. This thesis is also unmindful of the fact of history that while Kings and colonial powers have launched wars for their vested interests, the people of different regions and religions have interacted amicably resulting in the growth of Human culture and civilizations. In India the dominant political discourse presumes that Christians and Muslims are foreigners and that they are not having equal rights! This ignores the fact that Indian culture is a plural one, that people of different religions have lived amicably with each other and that it is due to the participation of people of all the regions and religions that we got Independence, and that the concept of India as a nation is all inclusive.

Violence in the name of Religion

The communal violence, more so from last two decades is leading to polarization of communities, strengthening of communal politics, and in turn ghettoization of minorities. The social links between communities are snapping fast and religion based localities are coming up in big number. In US and many other places Muslims are being looked at with suspicion and the gulf between religious communities is widening.

After the decades of 1950s to 1980s, when people from all religions came together for national liberation struggles and for marching towards democratic norms, the process seems to have been reversed and the aggressive slant of political and social powers is creating a situation where it seems that religious differences are the cause of problem.

Religion or Politics

The worst part of present social language is the abuse of religious identity for political goals. None of what is going on has any thing to do with the morality of religions. As a matter of fact the moral values of religions do supplement each other for better World. What has happened is that the global super power has in a shortsighted way promoted Radical Muslim groups and trained them in an insane ideology, which resulted in growth of terrorism. In India the RSS combine has similarly used the identity of Hindu religion to promote their agenda of Hindu nation, an agenda which is opposed to democratic values of society. The global scene due to this twin phenomenon is affecting the atmosphere of peace and is creating an impression of clash between religions.

Terrorism: Clash of Civilizations!

The main group which has created the impression that terrorism is due to religion is Al Qaeda. This group was propped up by Untied States to counter the Russian occupation of Afghanistan, in the decade of 1980s. To ensure the participation of Muslim youth in the battle, Madrassas were opened in Pakistan with the help of US money. The syllabus taught in these Madarassas was designed in US and it distorted the meaning of word Jihad and Kafir. In Koran, Kafir stands for the hidden person, who attacks the people of faith. The US designed syllabus presented Kafir as one who does not believe in Allah, a non Muslim. Jihad which means 'striving' effort for betterment was presented as war against non Muslims. In this direction Osama was brought in to lead the Al Qaeda and was supported by US with 8000 Million Dollars and 7000 tons of armaments, with the help of which he defeated Russian armies. The same Al Qaeda and its offshoots sprung up and survived over a period of time. Later in popular perception all acts committed by this group got associated with Islam and Muslims.

US media after the 9/11 2001, popularized the word Islamic terrorism for the acts of the group which they helped bringing up and which later turned against them. The demonization of Muslims Worldwide went on unchallenged, major sections of media propagated the word Islamic Terrorism and the whole community came under intimidation. Here the theory of Clash of Civilizations also presented Muslims as backward and aggressive, ignoring the fact that Muslims are as good or bad as any other religious community.

RSS Combine

In India RSS which began with the agenda of Hindu rashtra (Nation) began with the ideology that Muslims, Christians and Communists are a threat to 'our' Hindu nation. In pursuance of its politics RSS gave rise to many communal organizations, BJP, VHP, Vanvasi Kalyan Ashram, Bajrang Dal etc. These organizations built on the communal historiography introduced by British and went on adding more to it. They spread the canards that Muslim kings destroyed Hindu temples and insulted Hindu religion, converted people by force, did atrocities on Hindus, are eating beef while Hindu regard cow as her mother, are aggressive, are terrorists, have four wives and twenty children and the like. All this has been demonstrated to be totally false and based on half truths.

One knows that holy places were destroyed by the Kings of all religions for wealth and as a symbol of their victory over the defeated king. They also built holy places to respect the feelings of their subjects. The religions have not been spread by Kings, barring the exception of King Ashok and that religions spread by multiple mechanisms, interaction, influence of saints, expectation of reward etc. Also that, the victor King used to humiliate the defeated king by imposing various conditions on him, one of them being conversion to victor's religion. Kings' atrocities on their subjects, their humiliation of women in the areas defeated by them was done by all armies. Here selective presentation of such acts only by Muslim Kings was done by the British to win over people's loyalty to woo them away from the loyalty to Muslim kings.

Beef eating is a global phenomenon; also beef was the food item during the Vedic times is well known by now. Emperor Babur in his will to Humanyun advices him to desist from cow slaughter in deference of wishes to the Hindu subjects. Today the question of four wives does not arise as the sex ratio is adverse as far as number of women is concerned (All India average 932, amongst Muslims 936) The number of children depends on the level of literacy and social development. This number of children amongst Muslims is more a sign of their being marginalized from social development processes. Terrorism is not a religious phenomenon; it is due to political, economic and social reasons, Liberation Tigers of Tamil Elam, Irish Republican army, ULFA and 'Sadhvi Pragya-Dayanand Pande and associates' tell us that terrorists have come from all religions. The result of this propaganda has been demonization of Muslims and laying the ground for communal violence.

Anti Christian Propaganda

About Christians, RSS combine has been spreading that these groups are converting by force, fraud and allurement. As such this propaganda has been intensified from mid 1980s. Surely Christian missionaries have been here from last many centuries. Also during last four decades their percentage in population has been gradually declining (1971-2.60%, 1981-2.44%. 1991-2.34% and 2001-2.30%). Wadhva Commission, which went into the investigation of Pastor Stains brutal burning by Bajrang Dal's Dara Singh did conclude that Pastor Stains was not involved in the acts of conversions and neither has the percentage of Christians gone up in the area where he was doing his work amongst Leprosy patients. The real reason for targeting

Christian missionaries is not conversion or religion but their literacy work amongst the Adivasis, which is empowering them and leading to a shift in the status quo.

Religion: Dialogue and current times

Before we engage in dialogue we have to make two basic points clear. One, what are the issues involved, are they of religious nature or political nature. Second what is the implication of primary process on the intercommunity relations? Starting from this then we go on to explore as to how intercommunity relations can be improved, and bridges built for better and more amicable society.

As we have seen above globally it is the lust for oil which is the major cause of terrorism. It is not due to Islam. At home, in India it is the political outfit working for Hindu nation, which is spreading the lies and is doing propaganda against minorities. So we have to make it clear that the moral values of Islam, Hinduism and Christianity are not hostile to each other, they as a matter of fact complement each other. One is not talking of the theological, mythological issues, one is talking about the moral values propagated by these, like Vadsudhaiv Kutumbkam, (Hinduism), Love thy neighbor (Christianity) or take care of your neighbor's needs (Islam). To reemphasize the present problem is not with religions, it is the political interests of section of society which are being presented as being related to religion, the dialogue process has to make it clear that divisive force does not lie in domain of religion but in the arena of political interests. The problem has been imposed on societal, cultural and ideological spheres of society.

The moral content of religions has to be projected along the lines of the human rights of all in the society, and we have to help each other in enhancing the concept of morality and human rights. At the same time we can leave the issues related to identity, holy books, rituals and festivals to each religion, as their private-social matters. Here also one can encourage the participation in others' festivals and celebrations as far as the social aspect of festivals is concerned. Theological matters of the other religions should be left to them for sorting it out. Others should not pontificate on such matters except of their own.

Political-Social Dialogue:

The tragedy of communal violence has been creating the walls of separation amongst the communities. A dialogue is needed to overcome these artificial barriers created by the political phenomenon. For this the social workers, religious workers do form starting point of interaction where the matters are discussed from the point of community, keeping the politics aside. The basis of this interaction has to be three fold.

One, the moral values of religion, the syncretic values and traditions of people, to recapture the essence of that practice and to bring it back as the basis of social relationship. Second, we have to rededicate ourselves, to reaffirm proactively to the values of Indian freedom struggle. These values came to be enshrined in the Constitution of India. These are the values of Liberty, Equality and Fraternity. By equality one means the similar status as citizens, irrespective of one's religion caste and gender. To reaffirm that ours' is a secular democracy. To recommit that these values are the ground on which people of different faith will stand. Fraternity (community) teaches us that irrespective of our caste, religion or gender we are an Indian community. And that is the basis of our interaction. While picking this up we need to keep in mind that United Nations charter of Human rights is our guiding principle, which ordains for a dignified life as the right of all of us.

Promoting Affinity:

With these in mind we realize that negative propaganda is the root of hatred and it is the ground for violence. We need to work proactively to dispel the misconceptions, wrong perceptions about other communities. The bridges between communities are to be made stronger. Many a social effort is needed in this direction. To make ourselves aware of the truth about the history and the communities we have to develop platforms through which the truth is disseminated. It may be workshops, seminars, lectures, films or other cultural expressions.

The community leaders have to reach out to Human rights workers and those striving for plural values. Currently not much effort is being put to highlight their work. The major victims of the present attack on plural values of the society are dalits, women, workers, Adivasis and minorities. These sections have to be provided a platform where they exchange their ideas and grievances and raise forums for interaction and dialogue. It is through the dialogue of these sections that a positive force against the violence and retrograde politics can be made strong.

The country is continuing to be plural and secular because secular and liberal elements are much more in number. The problem is that they stand fragmented, and their voice remains in the background due to lack of cohesion. We have to talk in the terms of humane voices coming together and struggling for a composite society.

Since the society is in crisis of identity, let us define as to what is our primary identity, religious or national? We need to reassert our primary national identity at this juncture. Our efforts of dialogue have to be multilayered, starting from the school to the community, we have to spread he message of peace. The misconceptions about other communities/religions have to be negated by propagating the essential values of religions, the values related to love, compassion, peace and non violence. We also need to intervene at cultural level. For this, the specially designed programs involving people of the community, cutting across religions need urgent attention. The moral value classes in schools have to be enriched with the content of inter-religious understanding.

The prophets could inspire people as they stood for truth in a non compromising way. There cannot be peace without justice. Today the major section of population is unaware of the richness of Indian culture and plural ethos and has been frightened in the name of religion. Those doing politics in the name of religion or religious identity need to be re-educated in the norms of human values, with the focus that it is the goodness of different people which has kept human society on the path of progress.

Index

D

T